REPUBLIC OF LIES

REPUBLIC OF LIES

AMERICAN CONSPIRACY THEORISTS AND
THEIR SURPRISING RISE TO POWER

ANNA MERLAN

BOOKS

1 3 5 7 9 10 8 6 4 2

Random House Books
20 Vauxhall Bridge Road
London SW1V 2SA

Random House Books is part of the Penguin Random House group of companies
whose addresses can be found at global.penguinrandomhouse.com.

Penguin
Random House
UK

First published in the United Kingdom by Random House Books in 2019
First published in the United States by Metropolitan Books in 2019

www.penguin.co.uk

A CIP catalogue record for this book is available from the British Library.

ISBN 9781847948212

Printed and bound in Great Britain by Clays Ltd, Elcograf S.p.A.

Penguin Random House is committed to a sustainable future
for our business, our readers and our planet. This book is made
from Forest Stewardship Council® certified paper.

MIX
Paper from
responsible sources
FSC® C018179

Falsehood flies, and truth comes limping after it, so that when men come to be undeceived, it is too late.

—Jonathan Swift

CONTENTS

REPUBLIC OF LIES

PROLOGUE

In January 2015, I spent the longest, queasiest week of my life on a cruise ship filled with conspiracy theorists. As our boat rattled toward Mexico and back, I heard about every wild plot, secret plan, and dark cover-up imaginable. It was mostly fascinating, occasionally exasperating, and the cause of a headache that took months to fade. To my pleasant surprise, given that I was a reporter traveling among a group of deeply suspicious people, I was accused only once of working for the CIA.

The unshakable certainty that many of the conspiracy theorists possessed sometimes made me want to tear my hair out, how tightly they clung to the strangest and most far-fetched ideas. I was pretty sure they had lost their hold on reality as a result of being permanently and immovably on the fringes of American life. I felt bad for them and, to be honest, a little superior.

"The things that everyone thinks are crazy now," Sean David Morton proclaimed early in the trip, "the mainstream will pick up on them. Twenty-sixteen is going to be one of those pivotal years, not just in human history, but in American history as well."

Morton is a self-proclaimed psychic and UFO expert, and someone who has made a lot of dubious claims about how to beat government agencies such as the IRS in court. I dismissed his predictions about 2016 the way I dismissed a lot of his prophecies and basic insistence about how the world works. Morton and the other conspiracy theorists on the boat were confident of a whole lot of things I found unbelievable but which have plenty of adherents in the United States and abroad. Some of them asserted that mass shootings like Sandy Hook are staged by our own government with the help of "crisis actors" as part of a sinister (and evidently delayed) gun-grab. The moon landing was obviously fake (that one didn't even merit much discussion). The government was covering up not just the link between vaccines and autism but also the cures for cancer and AIDS. Everywhere they looked, there was a hidden plot, a secret cabal, and as the Gospel of Matthew teaches about salvation, only a narrow gate that leads to the truth.

I chronicled my stressful, occasionally hilarious, unexpectedly enlightening experience onboard the Conspira-Sea Cruise as a reporter for the feminist website Jezebel, and then I tried to forget about it. I had done a kooky trip on a boat, the kind of stunt journalism project every features writer loves, and it was over. Conspiracy theorists, after all, were a sideshow.

Yet I began to notice that they were increasingly encroaching on my usual beats, like politics. In July 2016, I was walking down a clogged, chaotic narrow street in Cleveland, Ohio, where thousands of reporters, pundits, politicians, and Donald Trump fans had massed to attend the Republican National Convention. I was there for Jezebel again and was busy taking pictures of particularly sexist anti–Hillary Clinton merchandise. There was a lot of it around, for sale on the street and proudly displayed on people's bodies: TRUMP THAT BITCH buttons, white T-shirts reading HILLARY SUCKS, BUT NOT LIKE MONICA.

I stopped a guy in his twenties, dark-haired, built, and jaunty, walking past wearing an eye-catching black HITLERY shirt: a photo of Hillary Clinton adorned with a Hitler mustache, smirking slightly.

"Can I take your photo?" I asked. He agreed, and then I noticed a bizarre sight: the guys walking with him. There were maybe eight of them, and they were enormous, muscle-bound, and heavily bearded. A couple were wearing camo pants and dusty boots. They looked like members of a militia, fresh from a training exercise in the desert, set loose in urban Ohio.

"Where are you guys . . . from?" I asked as delicately as I could.

One of them grinned at me.

"We're reporters," he said merrily.

"No, you're not," I blurted, without thinking. The biggest guy winked and showed me his press badge: they were from InfoWars, the mega-empire of suspicion—a radio show, website, and vastly profitable store of lifestyle products—founded by Austin, Texas–based host Alex Jones.

Later that night, I saw the enormous men again in a Mexican restaurant, quietly shoveling chips into their mouths with their bear-paw hands. After a few minutes, with a huge amount of bustling and self-important murmuring, a couple of them ushered in Alex Jones himself, installing him on a bar stool and pouring him shots of tequila.

I went over to say hello. The men looked concerned. One of them held up a hand: "You can have two minutes," he told me.

Jones was red-faced and effusive. We'd never met before and I was interrupting his dinner, but he greeted me warmly. We had a brief, scattershot conversation: we talked about Trump, whom he was there to support. I asked whether he thought vaccines cause autism. "I think they contribute to it," he said, nodding. (They don't.) I asked whether he considered himself "woke," the slang for a politically conscious, socially aware person.

"What?" he asked.

I explained what it meant.

"I'm one hundred percent woke," Jones replied in his signature growl. He beamed at me. "I am *woke*," he repeated. Everyone smiled at one another: the InfoWars guys, Jones, and me. One of them signaled that it was time for me to take my leave. I did.

As on the Conspira-Sea, my first reaction was to treat the exchange as a lark. It was the kind of interaction you might have with a harmless, nutty radio shock jock, because that's what Alex Jones was, for many years: a guy shouting into a microphone, warning that the government was trying to make everyone gay through covert chemical warfare, the homosexuality agents leaching into our water supply and from our plastic bottles. ("They're turning the freaking frogs gay!" he famously shouted. The clip quickly went viral and provoked mass hilarity on Twitter.)

Jones also made less adorably kooky claims: that a number of mass shootings and acts of terrorism, like the 1995 Oklahoma City bombing, were faked by the government; that the CEO of Chobani, the yogurt company, was busy importing "migrant rapists" to work at its Idaho plant; that Hillary Clinton is an actual demon who smells of sulfur, hails from Hell itself, and has "personally murdered and chopped up and raped" little children.

Jones was closer to the mainstream's attention than most people on the conspiracy fringe, largely thanks to the seminal 2001 book *Them* by British journalist Jon Ronson, one chapter of which chronicled the pair's extremely weird adventure of trying to get into a top-secret meeting of world leaders at Bohemian Grove in Northern California. (They made it inside; memorably, Ronson beheld a bunch of those world leaders putting on childish skits and peeing on trees as a sort of boys-cutting-loose weekend. Jones, meanwhile, has always maintained that the whole thing was an "occult playground" for the elites and that an effigy burned during the weekend was nothing less than a "bizarre pagan ritual" and that the world's most powerful people engage in "ancient Canaanite Luciferian Babylon mystery religion ceremonies," as a film he made about it declared.)

But while I was joking around with Jones, he was at the RNC on important business, it turned out: he was there to meet with Roger Stone, former Richard Nixon advisor turned dirty-tricks specialist and trusted ally of the Trump campaign.

Jones and Trump were in fact longtime mutual fans. After announcing his run, candidate Trump made one of his first media appearances on Jones's show, appearing via Skype from Trump Tower. Jones endorsed him early and often and, in turn, many of the radio host's favorite talking points started turning up in Trump's speeches. Jones began darkly predicting that the elections would be "rigged" in Clinton's favor, a claim that Trump quickly made a central tenet of the latter days of his campaign. At the end of September, Jones began predicting that Clinton would be on performance-enhancing drugs of some kind during the presidential debates; by October, Trump was implying that, too, and demanding that Clinton be drug tested.

Soon after, the United States narrowly elected a conspiracy enthusiast as its president, a man who wrongly believes that vaccines cause autism, that global warming is a hoax perpetuated by the Chinese "in order to make U.S. manufacturing non-competitive," as he tweeted in 2012, and who claimed, for attention and political gain, that Barack Obama was born in Kenya. And one of the first people President-elect Trump called after his thunderous upset victory was Alex Jones. In fact, Trump found time to call Jones along with a few—oddly prioritized—world leaders before he or any member of his transition team had contacted anyone at the Pentagon or the State or Justice Departments. Then, in a very short time, some of the most wild-eyed conspiracymongers in the country were influencing federal policy and taking meetings at the White House.

Here's the thing: the conspiracy theorists aboard the cruise and in the streets of Cleveland could have warned me that Trump's election was coming, had I only been willing to listen.

Many of the hard-core conspiracy theorists I sailed with weren't very engaged in politics, given that they believe it's a fake system designed to give us the illusion of control by our real overlords: the Illuminati, the international bankers, or perhaps the twelve-foot lizard people. But when they did consider the subject, they *loved* Trump, even the left-leaning among them who might have once preferred Bernie Sanders. They recognized the future president as a "truth teller" in a style that spoke to them and many other Americans. They liked his thoughts about a rigged system and a government working against them, the way it spoke to what they had always believed, and the neat way he was able to peg the enemy with sound bites: the "lying media," "crooked Hillary," the bottomless abyss of the "Washington swamp." They were confident of his victory—if the globalists and the New World Order didn't get in the way, and they certainly would try. Just as Sean David Morton said, they were sure that 2016 was going to change everything. (Although they perhaps didn't imagine that Trump would win as a result of the Electoral College while losing the popular vote by one of the biggest margins in American history.)

Trump's fondness for conspiracy continued apace into his presidency: his Twitter account became a megaphone for every dark suspicion he has about the biased media and the rigged government working against him, even, at one particularly low point, going so far as to accuse his political opponents of inflating the number of deaths in Puerto Rico caused by Hurricane Maria. His supporters became consumed by the concept of the "deep state," seized by a conviction that a shadow regime is working hard to undermine the White House. At the same time, Trump brought a raft of conspiracy theorists into his cabinet: among them was Secretary of Housing and Urban Development Ben Carson, who suggested that President Barack Obama would declare martial law and cancel the 2016 elections to remain in power. There was also National Security Advisor Michael Flynn (who was quickly fired), notorious for retweeting stories linking Hillary Clinton to child sex trafficking. Other conspiracy enthusiasts soon occupied positions in such staid government offices as the Department of Health and Human Services—where a Trump appointee named Ximena Barreto was hired despite her also claiming that Clinton was linked to a pedophile ring—and the National Security Council, where a senior aide and former Pentagon official named Rich Higgins sent out a furious, lengthy email on the various leftist conspiracies seeking to undermine the president.

With the candidacy and then election of a conspiracy peddler, conspiratorial thinking leaked from its traditional confines to spread in new, more visible ways across the country. As a result, a fresh wave of conspiracy theories and an obsession with their negative effects engulfed America. We all worried late in the election season about "fake news," a term for disinformation that quickly lost all meaning as it was gleefully seized on by the Trump administration to describe any media attention they didn't like. We fixated on a conspiracy theorist taking the White House, and then we fretted over whether he was a true believer or just a cynical opportunist. And as left-leaning people found themselves unrepresented in government, with the judicial, executive, and legislative branches held by the right, they too started to engage more in conspiracy theorizing.

But beneath the new conspiracy furor—talking heads worrying about it on CNN, Clinton's campaign sending out media blasts to decry Alex

Jones—the reality is that we've been a nation gripped by conspiracy for a long time. The Kennedy assassination has been hotly debated for years. The feminist and antiwar movements of the 1960s were, for a time, believed by a not-inconsiderable number of Americans to be part of a communist plot to weaken the country. A majority of us have believed for decades that the government is hiding what it knows about extra-terrestrials. Since the early 1990s, suspicions that the Clintons were running a drug cartel and/or having their enemies murdered were a persistent part of the discourse on the right. And the website WorldNet-Daily was pushing birther theories and death panels (the idea, first articulated by Sarah Palin in 2009, that under Obamacare bureaucrats would decide whether the elderly deserved medical care) long before "fake news" became a talking point. Many black Americans have, for years, believed that the CIA flooded poor neighborhoods with drugs such as crack in order to destroy them.

The Trump era has merely focused our attention back onto something that has reappeared with reliable persistence: the conspiratorial thinking and dark suspicions that have never fully left us. Conspiracy theorizing has been part of the American system of governance and culture and thought since its beginnings: as journalist Jesse Walker writes in his book *The United States of Paranoia*, early white settlers, including history textbook favorite Cotton Mather, openly speculated that Native Americans were controlled by the Devil and conspiring with him and a horde of related demons to drive them out. Walker also points to the work of historian Jeffrey Pasley, who found what he called the "myth of the superchief": the colonist idea that every Native-led resistance or attack was directed by an "Indian mastermind or monarch in control of tens of thousands of warriors."

The elements of suspicion were present long before the 2016 election, quietly shaping the way large numbers of people see the government, the media, and the nature of what's true and trustworthy. Sometimes, too, conspiracy theories *are* the "official story," the cause of real and far-reaching state action, as with the Red Scare, where a fear of Communists undermining the country led to life-ruining hearings and blacklists.

And for all of our bogus suspicions, there are those that have been given credence by the government itself. We have seen a sizable number of real conspiracies revealed over the past half century, from Watergate to recently declassified evidence of secret CIA programs, to the fact that elements within the Russian government really did conspire to interfere with U.S. elections. There's a perpetual tug between conspiracy theorists and actual conspiracies, between things that are genuinely not believable and truths that are so outlandish they can be hard, at first, to believe.

But while conspiracy theories are as old as the country itself, there *is* something new at work: people who peddle lies and half-truths have come to prominence, fame, and power as never before. If our conspiratorial world is a vast ocean, 2016 was, clearly, the year that Alex Jones—along with other groups, like anti-immigration extremists, anti-Muslim think tanks, and open neo-Nazis and white supremacists—were able to catch the wave of the Trump presidency and surf to the mainstream shore.

It seemed that something new could be learned by riding the conspiracy wave back out: from the stormy center of Trumpland to the farthest reaches of the conspiracy world, into the subcultures that most people never see. Traveling through the ecosphere of suspicion, I found a multiverse of alternate societies, humming below the surface of American life the way some people imagine an alien military base is doing just under Antarctica. I found decades-old belief systems that have never disappeared, new ones that are just starting to form, and strange, unlikely alliances coalescing among deeply improbable groups.

TO UNDERSTAND WHY PEOPLE BELIEVE THINGS THAT ARE AT ODDS WITH all provable truths is to understand how we form our views about the world and the resultant world we have made together. The riotous profusion of conspiracy theories in America shows us something about being American, even about being human—about the decisions we make in interpreting the complexities of our surroundings. Over and over, I found that the people involved in conspiracy communities weren't necessarily some mysterious "other." We're all prone to believing half-truths, forming connections where there are none to be found, finding importance in political and social events that may not have much significance at all. That's part of how human beings work, how we make meaning, particularly in the United States today, now, at the start of a strange and unlikely century.

I was interested, too, in understanding why this new surge of conspiracism has appeared, knowing that historically, times of tumult and social upheaval tend to lead to a parallel surge in conspiracy thinking. I found some of my answer in our increasingly rigid class structure, one that leaves many people feeling locked into their circumstances—in contrast with what we've been taught is the American dream—and desperate to find someone to blame. I found it in rising disenfranchisement, a feeling many people have that they are shut out of systems of power, pounding furiously at iron doors that will never open to admit them. I found it in a frustratingly opaque healthcare system, a vanishing social safety net, a political environment that seizes cynically on a renewed distrust of the news media.

Together, these elements helped create a society in which many Americans see millions of snares, laid by a menacing group of enemies, all the more alarming for how difficult they are to identify and pin down. I saw a disturbing thirst for vengeance, a willingness to punish enemies and vanquish evildoers that is then easily twisted by opportunists. These things were in the country around me, in my own life—shadows that seemed to grow longer and longer, even as people became increasingly aware of the destructive power of conspiracy theories and began doing their best to fight them. Still: we are the suspicious and the conspiracists are us, and there are more of us all the time.

FALSE TIMES

IT'S A TYPICALLY DISORIENTING WINTER DAY IN AN UNREMARKABLE part of Los Angeles, the palm trees bristling above the Walgreens and the tire shops, the golden light washing insistently over the slowly rotating sign above a twenty-four-hour burger joint, its paint peeled away into nonexistence. The sun doesn't penetrate into this vast, windowless ballroom out by the airport, where I'm learning about the secret pedophiles who make up 30 percent of the federal government.

"Some of the top D.C. elites are about to be prosecuted for pedophilia," David Wilcock promises. Wilcock is a popular filmmaker, researcher, and author in his forties, with shaggy blond hair fit for a boy band, a prominent forehead, and a matter-of-fact, deliberate way of talking about the moment all his dreams are on the breaking edge of coming true.

"We'll get prosecutions," he declares. "We'll get war crimes tribunals."

Much of the room, two hundred people or so, breaks into applause.

"They're now working for *us*," he adds a minute later. He means the government, or, anyway, its non-pedophile portion. "This is a very exciting time to be here. They're singing like songbirds." More applause and a few approving murmurs.

It's the second day of the 2016 Conscious Life Expo, a yearly conference attended by some fifteen thousand people devoted to all things New Age, spiritually refreshing, energy-healing, chakra-balancing, and aura-fine-tuning. Leaving the lecture, I stop in front of two beautiful women standing behind a table heaped with different kinds of gemstones promising to cure everything from anemia to depression to gout. A guy with full-sleeve tattoos offers me Starfire Water, a mere $6 for a bottle and capable of curing PTSD, he promises.

"It's just super, super intentional and positive," he says, beaming. The smell of the delicious Indian food being ladled from steam trays in a corner permeates the air, hanging over the display booths. There are many capacious scarves for sale and a variety of tiny crystal pyramids.

Conscious Life is held in the sterile marbled halls of the Los Angeles Airport Hilton, a chilly white expanse that feels a lot like spending the weekend in a large, spotless, flower-decked restroom. Besides being a great place to purchase a geode, the conference is also, more quietly, a surprisingly bustling hub for conspiracy theories. Anti-vaccine folks and CIA-mind-control experts and even a flat earther or two wander its halls, trading some of the most ferociously out-there claims over samosas and cups of very good coffee laced with vegan coconut creamer. There is maybe no more welcoming place to think about conspiracy theories in America and their freshly prominent place in our politics.

On that balmy February day, Donald Trump has just been inaugurated and the runaway hot air balloon of his presidency is beginning to lift off the ground. Pizzagate, the conspiracy theory alleging that Hillary Clinton's campaign chair is affiliated with a secret pedophile ring run out of a D.C. pizza parlor, is still burning up Twitter threads and message boards and leaking repeatedly into the mainstream press, where it's disbelieved but still covered. The environmental activist Robert F. Kennedy, Jr., a famous vaccine "skeptic," has announced that Trump asked him to chair a panel on vaccine safety. R.F.K., Jr. is pushing the debunked claim that mercury in vaccines causes autism, and he argues that the most prominent medical bodies in the nation are covering it all up, with help from a bought-off media.

It's a surreal time. Conspiratorial beliefs that usually simmer below the mainstream for decades at a time are suddenly, insistently pushing to the surface. The news is full of white supremacist groups and their suspicions of a shadowy Zionist world government. The concept of a Deep State—a shadow regime, a secret body that's *really* in charge—has become so pervasive that members of Congress are talking about it on national television, and its prominence hasn't even begun to reach full force just yet. Even those flat earthers—one of the most fringe sub-cultures there is, besides those who believe the world is ruled by twelve-foot lizards—have seen a real uptick in their numbers. The term "fake news" is everywhere, and there are acrid debates about misinformation, partisan news sources, bias, and lies. People I've been covering for years as a journalist devoted to subcultures are on the front pages and in Polit-ico headlines, achieving a hallucinatory new level of fame.

Even the most dedicated conspiracy theorists seem too stunned for words by their own sudden prominence. "It's a whole new reality," says Sean David Morton, my travel companion from the Conspira-Sea Cruise. He half chuckles. "The president of the United States has Alex Jones on speed dial! Alex Jones! I mean . . ." He trails off.

Along with his psychic skills, Morton is also a radio host on a pro-gram called *Strange Universe*, broadcasting daily from Southern California, which covers UFOs, get-rich-quick schemes, practical measures to achieve time travel, and conservative politics in pretty much equal measure. He has the booming, polished, confident cadence of radio stars everywhere, emanating from an incongruous body: he's maybe five-foot-six, stout and sandy-haired, with a big D-shaped belly and a bris-tly little mustache. He's forever in a navy blazer with what looks like a private-school crest on the pocket; he studs it with pins of Disney char-acters. TO SAVE TIME, ASSUME I KNOW EVERYTHING, his T-shirt reads. A string of beautiful women—thirteen, to be exact—stream by while we talk, kissing his cheek and stroking his shoulder delightedly.

Morton will tell you for many long minutes about the real power structure in these United States: that the government is controlled by the bankers and the British aristocracy and the Vatican. As he mingles with the Conscious Life attendees, Morton feels that all those entities are bearing down on him like never before. He and his wife, Melissa, are facing federal charges and a potential six hundred years in prison apiece for allegedly forging financial documents, a scheme that came directly out of their conspiratorial views about how the government and the financial system work.

If he's convicted, Morton is on the verge of seeing his personal belief system collapse and, by extension, his life. Meanwhile, people like Alex Jones, people he jovially detests, for professional, competitive reasons, are rocketing into the mainstream.

But Morton's worries aren't echoed by most of the Conscious Life attendees. Stalking the Hilton's halls, it's impossible to ignore the fresh energy in the air and the excitement of people like David Wilcock, the filmmaker convinced it's all on the verge of busting wide open: every secret government pedophile, every subtle plot, every dirty secret. Wilcock hosts a TV show on Gaia, a New Age video platform, with a cohost named Corey Goode, who claims to have served in a secret military space program for twenty years, fighting the bad kind of aliens. Later in the weekend, Goode will receive a standing ovation from an enraptured crowd for his galactic military service.

To BUILD A BOAT STURDY ENOUGH TO EMBARK ON THIS UNSETTLING voyage, let's pause to attempt to define a conspiracy theory. Splicing together a few different definitions offered by academics and historians, it's a belief that a small group of people are working in secret against the common good, to create harm, to effect some negative change in society, to seize power for themselves, or to hide some deadly or consequential secret. An actual conspiracy is when a small group of people *are* working in secret against the common good, and anyone who tells you we can always easily distinguish fictitious plots from real ones probably hasn't read much history.

The historian Frank P. Mintz coined the term "conspiracism," which he defined as a "belief in the primacy of conspiracies in the unfolding of history." Conspiracism works for everyone, in Mintz's view; it "serves the needs of diverse political and social groups in America and elsewhere. It identifies elites, blames them for economic and social catastrophes, and assumes that things will be better once popular action can remove them from positions of power." It is, in essence, a view of how we can vanquish the Devil and achieve Heaven right here on earth.

And conspiracism has been inextricably woven into the American experience from the beginning. As Jesse Walker writes in his book *The United States of Paranoia*, even before the colonists were fretting about the plots of secret super-Indians, the founding fathers accused England of plotting against them, trying to force the colonies into servitude or outright enslavement, what George Washington called "a regular Systematick Plan" to turn them into "tame, & abject Slaves, as the Blacks we Rule over with such arbitrary Sway." The Declaration of Independence lists the indignities and outrages England perpetrated against the colonies, but it doesn't stop there: it argues that those acts total up to a plot, what it calls "a design," to bring the colonies under "absolute Despotism."

Conspiracy theories tend to flourish especially at times of rapid social change, when we're reevaluating ourselves and, perhaps, facing uncomfortable questions in the process. In 1980, the civil liberties lawyer and author Frank Donner wrote that conspiracism reveals a fundamental insecurity about who Americans want to be versus who we are.

"Especially in times of stress, exaggerated febrile explanations of unwelcome reality come to the surface of American life and attract support," he wrote. The continual resurgence of conspiracy movements, he claimed, "illuminate[s] a striking contrast between our claims to superiority, indeed our mission as a redeemer nation to bring a new world order, and the extraordinary fragility of our confidence in our institutions." That contrast, he said, "has led some observers to conclude that we are, subconsciously, quite insecure about the value and permanence of our society."

It is worth noting that conspiracy theories frequently echo the spirit of the religious zealots who founded this country. Julie Ingersoll, a professor of religious studies at the University of North Florida, writes that such theories frame world events in monolithic, black-and-white terms: "Conspiracy theories seek to explain events not merely in terms of human actors but in terms of all-inclusive mythic narratives or worldviews, rooted in a fundamental division between Good and Evil."

Like religion, conspiracy theories don't just identify a common enemy, but outline a path to a better life and provide hope for the future. Numerous studies have noted that insecure and threatened populations— nonwhite people and unemployed people among them—show higher rates of conspiracy thinking. Joseph DiGrazia, then an assistant professor at York University, wrote in 2017 that "macro-level social conditions and structural social changes," like economic instability, could create "feelings of threat and insecurity," which, in turn, lead to higher levels of what he called "conspiratorial ideation."

Feelings of "threat and insecurity" are normal features of American life for plenty of people, and Joseph Uscinski and Joseph Parent, political scientists, argue that conspiracy thinking is like normal political thinking, but more so. "Where regular politicians highlight problems, advocate solutions and call for concerted action soon," they write, "conspiracy theorists highlight an abysmal state of affairs, advocate titanic policies, and call for concerted action right now." (And even on its best day, politics-as-usual frequently involves a sort of conspiracy-lite, with plots, alliances, hidden motives, and spin.)

Thus conspiracy theories, in the more sophisticated academic readings, look like a way to give corporeal form to hard-to-define anxieties, a foe on which to pin the varied worries and misfortunes of a group that senses marginalization, like conservatives during the 1960s and again in the Obama years, when they sensed power and cultural influence slipping from their grasp.

That sense of fragility and distrust are particularly noticeable again in the mid-2000s: huge swaths of people feel locked out of the political process, not even bothering to vote out of a belief that it won't make much of a difference. We have a stunning and increased lack of social mobility, a profound distrust of "elites" and those in power, as well as a persistent fear of "outsiders" and "others" taking what we see as limited resources. Combined with deep inequalities of race and class, all that makes for an environment that's conspiracy-saturated in a way that's unusual outside of repressive countries with authoritarian regimes and state-run media.

Conspiracy theories are, for example, wildly popular in the Middle East, many of them anti-Semitic or anti-Israel, holding either Jews or Israelis responsible for events at home (the most bizarre was in 2010, when an Egyptian government official claimed that a series of shark attacks at a Red Sea resort were directed by Israel, that the sharks themselves were "sent by Mossad") or events abroad (9/11, the assassination of U.S. presidents). In Israel, there are many competing conspiracy theories on the assassination of Prime Minister Yitzhak Rabin; they originate from the left and right alike, and focus on disbelief that a lone Jewish law student was responsible for the murder. Sometimes they originate from the state itself, as in Russia, where disinformation and elaborate conspiratorial explanations emanate constantly from both the government and respected public intellectuals. Russian conspiracies are as numerous as dandelions on a spring day, and a lot of them center on the United States; the so-called Dulles Plan holds that the CIA plotted to bring down the Soviet Union by promoting vice and sin through art and literature, among other things. The Hungarian government has a single-minded obsession with Hungarian-born liberal billionaire George Soros, who lives in the United States, accusing him of plotting to smuggle refugees into Europe. (The number of things pinned on Soros both at home and abroad could fill several books.)

The most famous writing on conspiratorial thinking in the United States is Richard Hofstadter's "The Paranoid Style in American Politics," a long essay that first ran in *Harper's* in November 1964, which posits conspiracism as a type of mental illness infecting a swath of Americans, particularly those on the far right. Hofstadter wasn't exactly engaged in diagnosis ("I am not speaking in a clinical sense, but borrowing a clinical term for other purposes," he wrote). At the same time, he bluntly pointed to a kind of feverish paranoia sweeping over political actors, wildly distorting their judgment, leading them to see hidden enemies everywhere, and convincing them that drastic action was not just necessary, but urgently justified.

As his examples, Hofstadter pointed to McCarthyism, anti-Masonic fervor, and fear of the Illuminati, which had been haunting the colonies since the 1700s. (The Illuminati were a real if short-lived secret society founded in Bavaria by one Adam Weishaupt, who liked the idea of a secret society but found the Freemasons too expensive. His organization's name, and their outsized reputation, long outlived the Bavarian Illuminati, which fell apart within a decade.) In the 1960s, Hofstadter saw paranoia as a pernicious and growing influence in American life, citing the rise of groups like the anticommunist John Birch Society. He laid out a blueprint for the paranoid style that, even after all these years, sounds familiar to anyone who ever watched Glenn Beck sweat onto his chalkboard.

"The central image is that of a vast and sinister conspiracy," Hofstadter wrote of the paranoid's view of the world, "a gigantic and yet subtle machinery of influence set in motion to undermine and destroy a way of life." He allowed that there were indeed actual conspiracies in American and world history, but the paranoid saw conspiracies as gigantic, apocryphal, world-ending: "The paranoid spokesman sees the fate of conspiracy in apocalyptic terms—he traffics in the birth and death of whole worlds, whole political orders, whole systems of human values. He is always manning the barricades of civilization. He constantly lives at a turning point; it is now or never in organizing resistance to conspiracy. Time is forever just running out."

It's easy to say that conspiracy theories present oversimplified narratives, that they're less messy than reality. Hofstadter claimed that "the paranoid mentality is far more coherent than the real world, since it leaves no room for mistakes, failures, or ambiguities." But that's not entirely true: very often, in practice, conspiracy theories don't seek to forge a single coherent narrative and are content to leave much ambiguity, creating chaotic narrative threads that don't quite add up or make sense. The point is more often to identify an enemy than outline precisely what they've done.

"The modern right wing," Hofstadter suggested, felt uniquely dispossessed: "America has been largely taken away from them and their kind, though they are determined to try to repossess it and to prevent the final destructive act of subversion. The old American virtues have already been eaten away by cosmopolitans." He was making that point as a coalition of movements—civil rights, second-wave feminism, anti-Vietnam War activism—aimed to fundamentally reshape American life. And his ideas about far-right discontent came before the conservative backlash of the 1970s, when aggrieved right-wingers began to mobilize and articulate a vision of social and familial "traditionalism" that became central to the Republican Party's vision of itself.

Hofstadter's analysis—that paranoia is an infection in the blood-stream of the body politic and an irrational way of experiencing world events—has been complicated in recent years by more culturally and socially sophisticated readings of conspiracy theorism. University of Florida professor Mark Fenster points out that conspiracy theories are often an exaggerated expression of American populism: our suspicion of authority figures, our fear of consolidation of power. Echoing that, journalist David Aaronovitch notes that a conspiracy theory is likely to be "politically populist, in that it usually claims to lay bare an action taken by a small power elite against the people."

It is true that while conspiracy theories are equally common in rural and urban areas of the United States, there's a distinct class element to them: people with only a high school education are more likely to believe at least one, and people who report a higher income are less likely to declare conspiratorial beliefs. The "elites" threatening the people tend to be the same foe by different names: Alex Jones uses the term "global-ists" as a catch-all for a vague and threatening global power elite, while others use terms like "New World Order." Sometimes the enemy is the U.S. government, sometimes it's the Jews, and sometimes—more rarely than I personally would like—the queen of England, believed by a sadly dwindling number of people to be the head of a brutal global drug cartel.

IN THE DARK OF THE NIGHT OF JULY 19, AD 64, A FIRE BROKE OUT IN the slums of Rome and, swept along by vicious winds, devastated the town, leveling several districts entirely. The fire burned for six days, died down, was reignited, and burned for three more. Hundreds of people were killed; many more were left destitute and homeless.

In the midst of it all, the famously conniving Emperor Nero—who was away in his holiday home on a cool hillside when the fires began—was reported by the historian Tacitus to have placidly watched the city burn as he nonchalantly played his fiddle or plucked his lyre. (Tacitus was writing years later; he was a teenager when Nero died, and histo-rians have argued since that we know little about his sources or biases.)

Per Tacitus, Roman citizens began to suspect that Nero himself had ordered the fires set, to consolidate his power and reconstruct Rome in the manner he saw fit. Or he had allowed the fires to keep burning for the same reason, even sending mobs to prevent citizens from quashing the flames. Nero, meanwhile, blamed the fires on an upstart religious group, the Christians, and used the pretext to merrily persecute and crucify them. Many parts of the story have been called into question by modern scholarship, but the Nero-fiddling-as-Rome-burns version is one of the earliest known examples of two things. First, it's a conspiracy theory about the government unleashing chaos to extend control; second, a government official used a conspiracy theory to realize political ends.

All these many centuries later, conspiracy theories relating to September 11 echo the Roman fire incident: that the Bush administration either passively allowed the attacks to happen or orchestrated them for political ends. (The two branches of 9/11 conspiracism have become so entrenched that they have their own acronyms: LIHOP, for "let it happen on purpose," and MIHOP, "made it happen on purpose.")

The Rome fire myth also illustrates something else: people historically developed conspiracy theories about local phenomena, things that happened right in front of them. As our world has gotten larger and more connected, we tend to theorize about distant people, places, and events. Our theories are so broad they encompass the galaxy itself and the most distant reaches of space: UFO conspiracism has been a beloved American pastime for nearly a century.

The local element hasn't disappeared, though; indeed, our communications have made conspiracism more intimate than ever. Social media allows us to fasten a conspiracy on a seemingly random or inconsequential person: the victim of a school shooting, say, or the owner of a pizza parlor. Self-appointed online detectives can use digital tools to contact, expose, harass, and occasionally terrorize the alleged plotters in ways that would have been impossible even twenty years ago.

Thus conspiracies have changed their form repeatedly over history, even in the relatively young history of the United States. A lot of conspiratorial hysterias in the early days of this country focused on what the historian Kathryn Olmsted in her book *Real Enemies* calls "alien subversion": a fear that disaffected outside groups—Jews, Catholics,

Freemasons, Mormons—were plotting to seize control for themselves. Sometimes, more rarely, the alien enemy was closer to home, as with the Salem witch trials, when a community turned on itself, neighbor accusing neighbor of serving the Devil in secret.

But as Olmsted points out, something significant changed in the twentieth century. Theories began to focus not on an outside, alien group seizing power, but on the existing power structure, the government itself; the Romans redirecting their attention back to Nero, as it were.

"No longer were conspiracy theorists chiefly concerned that alien forces were plotting to capture the federal government," she writes. "Instead, they proposed that the federal government itself was the conspirator. They feared the subversive potential of the swelling, secretive bureaucracies of the proto-national security state." As the government grew larger, particularly its military element, the number of conspiratorial ideas about it expanded proportionally. And some of those suspicions weren't unfounded: the country has innumerable examples of actual government conspiracies, which became more outlandish and horrifying as we approached the present day.

In 1954, the CIA directly assisted in overthrowing Guatemala's president, Colonel Jacobo Árbenz Guzmán, in large part to protect the interests of the American-owned United Fruit Company. In 1973, the agency did the same in Chile, to destabilize and drive out of power Salvador Allende, the country's democratically elected Socialist leader.

In the 1960s, the federal government engaged in systematic covert harassment of such activist groups as the Black Panthers and the American Indian Movement, and of Martin Luther King, Jr. and other members of the Southern Christian Leadership Conference, conspiring to ruin the lives of their leaders, set the membership against one another and against other activist groups with whom they might have formed ties, and drive them to despair, ruin, and suicide. The feds also engaged in long-term secret programs to test the effects of radiation on poor people, carrying out medical experiments that sickened and sometimes killed women, prisoners, and even children in state care.

Beginning in the 1970s and continuing through the 1990s, investigative journalism, along with declassified FBI and CIA files, revealed a series of appalling secret government programs. To pick just one: in

MKUltra, the CIA and the army explored the use of mescaline and LSD
by dosing unwitting civilians, including mental patients, prisoners, and
johns visiting sex workers at covert CIA-run brothels. The records of
that program were deliberately destroyed by the government in 1973.

But all those plots were, in the end, exposed, as were Watergate, the
Iran-Contra scandal, and the NSA's spying on Americans. Antigovernment conspiracy theorists tend to overestimate the ability of bureaucrats
to scheme in secret. Grand conspiracies are hard to conceal. Yet it's not
unreasonable—at all, even a little bit—to believe that the government
is still engaged in nefarious and secretive behavior, because we know
that it has done so in the past. Timothy Melley, an English professor
at Miami University, has written in recent years about the growth and
alarming secrecy of the national security apparatus, which we glimpse
through redacted FOIAs and anonymous whistleblowers, and reflect
back onto ourselves in the form of TV shows like *Homeland* and *House
of Cards*.

"Twenty-five years after the end of the cold war, the U.S. has 17 intelligence agencies employing hundreds of thousands of workers at a cost
of some $70 billion per year," Melley wrote in the *New York Times* in
2015. "But most of our ideas about U.S. intelligence work come from
the endless stream of melodramatic entertainment in movies and on TV.
The public thus finds itself in a strange state of half-knowledge about
U.S. foreign affairs. When 'top secrecy' and 'plausible deniability' are
widely accepted ideas, is it any surprise that so many people believe
political power is wielded by powerful, invisible agents?"

We have found ourselves at a point in history where both real government conspiracies and their shadows loom large in our collective
imagination. Those two things, working in tandem, destabilize the public
perception of what's true, what's possible, and what we're ready to pin
on those running the country. But the problem goes beyond how civilians feel about the government; it also works, more alarmingly, in
reverse. There are dozens of examples of feverish conspiracy thinking
driving *state* action, where imaginary enemies and nonexistent plots
have led to some extremely dark decisions. President Richard Nixon is
our best worst example of this: he was, for one thing, a genuinely paranoid person who kept a long and well-organized enemies list and, in a

double whammy of conspiracism, believed Communist-backed plots against him were orchestrated by Jews. That allowed him to justify his own conspiracies: tapping the phones at the DNC headquarters, the Watergate break-in, and bribing the burglary team themselves to stay quiet about their work.

During the Red Scare of the 1940s and 1950s, too, a fear of Communists infecting the country like termites in wood led to a shameful period of life-ruining witch hunts, hearings, and professional blacklists. (Richard Nixon, then a congressman, enthusiastically joined the House Un-American Activities Committee, which investigated suspected Communist sympathizers, to participate in the persecution.) Or, just a few years before, the incarceration of Japanese Americans in internment camps was based on nothing more than a racist suspicion that they were enemy agents organizing from within against the United States. When, beginning in the 1980s, right-wing extremists started to claim that the government planned to imprison political dissenters in camps run by FEMA, they used the Japanese internment as a reason why the theory was plausible.

More relevant to our own age is yet another phenomenon: politicians who willingly fan the flames of conspiracy either out of genuine belief or because it suits their political ends or some mixture of the two. Hillary Clinton blamed, with a straight face, a "vast right-wing conspiracy" for the women making sexual abuse claims against her husband, the president. The Bush administration infamously claimed that Iraq had weapons of mass destruction to justify its invasion of the country. Deputy Secretary of Defense Paul Wolfowitz enthusiastically promoted the idea that Saddam Hussein, not Osama Bin Laden, was the hidden hand responsible for 9/11. And beginning around 2010, with the rise of the Tea Party, we saw dozens of state and local politicians claim that Muslims were taking over their towns with the canny use of Sharia law. Many of the same politicians, including Republican senator Ted Cruz and now–Texas governor Greg Abbott, also claimed repeatedly that the United Nations had developed plots called Agenda 21 and Jade Helm, designed to invade the United States and take our guns. Whether they believed such things to be true (they weren't), the claims served as useful focal points for organizing their supporters.

With the arrival of Trump, politicians have also—in a twist reminiscent of Nixon conspiring against the imaginary enemies he feared—taken to generating what they themselves have scornfully termed "fake news." The Trump administration launched its own weekly news service on social media in 2017, dedicated entirely to positive coverage of the president. The same year, the Associated Press discovered that the Republican Governors Association created what looked a whole lot like a website for a news outlet: it was called The Free Telegraph and it shared positive news about—you guessed it—Republican governors, alongside negative headlines about Democrats. Until the AP started asking questions, the site did not disclose who was behind it.

EVEN IN THE UNITED STATES, WHICH, AS WE HAVE SEEN, IS A PERFECT petri dish for conspiratorial thinking, not everybody buys into every theory equally. Fairly common beliefs—that Lee Harvey Oswald didn't act alone in killing JFK, or that the government is hiding its knowledge of aliens—aren't shared by everyone.

One persistent question is why some people go further into conspiracy thinking than others. There are clearly psychological, cultural, emotional, and circumstantial elements at work and, predictably, a mess of slightly conflicting studies to tell us how much weight to lend to each. There is some balance here of nature versus nurture: at least seven different studies between 2011 and the present have looked at the idea that people can be predisposed to conspiracy theorizing.

Some people might indeed have a stronger innate tendency toward conspiracy thinking. A 2016 paper, also coauthored by Joseph Uscinski, explains that predisposition seems increasingly likely to be a real phenomenon, a mixture of "political socialization" and psychological factors.

As with many things, we tend to believe in the conspiracy theories we want to believe, drawn to the ones that satisfy and reinforce our view of how the world works. Researchers have linked that to a concept called motivated reasoning: we tend to give more weight to studies, news articles, and any other form of information that confirms our pre-existing beliefs and values, and find ways to reject things that don't line up with what we *feel* to be true, what talk show host Stephen Colbert memorably called "truthiness." Studies on motivated reasoning from both the early 1990s and 2000s show the same patterns: we're not particularly receptive to information that makes us feel defensive or attacked about our existing values or beliefs.

"When individuals engage in motivated reasoning," two professors from Appalachian State University wrote in a 2012 study, "partisan goals trump accuracy goals." They found that people would act as "biased information processors who will vigorously defend their prior values, identities, and attitudes at the expense of factual accuracy."

Uscinski and Parent, the Florida academics, have studied another clear example of motivated reasoning: their research indicates that the conspiracies you believe in tend to line up with your political beliefs. (In a 2017 YouGov poll, years after the birther conspiracy theory should have been dead and firmly buried, 51 percent of Republicans said they thought former president Obama was born in Kenya. People who voted for Donald Trump were particularly likely to believe it: a full 57 percent of them said it was "definitely" or "probably" true. Just 14 percent of Democrats believed that racist, repeatedly debunked lie.)

The one thing Americans have in common, though, is our profound, widespread suspicion. In 2014, Uscinski and Parent published *American Conspiracy Theories*, which presents the results of years of research and makes a pretty persuasive case that nobody in this country is *not* a conspiracy theorist, at least to some degree.

"Conspiracy theories permeate all parts of American society," they wrote, "and cut across gender, age, race, income, political affiliation, educational level, and occupational status." Some beliefs crossed class and political lines: between 60 and 80 percent of people surveyed agreed that the Kennedy assassination was part of a conspiracy that was covered up by the government. Others, surprising ones, were closely tied to party: the conviction that climate change is a government hoax is more common on the right, while suspicions about GMOs are more common on the left.

Uscinski and Parent's research revealed that people who believe in one conspiracy theory are likely to believe in others, a kind of domino effect of the mind. This isn't a new result: a much smaller survey in 1994

showed a similar pattern. Ted Goertzel at Rutgers University surveyed
348 people in New Jersey, finding that most of them classified at least
one of ten conspiracy theories as "probably" true. Fascinatingly, other
studies show that people are able to believe in multiple conspiracy theories even when they're logically contradictory: in my reporting, for
example, I've seen people claim that both vaccines and a weed killer
called Roundup are responsible for increased autism rates. (In an attempt
to split the difference, some folks say that Roundup somehow made its
way into the vaccines.)

Finally, a word about the term "conspiracy theory" itself. Taken on
its own, the phrase doesn't necessarily pronounce whether the theories
themselves are true or false. But there's no doubt that it has taken on a
negative cast, evoking a frenzied paranoiac sitting in a basement before
a wall of illegible, scribbled notes, his protective tinfoil hat firmly
clamped onto his head. Some of that impression comes from Hofstadter,
whose essay is incessantly cited and used, in my experience, to promote
a mocking and unsympathetic view of people who buy into conspiratorial ideas.

If you were paranoid, you might think there is something at work
in the use of the term "conspiracy theory." Something *sinister*, perhaps?
Most academics agree that the term came into academic use in the 1950s
and entered the popular lexicon in the 1960s, although Karl Popper's
The Open Society and Its Enemies, published in 1945, uses it ten separate times. According to Robert Blaskiewicz of the Committee for Skeptical Inquiry, there are instances of the phrase being used as far back as
1870, and in 1890 and 1909 it appeared in popular periodicals, medical texts, and the *Oxford English Dictionary*.

But if you spend any time at all in this conspiracy world, you will
hear that the term itself was created by the CIA to discredit people who
get too close to the truth. The notion was promoted most prominently
by Lance deHaven-Smith of Florida State University, who in a 2013
book proposed that the CIA came up with the phrase to undermine anyone who questioned the official story of the Kennedy assassination. It
was part of what he called "a whisper campaign against critics of the
Warren Commission," whose investigation JFK truthers have found

unsatisfactory and obfuscatory for decades. DeHaven-Smith and others point to a batch of Warren Commission documents released to the *New York Times* under a FOIA request in 1976. A CIA memo included in the documents showed that the agency was indeed concerned with alternate theories of the assassination, and with "countering and discrediting them," it said, "so as to inhibit the circulation of such claims in other countries."

Though the term was used long before he claims it was, there's still some degree of truth to deHaven-Smith's premise, according to Kathryn Olmsted. Public officials began adopting the term only "on a regular basis in the late '60s in reference to the Kennedy assassination," she said. "There might have been isolated incidents before then, but it wasn't widespread."

To this day, calling someone a conspiracy theorist remains a fast way to offend them and, as a journalist, confirm that you're part of the biased lamestream sheeple media planning a hit job on ideas they hold dear. I used the term on Twitter. That was a bad idea in that it led to the bizarre experience of being attacked for the contents of this book well before most of it existed. "At least we're trying to get to the truth," wrote one guy, the proprietor of a series of minor-league conspiracy-oriented websites as well as a clothing line of conspiracy T-shirts, modeled by pantless women. He sent increasingly outraged messages on every social media platform known to humans, imploring me to look beyond whatever my handlers/backers/government masters had told me to find.

"If there is fundamentally underlying foundations of information that the public believes to be true, I do not expect you to understand the cult that you may be a part of," he wrote, a little confusingly. "Science has turned into science fiction, history has been re-figured and you make fun of the people trying to heal. I believe in fair criticism, but find nearly only incredibly disingenuous hit pieces from the MSM sources you're connected with. They wouldn't run the pieces if you weren't making fun of us, but I'm seriously interested how far you are willing to deny some of the things you have researched."

This is a popular view: *they* will let me write about conspiracy theorists only if I make fun of them; the mainstream media and my handlers are all engaged in stigmatizing and discrediting people who get too close to the truth. People in the very deep end of the conspiracy pool have a Sisyphean view of themselves, perpetually rolling a boulder of truth up a hill, only to have the spiteful masses shove it back down again. One woman, named Raquel, a sixty-one-year-old Holocaust denier living in the Southwest, became a more-or-less friendly Twitter correspondent; she wanted to make sure I wasn't writing about "stupid conspiracies" or dismissing evidence out of hand.

"There's a lot of misinformation out there," she told me, much of it government-produced. Raquel also had theories about September 11, JFK, and the killing of his brother Robert F. Kennedy, but her main thing was the Holocaust; she was polite even after I let her know that I am Jewish and believe quite firmly that it happened. Raquel was at pains to show that conspiracism doesn't have to amount to pessimism or despair or inaction; she'd even come up with a scheme to save humanity. "My plan to save the world was to abolish money, law and the state boundaries," she wrote. That didn't work; she makes a living these days in a business connected to tax liens.

Conspiracy theorists prefer other descriptions, such as researchers, independent journalists, or seekers. A popular variant is members of the "truth community" or the "research community." And the truth community in the United States is very, very large, a size that is reflected in the rich ecosystem of conspiracy-centric "alternative" news that attracts significant audiences. Conspiracy theories became a hot product even more directly marketable with the rise of talk radio and more recently with YouTube, which has become a haven for armies of would-be Alex Joneses, pushing every conceivable narrative angle possible in winding videos for audiences that sometimes reach into the millions.

Between talk radio and YouTube, e-fields of conspiracy-peddling websites and message boards have sprouted: Before It's News, God-like Productions, corners of Reddit, The Conservative Treehouse, and WorldNetDaily, one of the very oldest conspiracy outlets, that's been able to keep a surprisingly loyal audience for a very long time. WND was founded twenty years ago by Joseph Farah, who wanted to make news from a "Judeo-Christian perspective." He envisaged WND serving the same function as any other news service: "The idea for WND was to return to what had once been the 'central role of a free press,' serving as a watchdog on government and other powerful institutions," Farah said.

In that watchdog role, WND spread stories about Obama's foreign birth, FEMA camps, and any number of other questionable ideas. Farah argues, though, that he's not the one making stuff up. "I deplore fake news," he wrote to me, "which is a real phenomenon in what you would call 'mainstream' sources like CNN, the New York Times and the Washington Post, as well as in the news media." He didn't consider that he himself promoted conspiracy theories—despite absolutely, definitively promoting conspiracy theories.

"Sometimes, they turn out to be right," he insisted.

The problem isn't that conspiracy theories are worse today than in the past, since they have more or less always been with us, waxing and waning in visibility through the decades. For their book, for instance, Uscinski and Parent analyzed a randomly selected 104,803 letters sent by readers to the New York Times and the Chicago Tribune between 1890 and 2010. They found evidence that conspiracy theories fluctuated in response to times of enormous social upheaval—the first spike was right around the year 1900, during a great acceleration of immigration, urbanization, and industrialization.

The issue, then, isn't the conspiracy theories themselves, which any healthy societal discourse can absorb; we've done so for generations, treating them as a natural and understandable outgrowth of social upheaval and (very) spirited public discussion. The real problem is that an ever-more-efficient conspiracy-information machine has coincided with a very real resurgence in nationalism and white supremacy. We're seeing unholy and shifting alliances of fellow travelers: conspiracy-oriented news sources, white supremacist groups, and so-called alt-right rising stars (generally, people who are willing to espouse nationalism and denounce political correctness but don't like being called Nazis) are all feeding into one another. They share tactics, interview one another, signal-boost one another on social media, and create a cacophonous, self-reinforcing ecology.

The worst corner of this flourishing conspiracy culture amounts to a deeply regressive view of the world. It denounces immigrants as the advance army of some hidden globalist agenda. It calls Black Lives

Matter activists liars and Soros-paid actors, while the victims of mass shootings and their grieving families are condemned as fakes. It confidently announces, as happened in July 2018, that liberals are planning to spring a "Second Civil War" on the country, attacking unsuspecting conservatives as they sleep. (The liberals apparently didn't quite get it together in time to strike, and the much-vaunted war didn't happen.)

And many of the biggest players are virulently sexist: Alex Jones denounced feminism as a globalist plot. Mike Cernovich, a juice-diet-peddling fitness blogger turned men's rights activist who ultimately morphed into one of the bigger conspiracy peddlers in the country, wrote several blog posts on how to coerce unwilling women into sex. He has argued that "date rape doesn't exist" and that men are the victims of a society-wide smear campaign: "Every man is under attack," he once wrote. "Everyone from school teachers, preachers, and media figures tell men we are garbage. We are privileged. We are sinners. We are potential rapists. Resisting the brainwashing takes an act of will."

The figure uniting these disparate groups—the white supremacists, the sexists, the die-hard nationalists—is Donald Trump. He legitimized certain conspiracy theories and theorists in a way that would have been unimaginable before the 2016 election, making "rigged elections" and the Deep State broad subjects of discussion. And nobody since Nixon has better embodied the concept of projection when it comes to conspiracy theories: the Trump campaign has, from the beginning, been dogged by allegations of a literal conspiracy with Russian governmental agents. Trump's brand of wild accusations and a new enemy to target every week looks, in this light, like a very familiar image, a classic defensive dodge of long standing.

But conspiracism won't die when the Trump era ends; it will persist and grow stronger, in large part because of our social stratification, our sense of disenfranchisement from the political system, our low trust in what we now derisively term the "mainstream media." An April 2017 Harvard-Harris poll found that a full 65 percent of voters believe "there is a lot of fake news in the mainstream media," including 80 percent of Republicans, 60 percent of Independents, and 53 percent of Democrats. Eighty-four percent of voters said it's "hard to know what news to believe online." The problem is not limited to the United States: A twenty-eight-country survey released in January 2018 found that twice as many people said they distrusted the media as trusted it, and many reported they were cutting back on news entirely. An erosion of faith in institutions, including media outlets, is global.

We've always been afraid of each other, fearful of the intentions of our neighbors, our government, our media. Some of us are especially prone to seeing ourselves as forces of good, fighting against whatever evil entities are trying to destroy society or religion. Conspiracy theorizing is part of the free exchange of ideas; suggestions that the government crack down on conspiracy thinking have been disastrous and inevitably given rise to new conspiracy theories.

And there's something else resurgent in recent years: conspiracy thinking isn't just for the politically disaffected, the powerless looking to make sense of their position on the social scale. We're seeing conspiracy theories wielded by the strong against the weak, by those in power against those without any. At the same time, politicians now accuse their opponents of being conspiracy theorists, of trafficking in "hysterical" and baseless ideas, even as they deploy similar thinking when it suits them (as in the concept of the Deep State).

Elsewhere, some precincts of conspiracy culture have reached a new scale: monetized, commercialized, and weaponized. There are more and more "conspiracy entrepreneurs"—as Harvard researchers Cass Sunstein and Adrian Vermeule have dubbed them—an army of people created by Twitter and Facebook and YouTube who make a living selling a heady blend of suspicion, hoaxes, and misinformation. Alex Jones and InfoWars is just the largest, most financially lucrative example, but there are thousands of others. They write blogs, teach seminars, promise quick-fix financial and legal packets, and sell nutritional supplements and other magical products meant to counteract the malicious effects of whatever "they" are doing to us.

Conspiracy theorists don't just gather to dissect the moon landing or the JFK assassination. They are deeply enmeshed in global politics, as they have been periodically throughout world history, sometimes to our serious universal detriment. To focus on just one strain of conspiracism, the anti-Semitic kind, think of the *Protocols of the Learned Elders of Zion*, the caricature of Jews as world-controlling "global bankers,"

or Holocaust denial: all are based on the ideas of Jews as secret manip-
ulators of the levers of power.

There is evidence that some disinformation peddlers are influenced
and fed information by governments that find them useful. The American alt-right participated enthusiastically in the dissemination of the
Macron Leaks, a set of partly real, partly forged documents released to
sway the French elections and put the nationalist anti-Semite Marine
Le Pen in power. (Le Pen has long toyed with conspiracy ideas to sway
her base. She's declared that the "enemy of the French people" is "the
world of finance," echoing Jewish-banker stereotypes that still have a
powerful hold in France.) The Macron Leaks failed to have any real
impact on French voters: Le Pen was resoundingly defeated, but her
party, the National Front, remains a legitimate force.

Around the same time, sites such as InfoWars and Before It's News
called chemical attacks in Syria into question, atrocities that were perpetrated by Bashar al-Assad's regime and which killed thousands of
civilians. Both sites suggested the White Helmets, a volunteer civilian
emergency-search-and-rescue organization, had carried out the chemical attacks. Those allegations, which were repeated by the Assad regime
and Russian-sponsored media, served one purpose: to create doubt or
plausible deniability for the Syrian regime against charges of mass
murder.

Global conspiratorial propaganda efforts also reached the United
States: Russian intelligence agencies created pages for fake activist
groups on Facebook and Tumblr, for example, designed to exploit and
exacerbate tensions over police shootings of unarmed black citizens, gun
control, and other hot-button issues.

Further, it became clear in 2017 that people serving in the Trump
administration were feeding information to far-right news outlets.
People such as once-marginal figure Mike Cernovich suddenly broke
news that could have been acquired only via someone in the White
House. The effect is twofold: a fringe figure becomes more credible, and,
more fundamentally, uncertainty proliferates about what is true, who is
trustworthy, who should be listened to. That uncertainty benefits the
reigning power structure and serves to deepen distrust of all blogs,

newspapers, and TV stations—the mainstream media the administration so vocally detests.

Our current conspiracy culture, then, is deeply entwined with the promotion of a radically right-wing and socially regressive worldview, one that elevates strongmen like Assad and Vladimir Putin to venerated positions and advances cherished conservative goals. Denying the death of mass shooting victims serves the gun lobby; denying Assad's chemical warfare supports a set of geopolitical interests; denying that rape and assault exist, are common, and that victims should be believed strengthens a retrograde, sexist culture. In nearly every case, contemporary conspiracy theories aren't random offshoots emerging spontaneously. They are politically useful.

The surge in the prominence of conspiracy sellers and the variety of wares they peddle shows they are a market that's been quietly building itself on the edges of society for decades. It should be no surprise, in the end, that it ultimately broke into the mainstream. The result is a chaotic wonderland where every conspiracy idea, no matter how long dead, dormant, or ridiculous, has a chance to return and flourish. The past couple of years have seen a resurgence of discredited medical treatments—like using apricot pits to cure cancer, or bleach enemas to treat autism—and old hoaxes, such as, again, the *Protocols of the Learned Elders of Zion.* At the same time, our trust in institutions and experts and authority figures—media, government, scientists—hovers at a historic low. No one can be trusted. Everything and every possibility is equally plausible. We no longer have a common set of facts on which to agree, not even the shape of the Earth. That amounts to a power vacuum, which creates an opportunity for someone—or many someones—to seize control and promote their own narratives and their own truths.

2

"NONE OF IT IS CRAZY"

In December 2005, just four months after the levees failed in New Orleans, Dyan French "Mama D" Cole took her seat before a congressional panel and told the representatives that there had been a bomb.

"I was on my front porch," she said. "I have witnesses that they bombed the walls of the levee. *Boom! Boom!* Mister, I'll never forget it." She added, a few moments later, "Debris that is in front of my door will testify to that. So what do we mean," she asked, "when we say the levee was 'breached'?"

French was a beloved and well-known New Orleans community activist, and at her appearance before Congress she was a fearsome vision in purple: a deep eggplant sweater, a lavender scarf wrapped around her waist-length graying dreadlocks, and, as the hearing wore on, a look of quiet contempt for Republican Christopher Shays, who didn't appear to believe her.

"I don't want to be offensive when you've gone through such incredible challenges," Shays told French and a group of other black New Orleans residents who had come to testify on the government's response to Hurricane Katrina. With his face pinkening to match his pink shirt, he did, in fact, sound pretty condescending. Referring to claims the panelists were making about the events following the storm, he declared, "I just frankly don't believe it." Mama D's expression was stony.

Right up until her death in 2017, at age seventy-two, Mama D insisted that the levees had been deliberately bombed as Katrina raged. While there's no evidence that the levee was bombed, and far more persuasive proof that it failed to hold at a number of different points, the bombing theory has retained currency in parts of black America. The idea is rooted in two things: an infamous 1927 decision in New Orleans to dynamite the levees; and a long-standing, multipronged suspicion that the federal government has engaged in depopulation schemes aimed at black citizens. In a TV interview a couple of years after Katrina, filmmaker Spike Lee said plainly, "I don't find it too farfetched that they tried to displace all the black people out of New Orleans."

Some people who propagated the levee-bombing theory explicitly cited the Great Mississippi Flood of 1927, when levees were blown up—but to save New Orleans, not to drown it. As the flood threatened the city, local leaders decided to take drastic action: to relieve the threat of a levee break within the city proper, engineers used several tons of dynamite to destroy the Mississippi River levee in the unincorporated community of Caernarvon, Louisiana. They promised to reimburse the people in the region who would lose their homes.

The explosion sent the floodwaters surging across the lower St. Bernard and Plaquemines Parishes, where thousands of poor black people lived, many of them sharecroppers eking out a subsistence living. As predicted, their homes and everything they had managed to scrape together were washed away. Blues legend Charley Patton captured what happened next in "High Water Everywhere, Part 1," recorded in 1929:

I would go to the hill country / But they got me barred.

Dr. Luther Brown, retired founding director of the Delta Center for Culture and Learning at Delta State University in Mississippi, explained to NPR that Patton was referring to the segregation laws of the time:

"He'd like to get out of the Delta and find higher ground, but he's not allowed to." While white citizens were free to seek safety, black families huddled together as the storm drew closer:

> Backwater at Blytheville, backed up all around
> Backwater at Blytheville, done struck Joiner town
> It was fifty families and children. Tough luck, they can drown

More than half a million people living along the lower Mississippi were left homeless. While many, often white, families began to rebuild or moved into indoor relief camps, black families found themselves crowded into desolate outdoor camps, often with inadequate food and shelter. According to the Colored Advisory Commission, many black displaced people said they were prevented from leaving the camps by armed members of the National Guard, something that didn't happen at the camps for white families. In other cases, homelessness and hopelessness forced people to leave the region entirely. The Great Mississippi Flood triggered one of the largest mass migrations in U.S. history and is cited in scores of blues songs. Across the region, between two hundred fifty and one thousand people are estimated to have died in the flooding; we don't know how many of them were put in harm's way by the decision to dynamite the levee at Caernarvon. One prominent black businessman, Sidney Dillon Redmond, later complained in a letter to President Calvin Coolidge that black workers were forced at gunpoint to keep working atop the levee, even as white people and mules began to be evacuated.

The Great Mississippi Flood lives vividly in the collective memory of the region: in 1965, during Hurricane Betsy, when the levees were breached by storm waters surging into Lake Pontchartrain, some New Orleans residents again felt certain that city leaders had blown the levees to save the wealthier parts of town. Then, too, according to local lore, survivors said they heard explosions that sounded like dynamite. In 2006, New Orleans rapper Lil Wayne released "Georgia . . . Bush," a song in which he made the suspicion plain:

I know some folk that live by the levee
That keep on telling me they heard explosions
Same shit happened back in Hurricane Betsy

It was natural that in the aftermath of Katrina, the past would come to mind, especially for people who felt sure they had heard the sound of an explosion. History repeated itself in the most traumatic ways: even the desolate relief camps of the Great Mississippi Flood were echoed during Katrina at the Morial Convention Center and the Superdome, which in the days following the storm were notoriously overcrowded, poorly staffed, and squalid, with substandard sanitation and medical care. New Orleans resident Leah Hodges told the House Committee that her family was taken to a camp that was even worse.

"We were dropped off at a site where we were fenced in and penned in with military vehicles," she testified. "The armed military personnel brought in dogs. There we were subjected to conditions only comparable to a concentration camp." Hodges added, "People died in the camp. We saw the bodies lying there. They were all about detention, as if it were Iraq, like we were foreigners and they were fighting a war. They implemented warlike conditions. They treated us worse than prisoners of war. Even prisoners of war have rights under the Geneva Convention."

And then there is the uncomfortable fact that after the storm, people from historically black neighborhoods were indeed displaced. Post-Katrina New Orleans was rebuilt with a focus on the wealthier, whiter areas. An Army Corps of Engineers map showed that only twelve out of twenty-eight flood-prone (mostly black, mostly poor) neighborhoods were less likely to flood than they had been before the storm. Public housing, which served a lower-income, predominantly black population, was, in several neighborhoods, not reopened even after being declared safe.

"There is a real question of equity and justice in terms of what neighborhoods are being assisted," William P. Quigley, a civil rights activist and law professor at Loyola University of New Orleans, told the *Chicago Tribune*. "There is a sense that by their actions, our public officials are indicating that some people are more welcome back to New Orleans than others."

THE ATTENTION TO CONSPIRACY THEORIES AND THEIR IMPACT TENDS TO focus on those believed by mostly white Americans: Pizzagate, for example, is a very white phenomenon, as is birtherism and the claim that climate change is a hoax. The most visible aspects of conspiracy culture can seem overwhelmingly white: people like Alex Jones and Glenn Beck, or sites like Drudge Report and WorldNetDaily, don't explicitly appeal to white audiences. But their fulminations about "thugs" or President Obama or organizations like Black Lives Matter (Jones has said the activist group is designed to "destroy America") make it difficult to imagine black Americans feeling welcome.

Yet a variety of studies going back decades show that in the past, at least, conspiratorial beliefs were slightly more common among black and, to a lesser extent, Latinx communities. In 1994, Rutgers sociology professor Ted Goertzel wrote that "minority status" was strongly correlated with a belief in conspiracy theories. So was what he called "anomia," a belief in the breakdown of the social order, characterized by three attitudes: "The belief that the situation of the average person is getting worse, that it is hardly fair to bring a child into today's world, and that most public officials are not interested in the average man."

Goertzel found that black and Latinx people were more likely to display anomia and what he called "low levels of interpersonal trust," which are positive indicators of a belief in conspiracy theories; so was answering affirmatively to the question, "Thinking about the next 12 months, how likely do you think it is that you will lose your job or be laid off?" That pattern has more or less held true. "In relation to whites," Uscinski and Parent wrote in 2014, "being black or Hispanic is a significant and positive predictor of conspiratorial predispositions when accounting for level of educational attainment and family income."

Uscinski and Parent have also argued that conspiracy theories are for "losers," meaning they are coping mechanisms to deal with perceived threats that "tend to resonate when groups are suffering from loss, weakness or disunity." Thus it would make sense that marginalized ethnic or religious groups would be predisposed to conspiracy thinking: their experiences of the social order make them more inclined to see conspiracies as possible.

But Uscinski and Parent claimed that the predisposition among African Americans seems to have faded over time. "We find that older blacks are more conspiratorial than younger blacks, presumably because they experienced more discrimination and were socialized by parents who experienced more discrimination," they wrote in 2011. "With the election of Barack Obama and the other strides blacks have made up the social ladder, we expect blacks to become less conspiratorial over time as they gain power." But that logic is, frankly, naive: it relied on the assumption that American society was steadily becoming more just and that young black and brown people would naturally face less discrimination and institutional injustice than their parents and grandparents.

Richard Hofstadter was inclined to pathologize conspiracy thinking: he talked about the "paranoid style" as a fundamental sickness of the mind. It was distinguished from the paranoia of individuals—"a chronic mental disorder characterized by systematized delusions of persecution and of one's own greatness"—but only by degree. The spokesman for the paranoid style, he wrote, sees not himself as under attack, "but a nation, a culture, a way of life whose fate affects not himself alone but millions of others."

But Hofstadter never quite reckoned with groups of people who have well-founded grounds for mistrust, even as he recognized America's tendency to demonize and scapegoat Jews, Catholics, Masons, and "Negroes." There's often (though not always) some relationship in America between conspiracy theory and actual conspiracy, between the shadows on the cave wall and the shape of the thing itself. But that relationship tends to be more direct where black America is concerned. Like many conspiracies particular to black Americans, the levee-bombing idea has its roots in generations of genuine injustice, cover-ups, and human rights abuses so horrific the wounds are still open generations later.

We have only to look at the early 1960s, when Hofstadter himself was writing, for proof. We now know that the federal government plotted to undermine its own citizens, with the FBI secretly plotting against black activists, fearful of the political and social power those groups could amass if left unchecked. In 1964, Martin Luther King, Jr., received an anonymous letter that called him evil, abnormal, and an animal, and threatened to expose his sexual affairs.

"There is only one thing left for you to do," the letter read. "You know what it is. You have just 34 days in which to do it (this exact number has been selected for a specific reason, it has definite practical significance). You are done." He was warned: "There is but one way out for you. You better take it before your filthy abnormal fraudulent self is bared to the nation."

King understood that the letter was urging him to commit suicide. He quietly told his friends and advisors that he believed it had been sent by the FBI at the direction of J. Edgar Hoover. King was right: in the 1970s, evidence suggested that the agency was behind the letter, and in 2014, reporter Beverly Gage found a copy, "a full, uncensored version," she wrote, tucked away in Hoover's official and confidential files at the National Archives.

King was far from the FBI's only target during the civil rights era. As the Black Panthers rose to prominence in the 1970s, the agency used disinformation, plants, and informants to create division within the group and with other activist organizations such as the Young Lords, with whom the Panthers had begun to form an alliance. In March 1971, the FBI's outrages were exposed by a group of burglars who broke into an agency field office in Pennsylvania, where they found proof that the Panther operation was part of what the FBI dubbed COINTELPRO (Counterintelligence Program), a grim and extensive campaign to sow distrust among activist groups and undermine civil rights leaders, political organizers, and suspected Communists. The burglars also found proof there that the King letter was written by the FBI.

Additionally, the FBI used paid informants to infiltrate the American Indian Movement throughout the 1970s. The AIM accused the FBI of using agents provocateurs to disrupt the movement, fomenting violence and division and suggesting illegal activities—that was one of the hallmarks of COINTELPRO. And in 2012, in an interview on National Public Radio, AIM member Milo Yellowhair talked about the movement's suspicions that the feds were behind a string of deaths on the Pine Ridge reservation in South Dakota throughout the 1970s and his belief that during that time they had worked with the tribal police to assault, murder, and disappear activists. "There had been a tremendous amount of carnage on the reservation . . . it was almost a daily occurrence, when people were disappearing or died or were found dead," Yellowhair said. "We always called it a 'reign of terror.'" (The FBI denied any role in the deaths, many of which remain officially unsolved. One, the execution-style shooting of Anna Mae Pictou Aquash, a thirty-year-old AIM leader, was eventually semi-solved when two AIM members were convicted of her murder. Arlo Looking Cloud confessed to the crime, while John Graham maintained his innocence and tried unsuccessfully to appeal his conviction.)

A Senate investigation in the mid-1970s revealed more information about COINTELPRO's activities and generated fairly widespread public fury. According to the FBI, everything changed after that. In 2014, the agency told the *New York Times* that such mass surveillance and interference with the lives and civil liberties of activist groups wouldn't happen today. The exposure of COINTELPRO, a spokesperson told the paper, "contributed to changes to how the F.B.I. identified and addressed domestic security threats, leading to reform of the F.B.I.'s intelligence policies and practices and the creation of investigative guidelines by the Department of Justice."

Not that many changes, though: in 2010, the Department of Justice's Office of the Inspector General released a report revealing FBI investigations into several activist groups initiated on "factually weak" grounds. The groups included PETA, the Thomas Merton Center in Pittsburgh (a social justice hub), Greenpeace, the Catholic Worker Movement (a long-standing pacifist organization), and a Quaker peace activist named Glen Milner. The investigations were tagged as domestic terror probes, even when the supposed crimes were on the lines of trespassing or vandalism. This meant that people were improperly placed on terror watchlists for doing things like participating in First Amendment–protected antiwar protests. To investigate a 2002 antiwar rally organized by the Thomas Merton Center, the FBI had claimed it had evidence of a possible terrorism link. The OIG report derided the surveillance as "an ill-conceived project on a slow work day." And in 2013, Edward Snowden's revelations of the National Security Agency's warrantless wiretapping of American citizens were seen by many as yet more proof that state institutions were not to be trusted.

Under the guise of national security, the FBI and other agencies also made a point of targeting Muslims, among other minorities. Consider the way the government responded to Black Lives Matter and Native-led environmental activism, such as the opposition to building the Dakota Access Pipeline through the Standing Rock Sioux Reservation. The movement at Standing Rock was allegedly infiltrated by private security contractors from a company called TigerSwan, according to reporting from The Intercept; those contractors were hired by Energy Transfer Partners, the company building the pipeline, to gather information on the water protectors that would later be used to file a lawsuit accusing activist groups of conspiracy. The TigerSwan contractors also passed information on the protesters to state, local, and federal law enforcement agencies, including collecting photo and video evidence intended to be used in future prosecutions. A constellation of other federal agencies were, at the very least, monitoring the Standing Rock demonstrations and gathering information on the water protectors from social media, including the FBI, the Department of Homeland Security, the Justice Department, the Marshals Service, and the Bureau of Indian Affairs.

In the case of Black Lives Matter, the FBI engaged in a pattern of surveillance. In 2015, the agency used secret spy planes to film a large-scale protest in Baltimore waged in response to the death of a young black man, Freddie Gray, in police custody. The same planes were used to surveil protests in Ferguson, Missouri, over the death of Michael Brown, also an African American. Buzzfeed News reported that the FBI deployed secret spy planes some *thirty-five hundred times* in the second half of 2015. The FBI defended the legality of aerial surveillance, insisting that they weren't gathering footage of particular peaceful activists, but instead using planes to follow "terrorists, spies and serious criminals," per a statement by agency deputy director Mark Giuliano.

Sometimes the agency is more pointed: ahead of the 2016 Republican National Convention in Cleveland, per the *Washington Post,* at least six Black Lives Matter activists said they were contacted by the FBI and essentially warned not to come to the city to protest. The FBI characterized the calls and in-person visits as "community outreach." The FBI also directly contacted at least three people involved in the opposition at Standing Rock; all three people, according to reporting from the *Guardian*, asserted their Fifth Amendment rights against self-incrimination and would not respond to the agents' requests to talk, fearing they were trying to build a criminal case. Red Fawn Fallis, a water protector at Standing Rock, was arrested in October 2016 and charged with firing a gun belonging to her romantic partner, who was, as The Intercept reported, an FBI informant. (The informant, Heath Harmon, told investigators he was hired by the FBI to "observe" the Standing Rock movement, though there is no evidence that he induced Fallis to fire his gun; she fired three shots after being tackled and pinned down by law enforcement officers during a protest, hitting no one.)

State conspiracies involving minority communities have not been limited only to surveillance or disinformation. In the mid-twentieth century, respected national health agencies and institutions saw fit to operate and experiment on ordinary citizens who were too ill-informed, powerless, or poor to resist. Their unwitting subjects included convicts, the mentally ill, and even children in orphanages. In each case, the people disproportionately affected were black; nearly as often, they were Latinx or Native American.

One of the best known of these genuine conspiracies against people of color was forced sterilization, which took place in thirty-two states for most of the twentieth century, with funding from the federal government. In 1907, Indiana passed a law making it legal to sterilize the "feeble-minded," a law that California copied two years later, followed by a cascade of other states in what were usually dubbed "asexualization acts." This system of eugenics—which Hitler vocally admired and would later copy—targeted other undesirables, too.

Some women unknowingly had their reproductive organs removed during C-sections or were threatened with losing their welfare benefits if they didn't accept sterilization. Medical students in southern states carried out what became known as "Mississippi appendectomies," unnecessarily sterilizing mostly black women without their knowledge as a routine part of their training. In California alone, more than twenty thousand people had forced hysterectomies or vasectomies, and the procedure was banned outright only in 1979.

These practices have a long and disturbing half-life. The Urban Indian Health Institute found in 2010 that American Indian and Alaska Native women have higher rates of sterilization than white women, adding that more study would be required to tell them exactly why. The UIHI speculated that it was possible that some of the women surveyed had been "directly affected" by coercive sterilization practices, in which women may have been subject to "harassment or deceit" to get them to agree to the procedure.

The ostensibly voluntary sterilization of prisoners hasn't ceased altogether, either. In 2017, Tennessee judge Sam Benningfield ignited a firestorm of controversy when it was revealed that he offered to reduce inmates' sentences by thirty days if they agreed to a vasectomy or a contraceptive implant. (Curiously, he offered just two days' good time in exchange for taking a class on neonatal development and substance abuse.) The ACLU of Tennessee objected to the practice and pointed out its echoes of the forced sterilization acts of the past; Benningfield responded by saying he hoped to help inmates "get on their feet and make something of themselves."

Then there was the infamous Tuskegee experiment, in which hundreds of black men with syphilis in rural Alabama were intentionally left untreated to track the progress of the disease. The experiment ran from 1932 to 1972, continuing after syphilis was found to be treatable with penicillin in 1945. The Tuskegee victims didn't see justice until a 1973 class-action lawsuit and a subsequent out-of-court settlement awarded them $10 million. The federal government was also forced to establish a medical care program for Tuskegee survivors, as well as for their wives, widows, and offspring. Even then, nobody apologized for Tuskegee until President Bill Clinton did so formally in 1997. The notoriety of the program spurred a host of ethical reforms in how researchers are legally required to deal with human subjects.

Among black communities, Tuskegee became a byword for medical experimentation, neglect, and conspiracy—a particular betrayal that stands for the universal experience. It is not surprising that a history of enslavement, lynching, segregation, surveillance—along with unequal access to housing, education, and jobs—has produced a relationship of distrust between black Americans and their government.

To Dr. John L. Jackson, the dean of the School of Social Policy and Practice at the University of Pennsylvania, Uscinski and Parent's claim that black communities are growing less conspiratorial seemed like wishful thinking. A cultural anthropologist, Jackson has spent a lot of time around conspiracy-leaning black communities across the United States and in Israel (where he studied the African Hebrew Israelites of Jerusalem, a group of polygamous vegans who have thought deeply about ways to achieve eternal life). Jackson's rebuttal of Uscinski and Parent's theory is all of one word: Obama.

"The way African Americans read the eight years of Obama is as this unrelenting and unfair demonization of an otherwise squeaky-clean president," he says. "It almost feels for a lot of folks like it's the quintessential example of the impossibility of being accepted. If Obama didn't have any serious skeletons, yet could be so roundly demonized, the idea is that no one else has a chance."

The most egregious attack on President Obama was itself a conspiracy theory: birtherism, in which a whole lot of people, including the president who followed him, argued that Obama was a secret Kenyan Muslim who had stolen the presidency. It was the most literal (and racist) expression of the idea that an alien force had taken control of the country. Republican congressman Bill Posey even proposed legislation that candidates for president have to include their birth certificate with their filing materials. The birther claims became so loud—due in part to their enthusiastic promotion by Donald Trump—that Obama eventually held a press conference to release his long-form birth certificate.

Birtherism wasn't the only conspiracy theory surrounding Obama's presidency. At his inauguration, Chief Justice John Roberts bungled a few words of the oath of office, which prompted claims that Obama wasn't really president. (Roberts and Obama quickly staged a do-over, just to be on the safe side.)

Beyond the treatment of Obama, Jackson argues that even non-conspiracist black Americans are still aware of the outlines of the most popular suspicions. "There's two or three degrees of separation between a non-conspiracy theorist and conspiracy theorist in black America," he says. "Folks will at least be cognizant of what the claims are. Folks are trafficking in the discourse and know it enough." And, he adds,

"There are moments, even fleetingly, when something happens in the news or an inexplicable occurrence and they're willing to give a head-nod" to some conspiratorial ideas.

The reasons are fairly obvious. "Folks can draw on some pretty significant historical precedents for racialized conspiracies," Jackson noted. Being black in this country comes with a "cultural sensibility that says you have to be cautious." Those precedents explain "all the deep-seated distrust of the medical establishment and criminal justice system. There are ways that folks don't believe that mainstream American society has the best interest of black people at heart. That's not a cockamamie thing." In an interview with *Vice*, rapper Bun B echoed Jackson's view, saying that conspiracy thinking is the result of questioning American history. "If you think of ten things that seem strange and then find evidence for four of them, you start to question the other six," he said. "When people say, 'This is a result of systematic oppression of entire races of people' and then you look at the Tuskegee experiments, you look at Guantanamo Bay, it does give you pause about blindly assuming certain things."

Some groups seek to take advantage of that suspicion, like the Moorish Nation or the Washitaw Nation based in Louisiana, which claims Native American origins and tries to gain tribal rights, usually without success. Most notably there's the Nation of Islam, the black separatist group. In the 1950s and 1960s, its leader, Elijah Muhammad, warned repeatedly against vaccines and other forms of mainstream medical care like birth control, which he called a depopulation scheme and a "death plan." To this day, NOI members are instructed to give their doctors an exemption letter to keep them from mandatory vaccines.

The distrust of vaccines has continued and expanded. In 2015, the NOI teamed up with the larger, mostly white anti-vaccine movement to encourage black families to refuse to vaccinate their children. One California NOI leader, Tony Muhammad, was convinced there is a CDC cover-up of the vaccine-autism connection after meeting with Robert F. Kennedy, Jr. Vaccines are a depopulation scheme, he believes, both in the United States and in African countries. "We are a target," he told me. "The world can go to hell. Black people are a target and it's a shame nobody wants to admit it."

Muhammad's specific claims—that Bill Gates is funding the depopulation effort in Africa through his foundation's vaccine work there—are not remotely true, but his underlying logic was tough to argue with. "We have a *reason* to be suspicious," he said. "Until that situation is handled, I don't trust the government. I don't trust pharmaceutical companies to do their own studies, just like I don't trust police departments to do their own internal investigations. . . . It's all the same."

Others against vaccines—like white conspiracist Mike Adams, the self-appointed Health Ranger—repeat the claims about vaccines and public-health programs in Africa to amplify their U.S. campaign, in the process reinforcing the idea that black people have been targeted for death. In November 2017, Adams sent out an email blast claiming that a recent plague outbreak in ten East African countries was not what it seemed. "Evidence is mounting that the plague outbreak in Africa may be a weaponized depopulation program," Adams wrote. "Globalists everywhere are freaking out over the population explosion across Africa, with over 3 million new African babies born each *month*. Those same globalists are now calling for urgent action to reduce the population across Africa. The plague, it turns out, is the easiest way for them to accomplish that."

Besides vaccines, AIDS conspiracism has also taken deep root in black America. The most common theory is that the CIA created HIV and AIDS in a lab to wipe out black and gay people. (The agency has also been repeatedly accused of dumping heroin and crack in black neighborhoods to prompt addiction and ensnarement in the criminal justice system.) The CIA-AIDS narrative was furthered by a KGB disinformation campaign in the 1980s, Operation INFEKTION, part of the KGB's so-called active measures of disinformation. KGB agents spread the rumor that AIDS was created as a biological weapon in a lab in Fort Detrick, Maryland. The allegations first appeared in a pro-Soviet newspaper in India in 1983, and spread all over the world by 1987; an even more pernicious version of the lie alleged that the virus was spread through "AIDS-oiled condoms," potentially discouraging people from using methods of safer sex. In 1992, the director of the Foreign Intelligence Service, Yevgeny Primakov, acknowledged the KGB had created and advanced those rumors.

The belief that AIDS was created to destroy black communities became widespread in various African countries, too: Zimbabwe's former president Robert Mugabe once described AIDS as a "white man's plot." In 2004, Wangari Maathai, a Kenyan biologist and the first African woman to win the Nobel Peace Prize, called AIDS a biological weapon created to "wipe out the black race." The disease is "not a curse from God to Africans or the black people," she told a group in Nyeri, Kenya. "It is a tool to control them designed by some evil-minded scientists, but we may not know who particularly did" it.

Once again, actual historical conspiracies lend credibility to claims that would otherwise be considered outrageous. "The conspiracy about AIDS is no more or less unbelievable than the Tuskegee experiment," Michael Harriot, a journalist for The Root, pointed out to me.

In 2005, a study published in the *Journal of Acquired Immune Deficiency Syndromes* found that 53 percent of African Americans surveyed said they believed the government was withholding a cure for AIDS from poor people; 27 percent thought AIDS was produced in a government lab; 48 percent called HIV a "man-made virus." However, more intentional conspiracy theories were less common: just 15 percent called AIDS a form of genocide against black people, and only 16 percent said the government created AIDS to control the black population.

But AIDS conspiracy theories are particularly dangerous in that they can lead directly to unsafe sex. The 2005 study found that black men who held conspiratorial beliefs about AIDS were less likely to use safer sex practices. The more a man supported one of these theories, the less likely he was to use a condom. (Women didn't show that tendency.) The researchers also suggested that for men who didn't particularly want to wear a condom in the first place, the conspiracy theories helped serve as justification for declining to slip one on.

AIDS conspiracies in black America are so entrenched that one researcher, Jacob Heller, found people in focus groups making virtually the same claims in 2012 as were made in 1992. "To find a rumor faithfully repeated after two decades demonstrates remarkable durability," he wrote. Heller pointed out that even respected celebrities repeated beliefs in conspiracy theories, sometimes intentionally and sometimes perhaps not: comedian Bill Cosby, in 1991, and actor Will Smith, in 1999, both suggested HIV could have been manmade, while Obama's onetime preacher, Reverend Jeremiah Wright, stated it outright. "The government lied about inventing the HIV virus as a means of genocide against people of color," he roared during a 2003 sermon. "Governments lie!"

Wright repeated those claims in a 2008 appearance at the National Press Club. "Based on this Tuskegee experiment and based on what has happened to Africans in this country, I believe our government is capable of doing anything." (Around then, Wright became such a headache for Obama that the future president denounced his views and cut ties with him. The following year, Wright told an interviewer he hadn't talked to Obama in some time: "Them Jews aren't going to let him talk to me. I told my baby daughter that he'll talk to me in five years when he's a lame duck, or in eight years when he's out of office.")

Beyond medical fears, recent conspiracy theories in black America have focused on the suspicion that the white establishment will cut down any black leader who threatens the status quo. During his confirmation hearings in 1991, future Supreme Court Justice Clarence Thomas thus explained accusations of having sexually harassed Anita Hill, a female subordinate. Thomas told then-senator Joe Biden that the whole thing was a setup, testifying that "someone, some interest group came up with this story" to discredit him. Other people called Hill a "pawn" for some shadowy white cabal focused on destroying a black man before he could rise to power. (The fact that Hill herself was black was somehow elided from the discussion.)

Virtually the same narrative played out in 2015, when accusations mounted against Bill Cosby for what ended up as more than sixty allegations of sexual assault. Cosby eventually stood trial for his alleged crimes against a single accuser, Andrea Constand, and, after a mistrial, was found guilty the second time around. But the Cosby truthers—easily findable on YouTube and Twitter—opined that the allegations were revenge for Cosby having tried to buy NBC in the mid-1990s. "The world really fears black power!" one person wrote in a typical tweet. "Like the Bill Cosby shit and him trying to buy NBC then all of a sudden that rape shit came out." Even Phylicia Rashad, who played Cosby's wife, Clair Huxtable, got in on it. "What you're seeing is the destruction of a legacy," she told *Showbiz 411* blogger Roger Friedman in 2015.

"And I think it's orchestrated." Someone, she added, "is determined to keep Bill Cosby off TV. And it's worked."

The assumption that white America will respond violently to black economic power is, of course, rooted in reality. In Tulsa, Oklahoma, in the early 1900s, a neighborhood called Greenwood became known as the Black Wall Street; it was thriving thanks to the discovery of oil. In 1921, the area's white occupants decided they could no longer endure the sight of financially independent black people. In a horrifying massacre, they used private planes to firebomb the neighborhood's buildings, then killed the fleeing residents with machine guns. More than thirty-five city blocks were leveled, eight hundred people were hospitalized, and at least six thousand people were detained. The National Guard declared thirty people dead, but the Red Cross put the real number at more than three hundred. Even today, the incident is often referred to as the Tulsa Race Riots, suggesting an equal fight between two equally culpable sides.

Every shocking incident in the history of black America has thus paved the way for a related conspiracy theory alive today. The very real government violence against black activist groups in the 1960s—such as the killing of Black Panther leaders Fred Hampton and Mark Clark by the FBI and Chicago police—implanted fear that the state is not above doing the same thing to contemporary activists. Those concerns were urgently heightened after three Black Lives Matter activists from Ferguson, Missouri, were killed in similar ways: Deandre Joshua was found dead in his car in 2014, as were Darren Seals in 2016 and Edward Crawford in 2017. Both Seals's and Joshua's cars had also been lit on fire; local authorities said Crawford's death looked like either an accident or a suicide.

Missouri state senator Maria Chapelle-Nadal, who represents Ferguson, found the deaths troubling. She addressed Crawford's death on the Missouri Senate floor: "I found out this morning another young man from my district died in the same fashion as two or three other people who were active in Ferguson," she said. "The people who were murdered at this point, they were all people who have been seen prominently in the media." In an interview with The Root, she suggested that local militia groups could have targeted the men. And Root columnist Jason Johnson wrote that, at the very least, the killings needed a more serious investigation than he suspected the Ferguson police had given them.

"It is possible to believe that Crawford's death was just an accident," Johnson wrote. "It is possible to believe that he decided to take his own life in full view of other people in the car." (According to a police statement, two witnesses who were in the car with him told police that Crawford was "distraught over personal matters relating to witnesses," rummaged in the backseat, and shot himself in the head in front of them.) "It is also possible," Johnson wrote, "in a town where police claimed that 19-year-old Michael Brown punched out a cop and then charged into a hail of bullets from 30 feet away in broad daylight, that police could be completely lying to cover up some more nefarious cause of death." He added, "There is a long history in America of the police jumping to the conclusion that everything, from shootings to hangings of black people, is a suicide so as not to tug too hard on the strings of violent white supremacy that hold communities together."

Conspiratorial thinking also furnished an explanation for killings in Flint, Michigan, where a mostly black populace was exposed to staggering levels of lead in their drinking water beginning in 2014, when the city started sourcing its water from the Flint River without properly treating it. City and state officials denied there was a problem well after Flint residents began to notice that their water smelled, tasted, and looked peculiar. "This is not an emergency," read a notice from the city sent to residents in July 2015. "If a situation arises where the water is no longer safe to drink, you will be notified within 24 hours."

It took until December 2015—after a battery of tests from independent organizations showed high lead levels in the water and in children's blood—for the governor of Michigan to declare a state of emergency, followed by the federal government. In response, residents began suing the city and the state. One of the first was nineteen-year-old Sasha Avonna Bell, who claimed her toddler had contracted lead poisoning. In April 2016, Bell was found shot to death in her home, along with a friend, Sacorya Renee Reed. This came just three days after a Flint water treatment plant foreman named Matthew McFarland was found dead in his own home by a friend.

Natural News, the conspiracy-oriented, increasingly unhinged "natural health" site edited by Mike Adams, the Health Ranger, baldly called both deaths a cover-up, indicating that the FBI had killed people to conceal the extent of the water crisis. Adams added, "For those who wonder why, as the editor of Natural News, I carry a loaded weapon with me at all times, consider how often whistleblowers who threaten to expose government conspiracy crimes end up dead."

But even mainstream outlets like BET struck a conspiratorial note, running with the headline "Something Terrible Happened to the First Person to Sue Flint Over Water," and saying that Bell's death was "raising concerns." Buried in the piece, one sentence noted that "a suspect" had been arrested, namely Bell's ex-boyfriend Malek Thornton. Thornton pleaded guilty in October 2017 and agreed to testify against a codefendant, Toron Fisher, who he said came with him to the apartment. McFarland, the water treatment foreman, was later found to have died from drug intoxication combined with hypertension; Natural News didn't bother to cover those developments other than to call Thornton "obviously a patsy in all this."

In fact, if you're not looking for strict accuracy, the best, deepest, weirdest discussion of conspiracies and conspiracy theories in black America is just inches away, with the turn of a radio dial or down a YouTube rabbit hole. Conspiracy theories are prevalent in hip-hop, which makes sense: the genre has functioned as a voice, mirror, and social conscience for African Americans for decades. In 1998, in his song "Channel Zero," the rapper Canibus gave a breakneck recitation of fifty years of conspiracy theories. The song manages to touch on mind control, brain implants, and all of our presidents being Masons, as well as containing one of the most incredible rhyming couplets in the history of rap and conspiracy writing:

> *Responsible for launderin' trillions of dollars from the nation*
> *for the construction of underground military installations*
> *Abductions and cattle mutilations*
> *Experiments on human patients*
> *Can take place in several subterranean bases . . .*

Elsewhere in hip-hop, Chris Brown speculated that Ebola might be used as a biological weapon; in the song "Heard 'Em Say," Kanye West claims that the government "administered AIDS"; and Snoop Dogg made a video decrying flu shots. "Fuck that, I'm not getting no flu shots 'cause it's flu season," he declared, adding that he'd be sticking with honey, oranges, and lemons. "I think they're shooting some control in you, some shit to take control of you," he added. "When they have your mind, body, and soul, they going to slow you down a bit. I don't trust it. I'm cool." Another rapper, TI, joined the Nation of Islam and began toting Tony Muhammad, the Nation of Islam's anti-vaccine spokesperson, around with him to radio interviews.

Rap, according to John L. Jackson, is "a medium that can carry conspiracy because it's operating on multiple levels." Although Chuck D of Public Enemy called hip-hop "the black CNN," Jackson cautioned that the lyrics are usually more nuanced than a rookie listener understands. "It's a way to talk about the real world and experiences that don't get thematized," he says, meaning experiences that aren't often reflected in popular culture or dialogue. "But what that obscures is that hip-hop is also a genre where there's a surface meaning that can be sometimes easy to grasp, and—because of the dense use of metaphor and how they use vernacular—there can be latent levels of meaning, and if you listen as a casual fan you won't catch it at all. Embedded all the time is stuff you don't know unless you're very initiated."

The overriding message is that no one could possibly tell black Americans they don't have the right to reasonable suspicion of the government. ("A right to be hostile," too, as Public Enemy put it.) Although the distrust can have grave consequences (as with the rejection of AIDS and vaccines), black Americans and other disenfranchised groups see no reason to let their guard down. "A weird thing about being black is some of it is true and some of it is not," Michael Harriot told me reflectively. "But," he said, "none of it is crazy."

IN A NEW WRINKLE, WE HAVE SEEN EVIDENCE THAT FOREIGN POWERS have harnessed this interplay of truth and suspicion among minorities to exploit for their own ends. In a series of stories, the Daily Beast, the *New York Times,* and Buzzfeed News revealed that the Internet Research Agency, the Russian troll farm, set up fake black and Native activist groups online as part of an apparent effort to stoke division and distrust of the government and each other. During the 2016 elections, Buzzfeed found, the agency backed a website called BlackMattersUS, which positioned itself as a social-justice news site focused "mostly on racism and police brutality."

The *New York Times* reported that a number of Russian-backed Facebook pages were dedicated to stoking every minority-related divide in the country. The pages, which used locally produced articles and news segments, focused on black issues or spread anti-Muslim fake stories, such as one that claimed Muslim immigrants in Michigan were living high on the hog on welfare, providing lavishly for themselves and their multiple wives.

The pages had names like Blacktivist and Being Patriotic, and they paid Facebook to sponsor posts, blasting them directly into the news-feeds of people who were likely to be most receptive to them. Jonathan Albright, research director at Columbia University's Tow Center for Digital Journalism, told the *Times* that the practice amounted to "cultural hacking."

The existence of such fake sites confirms one distressing, permanent point: actual government conspiracies have generated a long afterlife. They linger in the collective memory, give rise to new conspiracy theories, and lay out a detailed, easy-to-follow playbook for fomenting further division and distrust.

The federal government has done little to dispel that distrust. In the Trump administration, with Nazi-affiliated and white supremacist groups indisputably on the rise, the Department of Homeland Security gutted funding for Countering Violent Extremism, an Obama-era program that devoted resources to organizations that fight white supremacist groups and help former members leave the movement. At the same time, the FBI has poured more resources into following those whom they label "black identity extremists."

A leaked memo from the agency written in August 2017 warned that such people might be angry about police officers killing African Americans. "Police brutality against African Americans spurred an increase in premeditated, retaliatory lethal violence against law enforcement," the memo claimed. "And will very likely serve as justification for such violence." The memo never clearly defined the meaning of "black identity extremism." Judging by the examples it cited, the category is an unholy mix of lawful protest against police violence, violent acts against police committed by members of such groups as the Moorish Nation, and lone wolves like Micah Johnson, an Army Reserve soldier who returned from Afghanistan and in 2016 killed five police officers in an ambush in Dallas. The FBI claimed that BIEs "proactively target police" and justify their actions with what the agency called "perceived injustices against African Americans, and in some cases, their identified affiliations with violent extremist groups."

In November 2017, in response to questioning from members of the House Judiciary Committee, Attorney General Jeff Sessions wouldn't say whether he considers Black Lives Matter an extremist group. "I'm not able to comment on that," he told Karen Bass, a black Democratic congresswoman from California. But, he added, "I'm aware that there are groups that do have an extraordinary commitment to their racial identity, and some have even transformed themselves into violent activists."

Bass asked whether the Ku Klux Klan or neo-Nazis would be identified as "white identity extremists." Sessions attempted to avoid answering. "I didn't follow that question," he responded. Eventually, after a pained few minutes, he admitted the FBI hadn't produced a report on any white extremist groups.

When *Foreign Policy* published the leaked memo, one former FBI agent, Michael German—putting wind in the sails of conspiracy theorists everywhere—said plainly that the agency had identified a movement that wasn't real to justify ramping up enforcement activities.

"Basically," he said, "it's black people who scare them."

3

NOCTURNAL RITUAL PIZZA PARTY

ON A STUFFY, WINDLESS MARCH DAY IN 2017, I HEADED TO LAFAYETTE Park in Washington, DC, to join a bunch of people attentively facing a tiny outdoor stage, where a self-proclaimed child-abuse investigator named Neil Wolfe was urging the hidden, unrepentant molesters in government to grovel for their lives.

"This is my message to you," Wolfe boomed. "If you want to be shown mercy by humanity when all this goes full fold, I strongly suggest that you beg for forgiveness!" Wolfe had on a pinstripe shirt, saggy navy pants, beat-up loafers, and wraparound black shades that he never removed. Over the course of the afternoon, his neck reddened, both from sunburn and from agitation.

"Only when those terms of surrender are met do I feel that it's even reasonable for some of us to ask humanity to please try to muster some forgiveness in your heart for these people," he roared, a little confusingly. His point was clarified by banners fluttering onstage around him, decorated with solemn black-and-white images of terrified children and further instructions.

TERMS OF SURRENDER, one read. RELEASE ALL CHILDREN, SURREN-
DER AND CONFESS TO AUTHORITIES, BEG FOR FORGIVENESS. The beg-
ging seemed to be key.

Lafayette Square is just across the street from the White House, and
the people in the crowd were die-hard believers in Pizzagate, the theory
(I would get in trouble several times that day for calling it one) that
Comet Ping Pong, a pizza place in northwest DC, was the site of a child-
sex-trafficking ring—one with ties to Hillary Clinton.

The day of the rally it had been five months since John Podesta,
Clinton's campaign chairman, had his email hacked. Soon after, a few
motivated and suspicious individuals combing through Podesta's missives decided that references to pizza and hot dogs were in fact code
words for sexually abusing children: "cheese" for a little girl, "pasta"
for a little boy, "map" for semen, and "sauce" for an orgy. ("Cheese
pizza," the theorists reasoned, does start with the same letters as "child
porn.")

Pizzagate, as investigative reporter Amanda Robb outlined in a story
in *Rolling Stone*, is a roaring and impossibly strange conspiracy theory,
born from the faint embers of a Facebook post written in October 2016
by a sixty-year-old Missouri attorney named Cynthia Campbell. The
day before before Campbell wrote her post, FBI director James Comey
had announced that he was reopening an investigation into Clinton's
private email server. Data from that server had been found on a laptop
used by Anthony Weiner, an ex-Congressman disgraced for sending sexually explicit texts to a fifteen-year-old. At the time, Weiner was married to Clinton's top aide, Huma Abedin, which explained the data's
appearance on the laptop.

But according to Cynthia Campbell, the real scandal, and the actual
target, was far bigger and worse than private servers and underage
sexting.

"My NYPD source said it's much more vile and serious than classified material on Weiner's device," Campbell wrote on Facebook under
the name Carmen Katz. She accused both Clintons, husband and wife,
of traveling with billionaire pedophile Jeffrey Epstein on his private
plane. Further, Campbell claimed that on these trips Hillary had participated in sexual crimes against children. "The email [*sic*] DETAIL the

trips made by Weiner, Bill and Hillary on . . . the Lolita Express. Yup, Hillary has a well-documented predilection for underage girls. . . . We're talking an international child enslavement and sex ring."

Campbell wasn't the original source for the various pieces of her story, however. The *Rolling Stone* report shows that aspects of it had appeared all over the Internet, seeded on message boards and Twitter. (And, for what it's worth, one piece of it was sort of true: Bill Clinton had, in fact, traveled on Epstein's plane, according to flight logs published by several media outlets; Hillary had not.) Campbell had likely picked up the different strands from posts on 4Chan and THEE Rant, a forum for NYPD officers that is also, at times, fertile ground for right-leaning conspiracy theories. One post on the Weiner investigation traveled from THEE Rant to a law-enforcement Facebook group and then to Twitter, where it was energetically shared by a group of users that experts believe were bots: accounts tweeting too frequently and too widely to be real people.

Campbell was the first actual, inarguably real human to weave all the threads together into a tale of sex trafficking, cover-ups, and Hillary Clinton's inextricable involvement in it all. After she shared her story, another probable bot account picked it up, adding, "I have been hearing the same thing from my NYPD buddies too. Next couple days will be interesting!"

They were indeed. Four days after Campbell put up her post, it started to spread across the Internet. Douglas Hagmann, a self-proclaimed private investigator and the host of a conspiracy-leaning podcast, took up the story. Hagmann came on conspiracy's biggest megaphone, InfoWars, to tell Alex Jones about the scandal. "The most disgusting aspect of this is the sexual angle," Hagmann said. "I don't want to be graphic or gross here. . . . Based on my source, Hillary did in fact participate on some of the junkets on the Lolita Express."

Google searches for "Hillary" and "pedophile" skyrocketed and the story stampeded forward at terminal speed. Online sleuths returned to Podesta's hacked emails, which had been made public on WikiLeaks, and after decoding the references to "cheese" and "sauce," they arrived at the conclusion that Clinton and Podesta were part of a global child-sex-abuse ring. Reddit detectives determined that its physical center was the

Comet Ping Pong pizza parlor, owned by James Alefantis, a restaurateur who once dated Democratic fundraiser and author David Brock and a friend of Podesta's mentioned in the emails. (Reddit's Pizzagate board was eventually shut down by the site for posting people's personal information—phone numbers, addresses—and soon migrated to Voat, another message board site, with even less oversight.)

Within the space of five weeks, *Rolling Stone* reported, Pizzagate "was shared roughly 1.4 million times by more than a quarter of a million accounts," a potent and bizarre mix of human actors and possible bots, until it had become an exceedingly volatile global phenomenon. And at the end of that time, one Edgar Maddison Welch, a twenty-eight-year-old from North Carolina, arrived at Comet's doors.

According to a federal indictment, on December 1, 2016, Welch was at home in Salisbury, North Carolina, when he texted his girlfriend, telling her he'd been watching YouTube videos about Pizzagate and that it was making him "sick." Later that night and the next day, he texted with a friend, identified in court documents as C.

At one point, Welch asked C whether he had any "Army buddies" nearby. When C said yes, Welch asked, "He down for the cause?"

It depended on the cause, C said. "Raiding a pedo ring," Welch responded, "possibly sacraficing [*sic*] the lives of a few for the lives of many. Standing up against a corrupt system that kidnaps, tortures and rapes babies and children in our own backyard . . . defending the next generation of kids, our kids, from ever having to experience this kind of evil themselves[.] I'm sorry bro, but I'm tired of turning the channel and hoping someone does something and being thankful it's not my family. One day it will be our families. The world is too afraid to act and I'm too stubborn not to[.]"

Over the next few days, according to text messages and affidavits, Welch fought with his girlfriend and his best friend; the girlfriend implored him not to do anything "stupid" and the best friend, C, told Welch to go in with a camera instead of a gun, if he insisted on visiting Comet at all.

In the end, for reasons that aren't fully clear, Welch went alone. On December 4 he began a grim solo mission, a three-hundred-fifty-mile drive from Salisbury to Washington, DC, which he later told police he'd made straight through. At 9:00 a.m. that day, his girlfriend, who is not the mother of his children, woke to discover that Welch had left them sleeping with her in her house. "I can't believe you left me here alone with them the first day I'm fully detoxing," she texted him. She called what he was doing "your selfish adventure."

At 11:00 a.m., Welch made a video while driving, balancing his cell phone against the dashboard. He wore a black beanie and a black jacket, looking solemn, two tree-shaped car fresheners bouncing as he spoke into the phone. He told his family he loved them, he hoped he'd showed that love, and he hoped he would be able to tell them again in person someday. "And if not," he added, staring into the camera, "don't ever forget it."

Welch covered the journey in about six hours. He later told a *New York Times* reporter in a jailhouse interview that he merely wanted to give the restaurant "a closer look" and "shine some light on it." But as he drove closer to Washington, his mood darkened. He felt his heart breaking, he said to the *Times*, "over the thought of innocent people suffering."

Welch entered Comet Ping Pong a little before 3:00 p.m. He had two guns with him, one an AR-15, which he pointed at an employee, who fled. As Comet's staff gathered the patrons from their tables and quickly led everyone outside, Welch stalked the restaurant with his guns. He tried to get into a locked room, and when that failed, fired a shot through the lock, hitting a computer tower inside.

Welch searched the restaurant, but when he found no children there—indeed, Comet doesn't even have a basement, where they were rumored to be held—he put down his guns in two separate locations, stripped off his sweatshirt, walked outside in a T-shirt and jeans, and surrendered to the police.

"The intel on this wasn't 100 percent," he later told the *Times*. He refused to dismiss the stories entirely, the paper wrote, pointing out that "child slavery is a worldwide phenomenon."

FOR MOST PEOPLE, PIZZAGATE WAS AN ODD HEADLINE, A BIT OF LATE-night joke fodder that quickly receded, plowed under by the chaotic daily tide of the Trump presidency. As a movement of believers, it's small. But it is important if we want to understand the spread and reach of even the most far-fetched conspiratorial ideas.

We suspect the rumor that became Pizzagate—Cynthia Campbell's Facebook post—had sophisticated help to spread it across the country and the globe. But disinformation doesn't grow from a few smoldering embers into a bonfire only because of Twitter bots—or even through the encouragement of online conspiracy celebrities. Pizzagate represents a type of story to which Americans are particularly susceptible, a religiously based hysteria and conspiracism featuring the Devil and children and sexual horror. Different versions of the same scenario have dogged us from the Salem witch trials through the Satanic Panic of the 1980s and '90s.

This specific variant landed in fertile ground, and then mushroomed into something that, according to believers, had global implications. By the time of the gathering in Lafayette Park, Pizzagaters had taken to calling the scandal "Pedogate" and saw it not as a localized case of sexual abuse, or even a high-level cover-up among rapacious American politicians, but as a vast global conspiracy of child molesters embedded in government, the police, the armed forces, and the United Nations, with some ritual abuse thrown in to make it even more horrific. They wanted action from President Trump, and they wanted it fast. Their suspicions had spread far: in my travels through the conspiracy-leaning world, I heard over and over that the government was full of secret pedophiles; the rumor became an article of faith for those who considered themselves truly in the know.

If you heard about any of this beyond the saga of Edgar Welch, it might have been thanks to the tireless vlogging of David Seaman, a young independent journalist. Seaman used to write mostly about Bitcoin, but in the months before the DC rally he developed a large and rabidly devoted following as the king of Pizzagate. He was, once upon a time, an Internet-marketing expert—he wrote a book called *Dirty Little Secrets of Buzz: How to Attract Massive Attention for Your Business, Your Product, or Yourself.* He subsequently became a reporter for *The Street*, a financial publication, and then a contributor to the Huffington Post, a time he now refers to, a little derisively, as his stint in "corporate media." (Curiously, he was also briefly an intern at Jezebel, the feminist site where I also worked, though our time there didn't overlap.)

Seaman gets very angry if you mention any of that; he sees it as an attempt to discredit him and distract from his intense crusade to take down pedophiles. He made YouTube videos proclaiming that Podesta and a myriad of other public figures were child abusers, and set up a website called FULCRUM, which, as best I could tell, was a news service consisting solely of himself, with content composed of links to his YouTube videos. In the videos, which were fascinating to watch, Seaman alternates between calm, almost monotonal delivery and barely concealed rage, denouncing his targets as "baby rapists," "sick people," and—referring to the media and anyone who argues with him online— "hysterical paid trolls."

In terms of Pizzagate's spread across the web, though, no one had bigger influence than Alex Jones, who promoted the theory right up until the moment it threatened to get him in legal and financial trouble. "The notion of members of the elite being connected to child pedophile rings," wrote Paul Joseph Watson of InfoWars, "is a manifestly provable fact."

Provable or not, Jones, facing the threat of litigation, eventually retracted his story about Comet Ping Pong's connection to Pizzagate. "I want our viewers and listeners to know that we regret any negative impact our commentaries may have had on Mr. Alefantis, Comet Ping Pong, or its employees," he said on air, in an uncharacteristically sober tone. Jones also deleted several Pizzagate-related videos from InfoWars, including one in which he encouraged people to "personally investi-. gate" Comet Ping Pong. (This was one of two retractions he was forced to make in the space of two months: in May 2017, he apologized for his false claim about Chobani importing Syrian rapists to Idaho.) Jones's separation from the Pizzagate faithful came just one day before the DC rally, but the event showed no sign of demoralization.

THE ATTENDEES IN LAFAYETTE PARK WERE ABUZZ WITH THE NEWS THAT Seaman would be there to deliver a speech. His fans recognized the urgency of his quest.

"We need an investigation," a woman named Angel told me patiently. A casino worker in her midforties, she'd driven all the way to DC to hold a neat hand-lettered sign featuring a picture of a Comet staff member's toddler daughter, her hands taped to a table with heavy white masking tape. "We can't call people innocent without an investigation."

Given that she believes the federal government is involved in the sex-ring cover-up, who should do the investigating? I asked her.

"We need an unbiased investigator," she said, just as patiently.

Like a lot of people I spoke to, Angel was fairly certain there are no longer any children in the basement or back rooms of Comet Ping Pong.

"I'm sure they've cleaned themselves up to the point where if you look, there's nothing there," she told me.

"They use the word 'conspiracy' as a catchall to delegitimize any questions about anything," complained a woman standing next to Angel wearing a black BENGHAZI MATTERS T-shirt and an NRA hat. Refusing to tell me her name—I was instructed to call her "LaLa"—the woman went on, vacillating between rage at the press and a slightly irritable but basically kind desire to set me on the right path.

"This is why Trump has emerged as someone people trust," she said. "He calls things out as he sees them. And maybe these conspiracies aren't just theories, they're actually truths? That have been going on since the beginning of time?"

"*Amen,*" Angel responded forcefully. "Having sex with babies and children, they say it gives them power." She shook her head. "They get what they want in life."

She produced a list of primary sources: an *Oprah* episode from the 1990s about a woman who was sexually abused by a cult virtually her whole life, a *Dr. Phil* episode from earlier in the week, and the "pedo rings" in England, by which I think she meant the very real sex abuse scandal uncovered a few years ago implicating some of the most famed presenters at the BBC. There's absolutely no denying that sex trafficking is real, we agreed, that child abuse is sadly common, that rape and sexual violence are constant, daily realities for a lot of people, especially women and children.

It was at that point that I noticed a man in his late thirties hovering very close to us, filming us with his phone and talking quietly to himself; I realized after a moment that he was livestreaming, telling his viewers what he was seeing. When LaLa mentioned Trump, he laughed out loud, a short, sharp bark.

"Controlled opposition," he said loudly, pointing the phone at LaLa. "*Controlled. Opposition.*"

"What?" I said.

"What?" LaLa and Angel asked.

"Controlled by what?" LaLa inquired.

"Nothing," he said. And then, to me: "I'll talk to you about it later."

He couldn't quite help himself, though. "You love Trump," he told LaLa. "You love David Seaman." The crisp NRA hat, the BENGHAZI shirt—it all looked to him as if she was a plant, sent to the rally to discredit the movement. (Later, in an online video dissecting the event, he zoomed in on her purse, which looked barely used. A sign that it was freshly bought and contains a hidden camera, he speculated.)

"Why follow David Seaman?" he said to her.

"I don't know who that is," LaLa responded. "I'm some kind of plant? That's insane. I don't even know her." She pointed at Angel.

"I came with my friend over there," Angel said. They looked at him together, baffled and offended.

"All right." The man's hands were shaking so violently I was concerned he was going to drop the phone. Then, to his viewers, "They're telling me I'm wrong, guys." He didn't sound convinced. He drifted away.

David Seaman took the stage to cheers. He was tall and thin and mild-looking, with sandy brown hair and big glasses and a blue hoodie, like a Facebook employee or your company's quietest IT guy. "According to *Newsweek*, I'm a mentally unstable con man," he told the crowd. They booed sympathetically.

"There's a man here who's been recording me all morning, who attacks me on YouTube," Seaman said next. "I can't think of anything lower." He pointed dramatically at the man who was filming LaLa, Angel, and me. His name, it turned out, is Nathan Stolpman, and he ran a conspiracy-oriented podcast called *Lift the Veil*. He and Seaman were mortal enemies, each of them accusing the other of being plants, sent by God knows who.

With a rush, much of the crowd surrounded Stolpman.

"What's your endgame?" someone yelled in his face.

"You're protecting child molesters, bro!" screamed a tattooed, heavily muscled man with the sides of his head shaved.

"Asshole!" an older woman cried. They were filming and photographing Stolpman, pressing in on him from all sides. The potential for violence seemed high; I could almost feel the air thicken.

Then, as if responding to a signal I couldn't hear, they stepped away. The tension dissipated. The rally continued. Stolpman was smiling slightly, looking calm, still holding his phone aloft. Onstage, Seaman dropped to his knees and led a prayer for the abused, captive children. (Like me, Seaman is Jewish; I briefly wondered where he got into the Christian habit of kneeling in prayer.)

After Seaman and Wolfe finished their exhortations to arrest the unnamed molesters, anyone was free to speak. A winding and sometimes ragged group of people took the stage, one after another, for hours. There were impassioned pleas against child abuse, rants against CIA mind control, heartrending personal tales of sexual assault and child neglect, a guy who talked about the family court system being biased against dads.

"The American Bar Association is behind all this child theft!" a man yelled at one point, to considerable applause.

For many of the people in attendance, the only hope in this morass of baby-abusing corruption lay in the New York Police Department, who they believed wasn't beholden to the same pedophilic interests as the feds. They trusted that the NYPD was investigating Weiner, whose sexts with that fifteen-year-old girl could be the key to bringing the entire child-molesting house of cards crashing down.

I wandered the crowd, getting a sunburn in the crisscross pattern of the shirt I was wearing, sweating through my coat, trying to figure out what I was hearing. As chaotic and bizarre as the rally was, the common thread was clear enough: abuse, secrecy, and cover-ups, a government rife with pedophiles, and a media that refused to take a word of it seriously. A minor-league neo-Nazi podcaster was roaming the crowd, yelling intermittently at the stage about "Jewish ritual murder," but he was there alone and nobody was taking him seriously. LaLa pulled me aside and assured me the Nazi, too, was a plant to discredit the Pizzagaters.

PIZZAGATE ADHERENTS BREAK DOWN INTO A NUMBER OF SUBGROUPS. Among them are survivors of child sexual abuse who know firsthand the pain of that kind of violence. There's also what I think of as the chaos arm: people like Mike Cernovich, brought in by the alt-right and prone to pushing anti-Democratic conspiracies (and who saw the lack of coverage by the mainstream media as evidence of their having been bought off by the Democrats). And then there are deeply religious Christians, often evangelicals, to whom Pizzagate is proof that the Devil is real and working hard on Earth.

If all this is beginning to sound unpleasantly familiar, it should. Medieval historian Michael Barbezat pointed out that Pizzagate looks a lot like the "nocturnal ritual fantasy," a phrase coined by Norm Cohn, another historian: a belief that shadowy groups are gathering at night to plot the overthrow of society while participating in the ritual abuse, torture, and/or murder of innocents, usually children. Throughout the Middle Ages, it was popular to charge supposed heretical groups with meeting at night to solidify their bonds of friendship with orgies, black masses, and baby murder. Medieval Jews, Barbezat writes, were persistently accused of conducting rituals involving the abuse of children, beginning in England in the early 1150s.

"The belief that Jews tortured Christian children, which has come to be known as the blood libel, often featured a sexual component as well," he explains. "In some versions of the blood libel accusation, kidnapped Christian boys were reportedly circumcised against their wills as depicted in a woodcut of the martyrdom of Simon of Trent in 1475. The Jews supposedly used the blood from this circumcision and other tortures to make the matzos for Passover."

In all such accounts, the nocturnal ritual fantasy is used as justification for violence against the suspected group, Cohn and Barbezat write, a way of quantifying its wickedness in terms that justify any means to stop it. Writer and activist Chip Berlet calls the fantasy "coded rhetoric" meant to incite "scripted violence." Accordingly, accusations of ritually killing Christian and Muslim children have been used to justify mass executions of Jews across Europe and the Middle East.

Claims of blood libel persisted throughout the twentieth century, intensifying with the 1903 publication of the *Protocols of the Learned Elders of Zion* (the forgery of minutes of a secret meeting of hand-rubbing Jews plotting world domination). The *Protocols* and the idea of ritual killings or blood libel are cited even now. In 2013, to pluck one disturbing example out of dozens, Khaled Al-Zaafrani, founder of the Egyptian Justice and Progress Party, declared, "It's well known that during the Passover, they make matzos called the 'Blood of Zion.' They take a Christian child, slit his throat, and slaughter him. Then they take his blood and make their [matzos]. This is a very important rite for the Jews, which they never forgo. . . . They slice it and fight over who gets to eat Christian blood." At the Pizzagate rally, then, the neo-Nazi yelling about "Jewish ritual murder" was making a connection between Pizzagate and the blood libel, although he might not have known the historical and cultural roots of what he was doing.

Pizzagate also looks chillingly like a revival of a more local paranoid fantasy, the Satanic Panic of the 1980s and early 1990s, when dozens of childcare workers, teachers, and parents were accused of engaging in the ritual abuse of children. The panic was partially set off by the publication in 1980 of a book called *Michelle Remembers*, co-written by Canadian psychiatrist Lawrence Pazder and Michelle Smith, his patient and eventual wife. The book purported to be a chronicle of Smith's recovered memories of horrific Satanic ritual abuse in the 1950s, and it initiated some two decades of procedures in which self-proclaimed experts guided vulnerable patients through "recovering" similar memories.

Satanic Panic was an irresistible blend of sex, black magic, and crime, and stories about it soon pervaded the culture: huge media outlets from *Oprah* to *20/20* ran straight-faced stories on Satanic ritual abuse. (Angel had referred to the *Oprah* episode in our conversation, remembering it as the story of a woman abused by a Satanic cult for generations. I later figured out that the specific episode she was likely referring to recounted the case of a woman named Laurel Rose Wilson, who under the name

"Lauren Stratford" claimed to have been used as a "breeder" in a Satanic cult, producing babies for sacrificial rites. Her stories were deemed unfounded by police, investigative journalists, and the Christian magazine *Cornerstone*, and her books on the subject were pulled from print.)

Heavy metal was also seen as a culprit and a signifier of Satanic activity, as was the game Dungeons & Dragons. Three teenage boys in Arkansas, the so-called West Memphis Three, were convicted on the flimsiest of evidence of the ritual murder of three little boys; one of the teens, Damien Echols, was sentenced to death, and all three would have died in prison had their case not been covered by a popular documentary series, which attracted intense celebrity support. The West Memphis Three were eventually released from prison after close to twenty years, as were several other people—daycare workers, babysitters, teachers—falsely accused of child abuse.

In the case of Pizzagate, the demonic aspect of the plot was enhanced by an additional thread discovered in John Podesta's hacked emails: "spirit cooking." Podesta and his brother, Tony, were purportedly attending Satanic rituals conducted by the artist Marina Abramović where guests dined on semen and blood consumed on "earthquake nights." "WIKI WICCAN: PODESTA PRACTICES OCCULT MAGIC," yelled the far-right aggregation site Drudge Report when the telling emails came to light. Alex Jones dubbed spirit cooking "black magic," and Mike Cernovich weighed in with "sick stuff" and "sex cult." Abramović's repeated rebuttals that "Spirit Cooking"—the title of an art installation—was just that, art, and that nobody ate semen, blood, or anything else unsavory, had no impact. Those who bought into spirit cooking as a real demonic activity are certain that Abramović and the Podestas and everyone else involved in this Satanic sex-and-death cult will face their judgment, sooner or later.

These outbreaks of religious hysteria recur so persistently in American life for a reason: they are, like so many conspiracy theories, a response to moments of social change and perceived societal fracture. Satanic Panic allegations first arose during a moment in the 1980s of intense concern over the number of women in the workforce and a subsequent rise in "latchkey kids" and paid caregivers. Pizzagate emerged during the 2016 elections, a time when Americans were relitigating, to an exhausting degree, our beliefs, our vision of America, and our sexual ethics. The paranoid idea of sexual predators hiding in the highest echelons of power was not so paranoid; Pizzagate, though, spun it through a nexus of faux black magic, imagined ritual, and nonsensical accusations that were somehow both unbelievable and yet, for a lot of people, unbelievably powerful.

I HAD ALL THIS IN MIND DURING ONE OF THE SADDEST MOMENTS OF the DC rally, when I spotted a child holding a sign: IF YOU SEE ME WITH JOHN PODESTA, CALL THE POLICE. The little boy carrying the placard was beaming, bouncing up and down on his heels.

"You have the best sign," a woman told him, leaning down for a high five. His father was next to him in a wheelchair and an InfoWars shirt, glowing as one person after another came up to take photos of his son.

I walked over. The man was Michael White from Pennsylvania; he retired from the Air Force after a workplace injury on a base in Kosovo.

"Tell the lady why you're here," he instructed the boy.

"I want to stop child murder once and for all," he said, carefully.

"And abuse?" his father prompted.

"Yeah," the boy murmured. "I'm eager to help everyone and stop the kidnapping of teenagers." He batted impossibly long eyelashes at me. I asked his name, wrote it down, and decided not to use it. I suddenly felt desperately sad.

"What else do you like to do?" I asked him. He looked up at me, confused, then at his father.

"She's asking what you do for fun," White explained.

"I like to write and draw and read," he said triumphantly. We talked for a while about a superhero series he's working on.

"He's so great at writing dialogue," White told me. He seemed so calm and good-tempered that I felt comfortable asking him about what was weighing on me.

"Don't you worry this is disturbing for him?"

"Well, he's not really paying attention," White said. "And I don't tell him specifics, you know. When we talk about this, I explain everything in a way he can understand."

White, like everyone else here, is out for the truth, he said. "All we want is an honest public investigation instead of a media blackout and law enforcement refusing to investigate."

A few minutes later, I was listening to a guy onstage reading from a woman's account of child abuse he found on the Internet. She described being "sold to ten men" a day, chained up in an attic, forced to drink from a dog bowl. I turned to look at White's son. He was still holding his sign—gripping it, really—his mouth slightly open, his eyes laser-locked on the stage.

Seaman was turning journalists away, several in a row. Figuring it was a lost cause, I still walked over and gave him my card. An hour or two after the rally, I was glumly eating a salad in some dim, charmless chain restaurant and trying to recover from the ordeal when he texted me on Signal, a secure messaging app.

"I want to befriend you," the text read. "You seem sincere."

An hour later, we met at a Starbucks. He came with two women in tow: one, in her early twenties, who was introduced as an intern for his one-man news organization, and an older woman, Liz, who lived in the DC suburbs and helped organize the rally. She said her husband works in government and declined to give her last name. She got into Pizzagate after learning about spirit cooking from a "credible, savvy study group" that she was part of, which used to meet regularly to talk about the election.

"I just froze," she said, when she heard about spirit cooking. "That kind of thing, you can't unsee." She's visited Comet, she added. "I found it disturbing, and I definitely thought there was something going on."

Seaman, meanwhile, claimed that the Department of Homeland Security is investigating Podesta. "I have a background source," he told me, "who's currently employed at DHS and who's in a position to know."

"Is there anything that could convince you this isn't real?" I asked.

Seaman replied that he'd like to see DHS and the FBI issue statements to that effect. "If DHS calls me and says there's no trafficking, that's it."

"Have you seen the art in John Podesta's house?" Liz interjected. She was referring to a couple of weird paintings belonging to Tony and John that the Pizzagate people seized on: some nudes and an oil painting in John's office of a guy on a table in a suit with two men looming over him bearing forks and knives.

There was a heavy, loaded pause.

"It's not really my taste," I told her. "But I wouldn't necessarily interpret it as evil."

All three of them looked at me, appalled, as though I'd vomited bile on the table.

The conversation never really recovered. I could see Seaman deciding that I'm one of them, the dishonest mainstream press who meant to paint him as crazy. He corrected me, stiffly, when I referred to Pizzagate as a "belief."

"They're not beliefs," he said pointedly. "I didn't join a church."

"Millions of us are talking about this online," he told me before taking his leave. "It's not going to go away."

Seaman's certainty seemed noteworthy: like a lot of people firmly enmeshed in a conspiracy community, Seaman dwelled in an echo chamber so complete, so hermetically sealed, that he seemed incapable of processing anything that might change his mind or believing that anyone who disagreed with him could be anything other than a child-abuse apologist or a pedophile. I doubt that a statement from the FBI or DHS would make a difference to him; instead, he would find a way to explain their roles in the conspiracy. Although there might not have been millions of Pizzagate adherents, the movement could not be totally ignored: it was a crystalline example of an Internet creation that leaked into the real world in ways that were, by turns, startling, comic, alarming, and violent.

Pizzagate shared other traits that are typical of conspiracy communities: it's both startlingly cohesive—thousands of people are willing to believe in the idea of a global elite sex-trafficking ring headquartered in a pizza parlor—and quick to fracture, breaking into pieces under the weight of mutual suspicion and internecine feuds. That happens in every corner of the world of the deeply suspicious. Conspiracy theorists' lives can be extremely lonely: the mythology of the lone hero on the hunt for truth, against a mountain of enemies and lies, almost demands it.

Nathan Stolpman, the phone videographer of Lift the Veil and enemy of David Seaman, was pretty sure most of the people at the Lafayette Park rally were plants and bad actors. A former actor and then a used-car salesman, Stolpman was living with his dad at the time of the rally and making Pizzagate videos out of his bedroom. "It's a suspicious community because there are so many infiltrators trying to make people look bad," he told me. "And then we make ourselves look bad." (He meant the yelling, the near fistfights, the online feuding, the dueling videos.)

LaLa, the woman Stolpman accused of being controlled opposition, was disappointed by the depth of the suspicion. She seemed to have come to the rally hoping to find a real-life community to complement the ones she'd found online. "It seems that the core element from everyone in this 'movement' is distrust for everyone around them," she wrote in an email. "Nobody knows who's on whose side, or what the truth is. And we have a circular firing squad of everyone telling everyone else they are the 'opposition.'"

LATER IN THE EVENING, AFTER THE RALLY ENDED, I PULLED TOGETHER a group of friends—all reporters, for some reason—and headed to dinner at Comet Ping Pong. When I arrived, some of the rallygoers were standing outside, holding INVESTIGATE PIZZAGATE signs.

"Are you going in?" I asked a woman from Fredericksburg.

"I want to take a look around," she said. She was particularly eager to see the art on the walls, which struck Pizzagaters as Satanic. "I've done enough research to know this is real."

"It seemed to happen more on concert nights," another demonstrator said, of the sexual abuse. "I've seen some of the band names. We believe there's a whole underlying music scene that's related."

After Comet was pinpointed by Reddit detectives as the center of a global sex ring, things got very bad for the staff. Even before Edgar Welch showed up, people posted Facebook videos with graphic threats. The general manager, Bryce Reh, received several: "I'm going to chainsaw you in your sleep," one read. "I'm looking at your house," read another. Reh was sent photos of his home. Gay staff members had it worse. "There was definitely a homophobic element to some of it," Reh says.

The afternoon of the Welch incident, Reh was driving to the restaurant when he got a call that a man with a gun had come barreling through the doors. In a panic, he called his wife, a concert violinist who moonlights as a waitress there, and told her to stay away. Then he called every other employee in his phone. He got to Connecticut Avenue, where Comet is located, only to find the police had roped it off. He parked on a random street corner and sprinted toward the restaurant, pausing to have a shouting match with a police officer who didn't want to let him through.

In the meantime, after the staff got everyone out the door to safety, they "went down the block to other businesses to warn them," Reh recounted. He still sounded proud.

In the weeks that followed, Comet brought in trauma counselors for the staff. They assured anyone who wanted to quit that it would be all right, that they'd get severance and no hard feelings. Only a couple of people took them up on the offer. The rest stayed and tried to adjust to their new reality, one where they had to walk past demonstrators and use the stockroom that Welch had shot his way into.

"I didn't sleep for three days," Reh told me. One night, he woke up to a loud noise, and was convinced that someone was trying to take a belt sander to the lock on his door. It was only the belt on his neighbor's air-conditioning unit malfunctioning.

Alefantis had stopped to sneer at the Pizzagate rally, Reh told me, speeding through its outskirts on his bike, but Reh himself was unable to. The most infamous of the Pizzagate photos—of a little girl with her hands taped to a table—bothers him the most. It's a staff member's child, and Reh knows that the picture was taken at a school hobby day when the girl's older sister taped her hands to the table as a joke. She's grinning into the camera in the photo, her eyes bright.

"They put this photo of her on YouTube videos," Reh said quietly. "To monetize it. They're profiting off children in a real way. She will grow up with that photo of her associated with the word 'pedophilia.' I can't see that and not get upset."

Reh said he and the rest of the staff have worked on adjusting to the threats, the social-media deluge, and the knowledge that someone like Welch could visit again.

"The world is more chaos than we like to imagine," he said stoically. "The faster we come to terms with that, the more fluidly you can deal with it." Anyway, he added, "What's the choice? Lay down and cry?"

We talked until my pizza got cold; eventually Reh stepped away, greeting a staff member and her toddler son with a big hug. I had a beer and then, as a result, a little woozy trouble locating the bathroom, whose door was part of what looks like a solid wood wall. In Pizzagate world, they would find something like that suspicious.

THE COMET PING PONG GUNMAN EDGAR WELCH PLEADED GUILTY TO state and federal weapons charges in March 2017. In June, in an imposing courtroom in DC, he entered in leg shackles and an orange jumpsuit to be sentenced, looking exhausted and pale, with short-buzzed blond hair and a neat goatee. His family and fiancée watched him from a front row, all of them looking exhausted, too. His sister, a tall blond woman, cried intermittently, silently holding a tissue to her mouth.

Welch's court-appointed defense attorney argued to Judge Ketanji Brown Jackson that Welch deserved just eighteen months in prison. She pointed out that in 2010 he'd gone to Haiti for three weeks with his church to work with children orphaned by the hurricane. She described him as a devoutly religious man, devoted to his children, who'd already been deeply damaged by six months of not speaking to them and five weeks in solitary confinement. She also suggested that he was a little naive.

"He's not as sophisticated as the people who reside in the District of Columbia and are aware of politics," she told the judge.

Several Comet employees had a chance to read victim impact statements, although none of them used their names in court, to protect their privacy.

"I'm trying to be as sympathetic and empathetic with you as possible," one, a tall, skinny guy with dark hair and a maroon collared shirt, told Welch. He had been pacing the halls of the courthouse before the hearing began, looking miserable.

"I'm almost sorry you were duped," he continued, telling Welch he'd "fallen into a trap" set by Pizzagate peddlers like Alex Jones. "And they now believe you're a hired actor," he added, not looking at Welch. "That's how misinformation works, and how the game is played."

He paused.

"I hope the God who inspired all your tattoos is as forgiving as I am," he concluded.

Comet's owner, James Alefantis, a stocky guy with dark curly hair and a blue blazer, spoke, too. He didn't glance at Welch, either, as he told the judge how proud he was of his staff for their bravery.

"So many of us have suffered because of the defendant's actions," he said. "For me, the only good thing that has come of this ordeal is that I now know that I am a member of a community that comes together and raises up any member who has fallen. I know that all the families who experienced such pain by this one man's decision will not allow their lives to be defined by fear. And I say this with no vengeance and an open heart—I hope that one day, in a more truthful world, every single one of us can remember this as an aberration, a symptom of a time of sickness, when some parts of our world went mad, when news was fake and lies were seen as real and our social fabric frayed."

Welch himself spoke only for a moment and—as the prosecution pointed out—he never exactly said that he'd been mistaken.

"I wish there was more that I could offer than an apology," he told the judge quietly, his hands behind his back. "I want to make sure the victims understand I'm sorry for anything I've caused."

"Yours is not an average case," Judge Jackson told Welch, before she pronounced his sentence. "I've never heard anything like the conduct that brings us here today." She sentenced him to four years in prison and thirty-six months of supervised release, plus $5,744 in restitution to Comet. Welch's fiancée, very young-looking, with long, silky brown hair and an orange dress with bell sleeves, bent over at the waist as the sentence was pronounced.

As Welch ground through the gears of the penal system, the Pizza-gate movement rushed swiftly on without him. By May 2017, "detec-tives" on the message-board website Voat had found suspicious behaviors in the bearded indie rocker Father John Misty, and the bleach-dipped celebrity chef Guy Fieri, and at a chain of children's dental offices in Alaska. (They didn't like the look of photos of the dentist's office: there were toys in there and cheerful drawings hanging in front of the dental chairs. Most people would argue those were an effort to distract kids having their teeth drilled, but the Pizzagaters saw something a lot more sinister.)

Meanwhile, out in objective reality, a true and ongoing revelation was taking place. Investigative reporting in the *New York Times* and the *New Yorker* published in October 2017 revealed that Hollywood producer Harvey Weinstein was accused of serial rape, while his alleged crimes had been covered up for years. Weinstein's story broke a dam, and the #MeToo movement came flooding through, in which dozens of powerful abusers in politics, media, and entertainment were outed by the brave survivors of their abuse. It was a world-shaking blow to a patriarchal system of sexual violence that was, inevitably, fed into the Pedogate machine.

"Is Pizzagate all still fake?" David Seaman, the Pizzagate researcher, exulted in a video soon after the Weinstein story broke.

Pizzagate never really ended, then, and none of its prominent mem-bers ever admitted that they might have been mistaken. The momentum created out of real people, bots, religion, scapegoating, the alt-right, and the evangelical right was strangely, uniquely, disturbingly unstoppable. Once again, as Americans, we lapsed into an occult hysteria, a persis-tent need to seek out new witches among us and burn them, one by one, even when they refused to be found.

But the movement was also one that was firmly tied to the chaotic, prismatic tides and ripples of the Internet, and it was as malleable as any other rumor you'd find there. Pizzagate repeatedly changed its form, absorbing, jellyfish-like, the most alluring conspiracy theories of the moment. Over the next year, as the US government's pedophile core stubbornly refused to collapse, the movement's truest believers started to believe the deception was even bigger than they'd ever thought possible.

4

FALSE FLAGS

THE BOMBS EXPLODED AT THE FINISH LINE AT 2:49 P.M. ON APRIL 15, 2013. The worst photos—the ones widely published on conspiracy websites—were taken during the immediate aftermath of the bombing: a woman sitting dazed in a pool of blood, her face smeared with grime; a man with both legs blown off, sliding around in a pool of his own viscera. One of his leg bones juts out, horribly white, pointing in the air like a mile marker. He's looking away from the camera, off into the distance. In another shot, he's being rushed toward medical aid in a wheelchair, what's left of his legs visible.

"We were told his name is Jeff Bauman," one conspiracy site wrote sarcastically soon after the bombing, referring to the man who had lost his legs. "But since that can't be verified and his survival is unbelievable to the point of being miraculous, we'll simply call him Miracle Man."

The Boston Marathon bombings killed three people, including an eight-year-old boy who'd been cheering at the finish line, and injured more than two hundred, among them Bauman, who lost both legs above the knee. (His difficult road to recovery was documented in a memoir and a movie, and his name can most definitely be verified.)

The country was captivated by the manhunt that followed and the identification of the suspects as brothers Tamerlan and Dzhokhar Tsarnaev, two young Al-Qaeda sympathizers of Chechen descent. Four days after the marathon, Tamerlan, the older brother, died in a bizarre confrontation with police—he was first shot by officers and then run over by Dzhokhar attempting to escape. Dzhokhar was taken into custody alive and is today one of the youngest people on death row in the United States.

The story was gruesome, as dramatic as a Hollywood thriller, and its aftermath was filled with mysteries. Some have endured. It's never been clear, for example, why an FBI agent shot and killed a friend of the Tsarnaev brothers during an interrogation at his apartment. (The agency claimed that the friend had a weapon; however, the agent who shot him had previous accusations of misconduct and assault. In 2017, the family of the victim sued two FBI agents and two Massachusetts state troopers.) Before the brothers were identified, before the strange killing of the friend—before any details were known—an alternate version had begun to play out, parallel to the official story, as the conspiracy community figured out what was *really* going on.

Conspiracy theorists converged on the Boston bombing within hours. One of the first questions at the initial press conference convened by the authorities following the bombings came from Dan Bidondi of InfoWars. Was the bombing, Bidondi demanded, "another false flag staged attack to take our civil liberties and promote homeland security while sticking their hands down our pants on the streets?"

"No," replied Massachussetts governor Deval Patrick. "Next question."

"Our hearts go out to those that are hurt or killed #Boston marathon," Alex Jones tweeted, less than an hour after the bombs exploded. "But this thing stinks to high heaven. #falseflag."

ONE OF THE MOST INTENSE AND IMMOVABLE AMERICAN FEARS IS OF subliminal, hidden government control. We're also worried about the other, more overt kind—armies marching down the street, doors kicked in, guns in our faces—but the murky circumstances behind several major military conflicts, combined with revelations of various secret FBI and CIA programs, have helped foster the suspicion that we might be controlled and manipulated through more subtle means, ones beyond our recognition. That's one reason for paranoia about such threats as mind-controlling fluoride in the water supply, subliminal messages in advertising and Disney movies, and brainwashing in schools through the Common Core curriculum. But the fear of invisible government manipulation is also largely accountable for the prevalence of theories of false flags: the idea that mass casualty events have been orchestrated or carried out by the government to consolidate its power.

In the years since 9/11, and intensifying after the 2012 shooting that killed twenty children and six adults at Sandy Hook Elementary School in Newtown, Connecticut, most major mass casualty incidents in the United States have been subject to accusations of having been staged by the government, done to keep an unsophisticated populace in line. The charges are always the same: the people supposedly wounded or killed are actors, the photos and videos of the event are doctored, the witnesses are paid government spooks. Each of these conspiracy theory–generating events creates months of television news coverage after the fact, along with mountains of photographic and video evidence. That evidence is dissected by "researchers," as they call themselves, in a way that's come to seem so familiar, it's sometimes used for comedic effect: an interlocking system of red lines, arrows, textual notes, and geometric angles, overlaid atop the images like layers of a chaotic cake, pointing everywhere and at nothing simultaneously.

Though false flag theories spring up routinely around any event in which a lot of people die and that is covered heavily in the news, the accusation is especially common in response to mass shootings; conspiracy theorists, particularly on the far right, tend to link such shooting attacks to the liberal campaign for gun control.

Sometimes false flag theories dovetail with anti-Semitism and Islamophobia; attacks are frequently attributed to Israel or ISIS. That happened in the days following the Boston attack, when anti-Semitic conspiracy sites blamed Zionists, Israel, or simply the Jews at large. ("Zionist Jews Strike Again, Murdering Three in Boston," a site called NoDisInfo blared.) Florida anti-Muslim pastor Terry Jones—best known for publicly burning a Quran—declared that Obama planned to cover up the crime in sympathy for his fellow Muslims. "Is it an Islamic attack? It looks like it," he wrote in a statement. "The bombing came on Patriots Day. It has all of the earmarkings of an Islamic attack but will there again be a great coverup by the Great Satan Obama? His Administration, the people he has surrounded himself with, are all some type of closet Muslims, heavily influenced by Islam because of their background."

The callousness of false flag researchers can be shocking and painful to witness, even when they're not dipping into outright hate speech. In November 2017, a gunman stormed into a church in the small town of Sutherland Springs, Texas, and killed twenty-five people, one of them pregnant. The gunman had a long history of domestic violence, and his estranged wife sometimes attended the church he attacked. During the shooting, he murdered her grandmother. Yet the conspiracy theories sprang up immediately, most of them politically tinged: he was a Bernie Sanders supporter, a Hillary Clinton voter, an antifa (shorthand for "anti-fascist") terrorist who claimed "this is a communist revolution" before murdering the parishioners. The killings were said to be an attack on Christianity itself: "Report: Texas church shooter was atheist, thought Christians 'stupid,'" Breitbart's headline blared.

In the months that followed, the church pastor, Frank Pomeroy, and his wife, Sherri, whose fourteen-year-old daughter, Annabelle, had died in the shooting, were viciously harassed, accused of participating in a staged Department of Homeland Security "drill" to frighten people into giving up their guns. One self-proclaimed journalist calling himself Side Thorn (real name Robert Ussery) took himself to Sutherland Springs with his partner Conspiracy Granny (real name Jodie Mann). They leaped out of their car and began berating Frank Pomeroy, who was sitting in his own car nearby. Ussery filmed the encounter.

"Your daughter never even existed," he told Pomeroy. "Show me her birth certificate. Show me anything to say she was here." The pair were arrested for trespassing and possession of marijuana, but Ussery declared the mission a partial success. "It was everything but an outright admission," he wrote on his website.

———

THERE ARE EXAMPLES THROUGHOUT HISTORY OF REAL OR SUSPECTED false flag attacks; the name supposedly comes from a mode of pirate warfare, in which a pirate ship would feign distress to draw another vessel closer. When the other boat came within attacking distance, the pirates would raise their—surprise—black flag. The most infamous example cited is the 1933 Reichstag fire, in which the German parliament building was burned down. Hitler's cabinet claimed the fire was the beginning of a communist putsch and moved to enact emergency laws; historians have long debated whether the arson was carried out by the Nazis themselves to consolidate power. The bombing of four Russian apartment buildings in 1999, which were blamed on Chechen militants, has been compared to the Reichstag fire: many believe the attacks were carried out by the FSB, the Russian security agency, to help Putin in his rise to the presidency.

In American history, the most heavily debated event as a possible false flag operation was the 1898 explosion and sinking of the USS *Maine*, an event that precipitated the start of the Spanish-American War. It's never been clear whether the *Maine* was destroyed by an external explosion, as one government investigation found, or by a coal fire belowdeck, but the incident was blamed on Spanish forces, particularly in the tabloids of the day, and used as an incitement to war.

Justifying military involvement is a common theme in real or suspected false flags, and it cropped up in 1962's infamous Operation Northwoods. A proposal from the Department of Defense and the Joint Chiefs of Staff, Northwoods baldly floated the idea that the CIA commit acts of terrorism against American citizens and blame them on Cuba to justify pushing a simmering conflict into a full-scale war. The attacks involved a riot outside Guantanamo, the US naval base in Cuba, as well as shooting down airplanes or setting off bombs in US cities. President Kennedy vetoed the operation, but just two years later, in the Gulf of Tonkin incident, American forces insisted they had been attacked twice by a North Vietnamese patrol boat. But the second attack never happened, as documents declassified years later showed. They also demonstrated that then Secretary of Defense Robert McNamara intentionally withheld evidence that might have led to a full investigation of the event and perhaps put a slight speed bump in the United States' rush into the Vietnam War.

As with every conspiracy associated with the government, Northwoods opened the door to new conspiracy theories. In subsequent years, the false flags and abortive false flags of the Vietnam era generated abundant suspicion of military action. That suspicion only grew after the September 11, 2001, attacks, which generated particularly widespread and tenacious accusations of false flaggery. As Kathryn Olmsted notes in *Real Enemies,* September 11 conspiracy theorists "embraced" the concept that Operation Northwoods was a precursor to 9/11. Some of that was a matter of serendipitous timing: memos about Northwoods were declassified and put online in 1998, just in time for conspiracy-minded people to connect them to 9/11. Northwoods, Olmsted writes, served as "unassailable proof" for conspiracy theorists "that their theories of U.S. government-sponsored terrorism were horrifyingly plausible."

9/11 truthers, as the suspicious are called, divide into two broad camps: those who believe the George W. Bush administration let the attacks happen on purpose and those who believe the administration made them happen on purpose (LIHOP and MIHOP, in shorthand). Both camps contain people who believe that the attacks created a reason for the administration to justify going to war and expanding its surveillance powers at home. The statistics on trutherism show that the numbers of believers were initially low, but they grew in the years following the attacks. This echoes the way the official story of the Kennedy assassination was increasingly questioned in the decades after, according to many polls, as the initial shock of the president's murder faded and people began looking, as we often do, for deeper meaning.

With 9/11, the statistics on how conspiracy theorizing grew in the subsequent decade are readily available and very stark. As Jeremy Stahl wrote in *Slate* in 2011:

In May 2002, with Bush's approval rating still well over 70 percent, fewer than one in 10 Americans in a CBS News poll said that the Bush administration was lying about what it knew regarding possible terror attacks prior to 9/11. By April 2004, 16 percent of respondents in a CBS News poll said that the Bush administration was "mostly lying" . . . while 56 percent said it was telling the truth but hiding something and 24 percent said it was telling the entire truth. By the five-year anniversary of the attacks, one in three Americans would tell pollsters that it was likely that the government either had a hand in the attacks of 9/11 or allowed them to happen in order to go to war in the Middle East.

Beyond their scope and persistence, the suspicions also generated one of the biggest conspiracy successes ever: the film *Loose Change*, made by independent filmmaker Dylan Avery, just twenty-one at the time; two decades later, hundreds of awful straight-to-Netflix conspiracy documentaries are still trying to replicate the phenomenon. Released in 2005, *Loose Change* argued that the 9/11 attacks were just the latest in a long string of false flags—Northwoods makes a pretty significant appearance in the film—and helped crystallize the theory that the Twin Towers were brought down by a controlled demolition. The attacks were, the film posited, an "inside job" meant to pave the way for a permanent, oil-grabbing war in the Middle East.

Both the impact of the film and the fact that "truther" beliefs continued to grow in the decade after 9/11 might be due to the same thing: some of the broader political points made by *Loose Change* are not actually all that far-fetched, for people on the right or the left. "In the aftermath of September 11, President Bush had and continues to have permission to do and say whatever he wants," the narrator intones toward the end of the film. "All under the pretext of September 11. The Patriot Act. The Department of Homeland Security. Afghanistan. Iraq. It's time for America to accept 9/11 for what it was: a lie which killed thousands of people, only in turn killing hundreds of thousands more, to make billions upon trillions of dollars." After a multigenerational conflict in the Middle East more than fifteen years later, it's hard to dispute that, at the very least, the attacks were politically beneficial.

In response to the success of *Loose Change* and other conspiracy-theorizing books and films about 9/11, the magazine *Popular Mechanics*

devoted itself to debunking the scientific claims made by the conspiracy theories. Those include the idea that "jet fuel can't melt steel
beams," by now such a well-known argument that it's become a jokey
shorthand for conspiracy thinking. The magazine eventually produced
a book of its research. Not that it helped. Some level of 9/11 conspiracism remains common across the political spectrum. In 2016, the Chapman University Survey of American Fears found that more than half of
those polled believed that the government is still hiding some of what
it knows about the attack.

Mostly, though, theories about false flags or government responsibility stay firmly relegated to the fringe, confined among people who,
for ideological reasons, very much want to find an alternate explanation for a violent event. The bombing of the Alfred P. Murrah Federal
Building in Oklahoma City by Timothy McVeigh in 1995 is a case in
point. The attack killed one hundred sixty-eight and wounded more than
seven hundred; it was even more shocking because the Murrah Building
housed a daycare center for the government workers' children, and nineteen of them were among the dead.

The bombing posed a particular challenge to anti-government conspiracy theorists because it was carried out as retribution for what
McVeigh saw as tyrannical government overreach: the deadly standoffs
at Waco and Ruby Ridge. McVeigh intended the bombings to be the
first spark in what he ultimately hoped would be a full-fledged revolution against the federal government. But the fact that civilians and
children died in the attack made it not especially sympathetic, even for
McVeigh's fellow ideological travelers. After all, one of the horrors of
the Ruby Ridge standoff was that it targeted a family, the Weavers, who
sympathizers argued were only trying to live peacefully on a hilltop
beyond the reach of a tyrannical Zionist government. During the standoff, the Weavers' son Sammy, fourteen, his mother, Vicki, and their dog
Striker were all shot and killed by FBI snipers.

It was, therefore, incumbent on people on the far right to come up
with an alternate explanation for the Oklahoma City bombing. Alex
Jones, the most famous and prolific spreader of false flag theories, got
his start as an Oklahoma City truther, which he argued was not an
attack by a lone, disgruntled domestic terrorist but a plot by a tyranni-

cal government to consolidate power. According to a 2013 *Esquire* profile, Jones claimed that the bombing was part of a string of assaults on right-wing patriot groups and had been staged to justify a further crackdown on those groups.

Jones lost his job at an Austin public radio station after diving too deep into the false flag pool, leading him to found InfoWars and colonize what became an improbably large section of the media landscape. (In his book *Them*, Jon Ronson describes Jones's early days broadcasting via an ISDN line out of one of his kids' bedrooms, with "choo-choo train wallpaper and an *Empire Strikes Back* poster pinned on the wall.") After 9/11, he had a lot more company: more and more events were labeled as false flags staged by the government by more and more people with blogs, YouTube channels, Twitter accounts, and websites. The targets of their investigations ranged from the mass shootings at Sandy Hook Elementary in Connecticut in 2012 and a San Bernardino community center in 2015, to the disappearance of Malaysia Airlines flight 370 in 2014 (which was speculated to have been carried out by the CIA or the Israeli government), and the 2017 suicide bombing at an Ariana Grande concert in Manchester, England (which some American conspiracy theorists thought was perpetrated to distract from the discussion around DNC staffer Seth Rich's death). Interestingly, the first major school shooting, at Columbine High School, wasn't a popular false flag theory when it took place in 1999, before the age of YouTube, easily buildable blogs, and widely used social media platforms. Instead, that shooting was retroactively identified as a possible false flag years later by the truther community.

On rare occasions, false flag theorizing can become so persuasive that it prompts real state action. Agenda 21, a conspiracy theory that rocketed to mainstream attention in 2012, was aided by then-prominent far-right TV star Glenn Beck. It held that the United Nations planned to invade the United States, seize everyone's guns, and supplant the country's sovereignty. (Agenda 21 was actually an entirely voluntary UN program for member countries that laid out various social improvements.)

Ted Cruz, then running for the U.S. Senate in Texas for the first time, appeared on Beck's radio show to fret about Agenda 21, warning that it would result in the end of single-family homes, ranching, private cars, and, as he put it, "the American way of life." That's not a false flag; it's just very, very stupid. (So stupid that the national Republican Party put an anti–Agenda 21 plank in its national platform: "We strongly reject the UN Agenda 21 as erosive of American sovereignty, and we oppose any form of UN Global Tax," the declaration read.)

When Agenda 21 didn't come to pass, its true believers decided that the UN planned to sneak it in the back door instead, disguising an armed invasion as something else entirely. In the summer of 2015, they identified their Trojan horse: Jade Helm 15, a massive military drill operation taking place across seven states.

The unabashed conspiracism that followed made its way to high levels of government. Texas governor Greg Abbott ordered the Texas State Guard to monitor Jade Helm, saying in a statement, "During the training operation, it is important that Texans know [that] their safety, constitutional rights, private property rights and civil liberties will not be infringed." Abbott had echoed the fantastical line of the Oath Keepers, a far-right militia group that worried that Jade Helm was nothing less than a "portentous government plan":

> a pre-fabricated and preconstructed umbrella under which a black op by the Deep State's compartmentalized agencies could possibly "Go Live" in a fantastic sort of Shock and Awe False Flag psycho-coup to jar the public mind of America through fear into acceptance of some nefarious policy the government desired, such as the establishment of Martial Law and the complete loss of individual liberty and our Constitution.

Jade Helm, then, was an exceptional example of a fake military exercise being twisted into a real one. It's striking for the wide spread of the belief, particularly in Texas. A poll taken that summer by the University of Texas and the *Texas Tribune* showed that 39 percent of Texas voters supported Abbott's plan to monitor the Jade Helm exercises. It also asked Texans about the probability of a military takeover: 44 percent thought the military would "likely be used to impose martial law," while 43 percent thought it would be used to "confiscate firearms from citizens."

Jade Helm was unusual, too, for its coherence. More or less every-one who believed in it seemed to agree that the invasion would be car-ried out in a particular fashion. That's not usually the case with false flag theories. An event tends to generate a multitude of different suspi-cions, branches of a gnarled tree forking in hundreds of directions. Of the recent mass shootings, the murder of fifty-nine people with hundreds more wounded at the Las Vegas Harvest Music Festival generated a par-ticularly high number and variety of conspiracy theories: it was orches-trated by an "Obama Administration intelligence contractor;" it was planned by the government, with the gunman brainwashed by psychi-atric medication; it must have been a cover for *something else*.

The abundance of suspicion is partly due to the timeline of the shoot-ing, which was deeply confused; the Las Vegas police revised it three times, and the order of events has never been entirely clear. One of the key witnesses, a security guard who was shot at by the gunman, went silent for five days and canceled several TV appearances. This of course fueled the conspiracy theories, though it seems likely he did so as a result of trauma rather than any suspicious motives. The gunman, Stephen Paddock, remained something of a mystery: his brother declared him "not an avid gun guy," and his girlfriend swore she had no idea he was planning the attack.

It is no longer a surprise in this country when an aggrieved white man buys high-powered weapons and kills a lot of people, but for some reason the Las Vegas attack, because of these minor quirks, was broadly marked as "strange" or "suspicious" by a notable number of people on both the right and left. David French, a senior writer at the *National Review* and usually a fairly staid example of mainstream Republican-ism, called the shooting "very, very strange," "flat-out bizarre," and "significantly different from virtually any other mass shooting in U.S. history," though he declined to make clear what he was getting at.

One theory even suggested that this was a false flag attack planned by a foreign government, a semiotic twist we don't usually see. Eric Gar-land, a self-described "futurist" and intelligence analyst who became infamous on Twitter during the 2016 elections for sprawling, apoca-lyptic threads, implied that the Las Vegas attack was somehow planned by Russian government sources. He claimed that Russia had prior knowledge of the attack, and that Russian trolls flooded the Internet with misinformation "minutes" after it took place. "Today's reaction to Las Vegas was coordinated throughout the Deza-sphere," he wrote, using the shorthand for *dezinformatsiya* (disinformation). "If you don't know how this is working, get educated."

Even a sitting Republican congressman got in on the action. Representative Scott Perry, a Republican from Pennsylvania, went on Fox News several months after the shootings to blame the whole thing on ISIS and Mexicans simultaneously. "I smell a rat, like a lot of Americans," Perry told host Tucker Carlson. "Nothing's adding up." Nonetheless, he added, "Even more troubling than that, recently I've been made aware of what I believe to be credible evidence, credible information regarding potential terrorist infiltration through the southern border regarding this incident." Perry never explained what the hell he meant, but he was following a classic, broad tactic in false flag conspiracizing: take a violent event that, on the surface, means one thing, and make it mean something entirely different—and much more politically valuable, given the climate against Mexican immigration.

Globally, false flag theories can have extremely sinister political uses. One particularly chilling international conspiracy theory claimed that the chemical attacks by the Syrian government against civilians were either staged or perpetrated by the White Helmets, a civilian aid and rescue group. That conspiracy theory built onto a broader skepticism of the attacks themselves: an investigation by the *Guardian* found that stories questioning how the attacks *really* happened began soon after Russia staged a military intervention in Syria in September 2015 to support the Assad regime, which was conducting airstrikes on opposition-held areas. "Almost immediately, Russian state media such as RT and Sputnik started falsely claiming that Isis was the only target," reporter Olivia Solon wrote, as well as "throwing doubt" on whether "infrastructure and civilian sites" had been bombed.

Soon enough, the White Helmets were called into suspicion; the fact that they speedily arrived on the scene to render aid was deemed suspicious. The accusations have toggled between suggesting that the White Helmets faked video footage of the attacks and that they actually carried them out, murdering civilians; in either case, the implication is that the attacks were an attempt to justify Western military intervention in Syria. The claims aren't very subtle: Russia's ambassador to the European Union, Vladimir Chizhov, called one chemical attack a "staged event," adding that the White Helmets were "already caught in the act with staged videos."

Russian state media—Sputnik and RT—as well as a conspiracy-leaning site called 21st Century Wire that's often described as sympathetic to the Russian government, began attacking the White Helmets as a terrorist organization in 2018, deeming them likely responsible for the chemical attacks in cooperation with the actual Syrian terrorist group Al-Nusra Front. (In June 2018, for example, both RT and Sputnik claimed that the White Helmets were preparing a "false flag chemical attack" in Idlib, Syria.) Drawing on their large volume of material, far-right bloggers in the United States started to echo the accusation.

The overall effect was to whitewash Assad's deadly attacks on civilians, casting doubt on their source, and to make it sound as if anyone who talks about the brutality of the Assad regime is a mindless warmonger. Roger Waters of Pink Floyd attacked the White Helmets onstage, calling them "a fake organization that exists only to create propaganda for the jihadists and terrorists," adding, "If we would listen to the propaganda of the White Helmets and others, we would be encouraged to encourage our governments to go and start dropping bombs on people in Syria." And Vanessa Beeley, a blogger at 21st Century Wire, claimed that the White Helmets' work rescuing civilians is actually a sinister act of imperialist control. "Led by the US and UK this group is essential to the propaganda stream that facilitates the continued media and political campaign against the elected Syrian government," she wrote in 2016, "and permits the US and NATO to justify their regime of crippling economic and humanitarian sanctions against the Syrian people."

THE TERM "FALSE FLAG" ITSELF HAS BECOME MORE COMPLICATED OVER time. Jones and lesser-known conspiracists, for example, have sometimes said that an incident is a "hybrid:" partly real, partly staged by the government—the Las Vegas shooting as well as the Pulse nightclub massacre have been described that way. How exactly that could be is mind-bending, but it's a way to point at a theory—the government had a hand in this—without having to interrogate it fully or prove it. (The theorizer might imply that the shooter was brainwashed or mind-controlled into carrying out the government's dark scheme, but they often decline to be quite that explicit. Jones, for example, speculated that Stephen Paddock was "a patsy" or a victim of CIA brainwashing; InfoWars claimed that an unnamed government source said the attack might have been intended to "increase the Shadow Government's Surveillance State.")

Additional events identified as false flags have come to include ever-more-insignificant and far-flung incidents: Robert Ussery, the conspiracy theorist arrested for trespassing at the Sutherland Springs church, claimed that a hot-air-balloon crash outside Austin and even a biker shootout in Waco were both government-orchestrated false flags.

The logic of false flaggery has become so convoluted that Ussery and other lesser conspiracy theorists have said that Alex Jones is *himself* a false flag, a government plant designed for a sinister purpose. "Alex Jones promotes the hoaxes as real," Ussery wrote darkly, and incorrectly, on his website. "He is a lying gatekeeper, a government sponsored traitor."

Even the maker of *Loose Change*, Dylan Avery, has expressed alarm at the rise of false flag thinking. He told the *Outline* in 2018 that he sometimes felt alienated from the movement that his film helped create. "Before, when you said you believed in 9/11 Truth, it meant the original investigation was shoddy," Avery said. "But you weren't a nut-job. Now, as soon as something happens, people say it's a false flag."

HOW DO IDEAS SUCH AS FALSE FLAGS—SOME OF THE MOST COMPLEX, unintuitive, hard-to-believe conspiracy theories on the planet—spread and gain such power and force? Kate Starbird, a researcher at the University of Washington, led a team that in 2017 released a study on the ways hoaxes and false flag theories proliferate online following mass shootings. They found that a few sites were central to sharing, spreading, and furthering hoax theories: BeforeItsNews.com, NoDisinfo.com, and VeteransToday.com (a normal-sounding site that frequently runs stories questioning the veracity of Sandy Hook and other mass shootings).

The team found that the conversation around false flags is, not surprisingly, fueled by "alternative" media sites, most of which have certain, easy-to-recognize themes and biases: hostility toward science and the mainstream media is common. "In addition to anti-globalist and anti-media views, we found content that was anti-vaccine, anti-GMO, and anti–climate science," Starbird and her coauthors wrote. "Most alternative media domains contained accusations about the activities of George Soros and the Rothschilds, and almost all hosted articles referencing "pedophile rings" of high-powered people around the world."

There was another important element: the same stories, sometimes verbatim, appeared on different sites, over and over again. "We found the same stories on multiple domains, sometimes as exact copies, but also in different forms," the team noted. "This means that an individual using these sites is likely seeing the same messages in different forms and in different places, which may distort their perception of this information as it gives the false appearance of source diversity."

I often saw the same thing in conspiracy news sources, the most intriguing source being a writer named Makia Freeman. That probably isn't his real name (nothing matching showed up in public records). For years his byline appeared across the conspiracy-verse, on a variety of little-known sites: ToolsForFreedom.com, Wake Up World, Paranoia Magazine, The Daily Sheeple, and The Sleuth Journal, as well as the slightly better-trafficked Before It's News. On one site, Freeman's online bio said that he writes on "many aspects of the global conspiracy, from vaccines to Zionism to false flag operations and more, and also including info on natural health, sovereignty and higher consciousness." As with the conspiracy sources Starbird studied, Freeman's articles frequently appeared identically or near-identically across multiple sites, populating an information world that is, on closer inspection, a lot like a hall of mirrors.

The motives of sites such as Before It's News or The Daily Sheeple can be hard to parse, beyond generating clicks through frightening, outrageous, and alarming headlines. Sometimes, though, the motives are a little clearer. That's the case with NewsBusters.org, a site run by the

conservative group Media Research Center. The MRC is funded
largely by the Mercer family, who backed Trump and a host of other
ultra-conservative causes. NewsBusters is focused on liberal media lies,
and it is prominently shared by other conspiracy sites.

Starbird's research also found that Twitter users who shared information from NoDisinfo and Veterans Today were more prone to sharing information from RT and Sputnik. In other words, there are unholy
and chaotic alliances among state-sponsored actors, bots, trolls, and
garden-variety conspiracy theorists to help advance untrue stories, fun-
neling them from the farthest fringes into the mainstream.

One particularly stunning example was covered by journalist Adrian
Chen, who wrote in 2015 about a "troll farm" in St. Petersburg, Russia,
where an army of employees paid by the Internet Research Agency sat
all day long, posting disinformation and trying to sow chaos around
catastrophic events in the United States. Some were real natural disas-
ters, while some were entirely false events: nonexistent fires, fake shootings. The Internet Research Agency, Chen found, possibly had ties to
an oligarch who was an ally of Vladimir Putin. The "troll farms," as
Chen explained in the *New Yorker*, were also part of an effort to knee-
cap Internet-based organizing and weaken people's confidence in what
they saw online. "Trolling has become a key tool in a comprehensive
effort by Russian authorities to rein in a previously freewheeling Internet culture," he wrote, particularly after massive anti-Putin protests were
organized on social media.

MOST OF THE TIME, FALSE FLAG CONSPIRACY THEORIES DO NOT HAVE
far-reaching global implications. Usually, the effect of the theorists is to
make the lives of mass casualty survivors very difficult, and the wider
world does not necessarily hear about it. The harassment of the families in Sutherland Springs, for example, amounted to a couple of tiny
national news blips.

Particularly painful for individual survivors is the idea of the crisis
actor. For close to a decade, even as false flag peddlers harassed and ter-
rorized people who had lost loved ones in mass shootings, much of the
United States had never heard that term. That changed in February 2018,

when a mass shooter killed seventeen people and wounded seventeen more at Marjory Stoneman Douglas High School in Parkland, Florida.

Some of the teenagers who survived the Parkland attack became immediate and well-spoken advocates for gun control, transforming their pain and grief into political action. As they became more famous, students such as David Hogg and Emma González were subjected to intense hostility and false flag suspicions. It struck many of the usual suspects as just too tidy and contrived that they were attacked (with a gun) and immediately began fighting for gun control. But Hogg and González and the other Parkland teens responded forcefully to accusations that they were tools of the federal government. "I'm not a crisis actor," Hogg told Anderson Cooper on CNN, a few days after the shooting. "I'm someone who had to witness this and live through this."

Thus the wider world discovered the concept of the crisis actor. It first appeared, however, years earlier, immediately following the killings at the Sandy Hook Elementary School, on a number of conspiracy blogs that seized on a press release issued by a company called Visionbox. Located in Denver, Visionbox is an acting studio; a little over a month before the Sandy Hook shootings, the company announced that its students were available to help with "active shooter drills and mall shooting full-scale exercises." They were clearly offering to help companies and law enforcement with such exercises, but conspiracy theorists seized on the phrasing, specifically a section that promised the students were willing to play civilians.

"The actors can play the part of the shooters, mall employees, shoppers in the mall, shoppers who continue to arrive at the mall, media reporters and others rushing to the mall, and persons in motor vehicles around the mall," the release read. "Visionbox Crisis Actors can also play the role of citizens calling 911 or mall management, or posting comments on social media websites." Two sites, Fellowship of the Minds and Memory Hole Blog, pounced on the press release as evidence that "crisis actors," a term they quickly co-opted, were being hired to carry out fake events like Sandy Hook. And if the events were staged, then the victims—the dead and the wounded—were also faked, alive and well, perhaps, or wholly invented. Soon, James Tracy, the publisher and main author behind Memory Hole Blog, became embroiled in a feud with a

Sandy Hook family over their murdered child, one that dragged on for
years.

Lenny and Veronique Pozner were the parents of Noah Pozner, the
youngest child to die in the mass school shooting. Sandy Hook conspiracy theorists insist that Noah never existed and thus never died. Or
else they sarcastically insist that he died twice, once at Sandy Hook and
again in Peshawar, Pakistan, two years later, where Noah's photograph
was displayed at a memorial for child shooting victims in Pakistan
(although he was not represented as a victim of that shooting).

A father of four, James Tracy was for many years a professor of
media studies at Florida Atlantic University. A syllabus for one of Tracy's
classes shows a very thoughtful reading list about the role of conspiracy theories in public life and conspiracy panics—the periodic sense we
get in the United States that conspiracies are swamping us, taking over,
and warping reality. But something changed for Tracy, and he went from
teaching a syllabus related to conspiracy theories to spreading some of
the most egregious ones. In December 2015, in an op-ed for the Florida
Sun-Sentinel, the Pozners wrote that Tracy had begun harassing them
after they demanded that conspiracy sites stop using Noah's image.

"Tracy even sent us a certified letter demanding proof that Noah
once lived, that we were his parents, and that we were the rightful owner
of his photographic image," they wrote. "We found this so outrageous
and unsettling that we filed a police report for harassment. Once Tracy
realized we would not respond, he subjected us to ridicule and contempt
on his blog, boasting to his readers that the 'unfulfilled request' was
'noteworthy' because we had used copyright claims to 'thwart continued
research of the Sandy Hook massacre event.'"

The Pozners also charged that Tracy was using his university credentials to bolster his assertions. In a response letter to the Pozners'
op-ed that was never published but that Tracy later read in court, he
wrote, "The Pozners, alas, are as phony as the drill itself and profiting
handsomely from the fake death of their son."

Tracy was eventually fired for his writing on the Memory Hole Blog
site, with FAU claiming that he hadn't properly disclosed the blog as an
"outside activity" that could potentially affect the university. Tracy
promptly sued FAU, alleging wrongful termination and an abridgment

of his rights to free speech, but he lost. He always maintained that he didn't discuss Sandy Hook in class, and that outside of work he was just asking questions the media refused to consider. In a statement to CNN, he wrote that his research "led me to conclude that the nation's media failed to provide an accurate, in-depth and sustained investigation of what took place at the school on the morning of December 14."

The unanswered questions are how did Tracy come to hold the beliefs that he does, and how did they come to control his life to the extent that he lost his job and a good deal of his public standing? Tracy appeared frequently on conspiracy podcasts but never submitted to an interview with an actual journalist. In response to an interview request, he referred me to his attorney, Louis Leo IV, who repeated that Tracy never discussed Sandy Hook with his FAU students and his firing was illegal. "Tracy's case has nothing to do with 'Pozner' (if that's even a real name) or Sandy Hoax," Leo wrote. "It's about the First Amendment."

In a phone conversation, Leo proved himself eager to join and even outdo his clients in mass-shooting denialism. "I think Sandy Hook was staged," he said, then paused, and corrected himself. "I don't like to use that because you can stage a real shooting. They were making things up. Nobody died." The theory Leo and other Sandy Hook truthers subscribed to was that the school had been closed for years before the attack took place. "If you look at some parts of the school, it was in disrepair," he said. "It was like a ghost school. It had been out of service. Hadn't been functioning as a real school in a long time."

"This category of recent conspiracy theorists is really a global network of village idiots," Pozner told me by phone. "They would have never been able to find each other before, but now it's this synergistic effect of the combination of all of them from all over the world. There are haters from Australia and Europe and they can all make a YouTube video in fifteen seconds." Pozner was, as *New York* magazine noted, mildly interested in the fun, lighthearted kinds of conspiracy theories before his son died: Bigfoot, Area 51, the one about how the Denver Airport is a secret Illuminati hub. He would sometimes tune in to InfoWars in his car, but he didn't take it, or Alex Jones, at all seriously.

After Noah died, when people like Jones started to call the attack suspicious ("I've looked at it," Jones declared in 2014, "and undoubtedly there's a cover-up, there's actors, they're manipulating, they've been caught lying, and they were pre-planning before it and rolled out with it"), Pozner took on a new mission. As Sandy Hook theories started ricocheting around the Internet, he thought he could probably talk some sense into the people spreading those theories, given that he was once a lot like them.

Pozner quickly found that trying to engage with conspiracy theorists just made him an object of threats and suspicion by an army of Internet personalities. For his trouble, Pozner was fixated on by two of the biggest Sandy Hook hoax peddlers, Tracy and Wolfgang Halbig. A grandfather from Florida, Halbig claims to be a former state trooper and "school safety expert." He became a Sandy Hook denier early, making a speech before the Newtown Board of Education in 2014, saying that he wished only to find the truth about the murdered children. He has since made dozens of trips to Newtown, spending all of his pension and $100,000 more, and returning even as a growing chorus of Newtown dads let him know he's in danger of an ass-kicking.

"I call it an illusion," Halbig told the BBC, referring to Sandy Hook. "The biggest government illusion that's ever been pulled off by Homeland Security." He added, "I'll be honest with you. If I'm wrong, I need to be institutionalized."

When Pozner tried to contact Halbig, before he stopped working to persuade the deniers, he got a response from a different Sandy Hook denier. "Wolfgang does not wish to speak with you," this person wrote, "unless you exhume Noah's body and prove to the world you lost your son."

Eventually, Pozner sued Halbig for invasion of privacy. Around the same time he filed the suit, he assembled what he called a "one-hundred-page book" about Halbig's life to demonstrate what Pozner sees as his habit of lying and misrepresentation.

According to Pozner, Halbig's interest in Sandy Hook was only the latest in a long line of similar obsessions. "[Halbig gave] other hoaxers and harassers copies of my TransUnion Comprehensive Background check, copies of my driver's license, social security numbers of myself and family members, and photos if they donated money to his 'Sandy

Hook Justice' nonprofit." Pozner says. "He has sent thousands of harassing emails over the years: to me, to my attorney, to other victims' families,
to the school board members, to the police, to government officials,
even to the FBI. I had to file charges with the police to get him to stop
contacting me, not just with claims about my son and my family but
about a whole host of other conspiracies that he was trying to raise
money to pursue."

Pozner points out that a retiree with grandchildren presumably has
better ways to spend his time. "He doesn't go fishing or get together
with his buddies. He starts blasting out these harassing emails to the
FBI, to governors, to police, to school districts, to crime victims, to my
attorney who then charges me because every email he has to read for
fifteen minutes. It's a nightmare." Pozner has spent, he says, thousands
of dollars in legal bills "just in Halbig sending spam. It's insane."

None of this seemed to bother Halbig, who maintained a cherubi-
cally sunny demeanor at every public appearance. He was even thrilled
when nine Newtown families brought suit against the manufacturers
of the AR-15, the gun that the shooter, Adam Lanza, used to kill their
children. "They'll have to exhume the bodies to prove it was the AR-15
that actually killed the children," he told *New York* giddily.

Halbig and Tracy are only the most well-known Sandy Hook deniers.
There is also James Fetzer, a professor emeritus at the University of Minnesota Duluth, who has written about conspiracy theories since around
2000, beginning with JFK and accelerating into Sandy Hook denialism.
His barebones blog has exposed everything he considers a false flag or
an operation by Mossad, Israel's intelligence service, which is a lot of
things. A Holocaust denier, too, Fetzer maintained that Sandy Hook
was "a FEMA drill to promote gun control," one in which nobody
died.

In an object lesson on the spread of conspiracism—and the ways it
can immiserate everyone involved—sites like Fetzer's succeeded in
converting fifty-seven-year-old Lucy Richards of Brandon, Florida, to
denialism. Richards was at one point a waitress, but according to court
documents had been living on disability payments for thirteen years, diagnosed first with agoraphobia and then obsessive-compulsive disorder. She

didn't have a computer, but she had a cell phone. At some point, she started reading, and that reading took her to some strange places, among them InfoWars and James Fetzer's website.

It's difficult to tell what about the story affected her, what button it pushed, what triggered an apparently volcanic rage. On January 10, 2016, Richards called and emailed Lenny Pozner. "Look behind you," one message read. "Death is coming to you real soon."

"Death is coming to you real soon and there's nothing you can do about it."

"LOOK BEHIND YOU, IT IS DEATH."

Richards made little effort to mask her identity, but it took almost an entire year for her to be charged. She told her lawyer that she was "reared in a hellhole." At the time she stumbled on Sandy Hook denialism, she'd been estranged from her family for years. In her mugshots, Richards is a ghastly figure, with stringy hair, a pasty face, and a desperate expression.

She was indicted on four counts of transmitting threats across state lines, a federal offense. A plea deal would have allowed her to serve her sentence of five months on house arrest, but Richards failed to show up for her initial sentencing hearing. She was arrested and sentenced to serve out her time in jail.

"I don't know where my head and my heart were that day when I made the calls, but they were not in the right place," Richards meekly told the court when she was sentenced. As part of her sentence, the judge forbade her from looking at conspiracy websites.

LENNY POZNER, MEANWHILE, FOUND THAT HIS LIFE HAD BEEN devoured—or shaped, if we want to put it more neutrally—by his crusade against the "truthers," a term he preferred not to use. (He dubbed them "hoaxers" instead.) A few years after Sandy Hook, he formed an organization called the HONR Network, devoted to fighting denial and other kinds of conspiracism he considered particularly toxic, the kind in which the families of murdered children are harassed. YouTube was where he focused most of his energy.

"The responsible parties are Facebook and Google and YouTube," he said. He would file copyright complaints or a terms of service violation whenever a website or a video used photos of Noah taken by the Pozners. As often as not, Google and YouTube refused to respond or sent polite auto-replies rejecting the complaints as having no merit. "Fighting with Google is a constant," he said.

Pozner made a case that he recognizes as unappealing for some: for more regulation and control of the Internet, arguing that this is the only thing that can pull us back from the brink. "I understand that the concept of greater user safety measures is unpopular with these social media platforms because of cost and ideology," Pozner told me. "But we can't sustain an Internet that is unsafe for users and overrun with content that causes mass delusion, violence, and a threat to democracy."

5

USEFUL MURDERS

Seth Rich was shot early on Sunday, July 10, 2016, not far from his apartment in northwest Washington, DC. In their grief and exhaustion, Seth's family bleakly joked that, upon dying, he got an immediate promotion.

Seth was twenty-seven years old, just starting a promising career at the Democratic National Committee as voter-expansion data director. He was on his way home at around 4 a.m. when he was hit by gunfire. He'd last been seen at 1:30 at a bar a forty-minute walk from his apartment. Phone records show that he called his girlfriend at around 2 a.m., and they spoke for more than two hours before he hung up abruptly. Police on patrol in the neighborhood, responding to the sound of gunshots, found Seth alive and breathing and discovered evidence of a struggle, including damage to his watch and bruises on his hands and face. Seth died later that day at an area hospital. Police told his family that they suspected a botched robbery, but nothing was taken from him, including his wallet. The perpetrator was never caught. It took less than thirty-six hours after Seth died for the situation to go from simply tragic to something much darker and more bizarre.

The story of Seth Rich—the way his murder became worldwide news, a set of interlocking accusations, suspicions, and purported schemes—illustrates a few things: One is the role of conspiracy entrepreneurs, those people who make a living and a name for themselves hawking speculation about Rich's death and Hillary Clinton's health and John Podesta's pizza habits. A lot of people used Rich's death for commercial ends, peddling a particular conspiracy narrative about how he died to boost their own fame, enhance their public profiles, and get themselves on TV, all of which they did quite successfully.

More important, Rich's death became a particular and gruesome illustration of the political usefulness of conspiracy theories in America. For a variety of reasons, Trump supporters—and quite possibly the president himself—were deeply invested in promoting their own version of how Rich died. His death shows the way in which self-interested political actors can lift a conspiracy theory out of obscurity and work to legitimize it, inspiring further "investigation" into a bogus idea. They use the results of that investigation to push the idea even farther, and what results is an endless feedback loop that creates an alternate reality.

The conspiracy entrepreneurs are by now well known to us. But what about the people who buy the information they're selling? What do these consumers choose to do with their newfound knowledge? In the *New York Times*, writer Jonathan Mahler dubbed the activity of serious conspiracy consumers as "not quite investigating" but "self-investigating." (The phrase comes from Pizzagate gunman Edgar Welch himself; not long after he was handcuffed and pinned to the pavement, he told police he'd come to Comet Ping Pong to "self-investigate" the Pizzagate allegations. In a jailhouse interview with the *Times*, a depressed and exhausted Welch said the same thing in a different way: he had gone there to "shine some light.") The Seth Rich story, an unsolved murder in the heart of DC, with its connections to the Democratic Party and a heated election, was tailor-made for the self-investigators and the people who profit from them.

"It had to have started on Sunday," the same day Seth was killed, his brother Aaron Rich told me almost a year later. When Seth died, Aaron's wife was out of town, and so his aunt and uncle and then a cavalcade of friends came to sit with him in Denver, where he lived. They followed the news in a daze.

"We're watching these stories come out, and it starts out as 'DNC staffer killed,'" Aaron said, remembering the news headlines. "Then it becomes 'DNC official,' then 'top DNC official.' We're watching this progress as he's moving up the ranks in the DNC in each article." Aaron thought bitterly that by the end of the day, Seth would be Hillary Clinton's running mate.

The next day, a friend looked on Reddit and told Aaron with alarm that Seth's death was the subject of speculation on a long thread. He said it was split about 50 percent condolences and 50 percent conspiracies, Aaron remembered. A little later, as the thread stretched to three pages, the balance had shifted all the way over to one side. The thread was reposted on several subreddits, including r/conspiracy and r/the_ Donald, a place where alt-right Trump supporters hang out to swap conspiracies as well as racist, anti-Semitic, and misogynistic memes. One r/conspiracy thread was titled "Young DNC voter database employee shot and killed with two shots to his back. Nothing was taken, no witnesses. He had allegedly talked about Hillary Clinton trying to buy voting machine companies with money and threats before." It linked to a New York *Daily News* story that accurately reported on Rich's death and didn't contain a word about him supposedly speaking about Clinton.

The thread garnered hundreds of comments and thousands of upvotes, even as numerous commenters noted the discrepancy and labeled it, in one person's words, "ridiculous speculative bullshit." At some point, Reddit moderators archived the thread, preventing anyone new from commenting, and flagged it as "misleading."

But the skeleton of a theory was there, in the suggestion that Rich's death was suspiciously and inextricably linked to Clinton. Other comments implied that perhaps Rich had been a disgruntled Bernie Sanders supporter or even—absurdly—a disaffected Trump fan who somehow found himself working for the DNC. Didn't it make sense that Clinton would stop at nothing to silence him? After all, someone noted, echoing dozens of others, "this is not the first person who has died with suspicious Clinton ties."

The whole thing struck Aaron Rich and his family as "insane." "Just the amount of loose connections people were pulling together, based on the fact that he worked at the DNC and his LinkedIn profile," he said. "It wasn't just a random wrong-place, wrong-time thing to them." Eventually, Rich's parents stated that Seth had just accepted a job with the Clinton campaign before he died, making it even less likely that he would be a leaker or the target of a Clintonian contract killing.

The family tried at first to cope with it all through "morbid humor," Aaron recalled. "We were joking that Seth would be happy if he envisioned a parade of people, his friends and family on one side of the street and conspiracy theorists on the other." But on July 13, three days after Seth died, the conspiracy theories started to coalesce into a more coherent story when a site called WhatDoesItMean.com claimed that he had been on his way to testify against Clinton before the FBI when he died. (Again, Rich was shot at around 4 a.m., and he was on his way home from a bar.)

WhatDoesItMean is almost indescribably weird. Visually, it's a chaotic riot of hyperlinks, Masonic symbols, and poorly photoshopped pictures. Textually, it contains the most farfetched allegations you can possibly think of—"FACEBOOK DECLARES ITSELF A RELIGION"—sitting next to perfectly sober aggregated headlines about world news. WhatDoesItMean claims to be authored by the "Sisters of Sorcha Faal," a purported ancient Christian order of nuns; archived versions of the site from 2004 identify its author as someone named David Booth, an "internationally known psychic, researcher, and author."

The site's most outlandish information is often attributed to "a Foreign Intelligence Service Report circulating in the Kremlin," which was also cited as the source for its Seth Rich information. (The Foreign Intelligence Service is a real entity, Russia's intelligence service for matters outside the country, although the site's purported reports often don't seem to show up anywhere besides WhatDoesItMean.)

The site's Seth Rich story had a special twist: the FBI agents Seth was on his way to meet were really hit men working for Clinton. And although WhatDoesItMean seems like obvious and crazed nonsense to most people, it gave the true believers on Reddit a sober conceptual framework on which to hang their Clinton body count, a story citing an official-sounding source. People shared the posts without adhering to basic fact-checking standards or noting the site's disclaimer, which reads, "Some events depicted in certain articles on this website are fictitious and any similarity to any person living or dead is merely coincidental. Some other articles may be based on actual events but which in certain cases incidents, characters and timelines have been changed for dramatic purposes. Certain characters may be composites, or entirely fictitious."

It's possible that the Seth Rich story would have stayed permanently in the distant, verdant jungles of the wildest conspiracy sites. To go truly viral, conspiracies need a famous name or a big media outlet as an accelerant, the connective tissue that connects the fringe with the power players, the obscure with the mainstream. Things began to feel "fully fucked up," as Aaron put it, a month later, when out of the blue Julian Assange of WikiLeaks began to imply that he knew something about Seth's death. Assange was holed up in the Ecuadorian embassy in London where he had received asylum when he gave an interview to a Dutch TV station. In the interview, he strongly suggested that Rich had been a mole for WikiLeaks, giving them hacked emails from the DNC and John Podesta that appeared on the site soon after Rich had been killed.

"Whistleblowers go to significant efforts to get us material, and often very significant risks," he told his interviewer. "There's a 27-year-old that works for the DNC who was shot in the back, murdered, just a few weeks ago, for unknown reasons as he was walking down the streets in Washington." WikiLeaks then offered a $20,000 reward for information on Rich's murder without confirming or denying that he was their source but hinting at it at every opportunity.

It is more likely, according to the American intelligence community, that WikiLeaks received the hacked emails from a Russian-backed Romanian hacking group going by the alias Guccifer 2.0. But the Rich story was instantly convenient for Assange, letting him distance himself from the accusation that WikiLeaks was little more than a conduit for damaging Russian information about the Democrats and Clinton. Over time, WikiLeaks' Twitter account found reason to comment on every tiny development in the Rich case, although its only official statement on the matter read, "As a matter of policy, we do not confirm or deny whether any person has ever been a source for WikiLeaks." The organization "treat[s] threats toward any suspected source of WikiLeaks with extreme gravity," the statement continued. "This should not be taken to imply that Seth Rich was a source to Wikileaks or to imply that his murder is connected to our publications."

Until this point, the Rich family had readily spoken to the media, mostly local DC outlets, emphasizing their desire to find any information that might help solve Seth's murder. That changed after Assange's involvement. "When WikiLeaks happened, we realized we would get completely different kinds of questions and that it would be a whole new world," Aaron said.

Sensing that they were out of their depth, the family asked Seth's friends if someone was available to help field media requests. Brad Bauman, the former executive director of the Congressional Progressive Caucus, who had represented various progressive and Democratic causes, volunteered to work with the family for free. WikiLeaks immediately attacked him as "Seth Rich's new 'family spokesman,'" with heavy sarcastic emphasis. Reddit detectives also smelled a rat. "The Clintons have gotten to Seth Rich's parents (Joel and Mary) and have completely silenced them," one wrote on r/Conspiracy. "They thought we'd been assigned a handler to keep us quiet," Aaron said dryly.

In just a few short weeks, the Rich family had been forced to grieve the loss of their son and brother while simultaneously processing a bizarre new reality. Seth—whom they knew as goofy, sweet, and talkative—was now at the center of any number of sinister schemes, and everything they themselves did looked suspicious. Then came the hucksters. Before long, private "investigators" and "journalists" of every stripe emerged from the woodwork with offers of help. One Republican lobbyist, Jack Burkman, put up a $130,000 reward for information on the case, papering the neighborhoods near where Rich died with posters reading, "Do you know who killed Seth Rich?"

Before the Rich case, Burkman was best known for claiming in 2014 that he was working on legislation that would "ban" openly gay players in the NFL—legislation that never actually materialized—and for working on both pro- and anti-Trump initiatives during the election. He wasn't habitually known as a conspiracy theorist, but it soon became clear that he was interested in promoting a baseless claim that Rich was killed by the Russian government, which he insisted on airing on several local news programs. "Somebody whacked him," he told a *Mother Jones* reporter. At one point, Burkman announced his curious intention to solve Rich's murder by staging a public reenactment of it with six to ten actors, something he eventually carried out on the street where Rich died, as Rich's disgusted neighbors clustered to watch.

For Aaron and the Rich family, the involvement of people like Burkman was the point at which it became hard to determine who sincerely wanted to help, who might have a real tip, and who was peddling self-interested, publicity-hungry snake oil. "We want to trust everyone and we can't," Aaron said at the time. The Riches had to accept that some people might have been offering a lifeline, but the family could not "necessarily trust them enough to take it anymore."

The Rich family was right to be wary, as the strange moths flitting around the morbid light of Seth Rich's death got a little more numerous over the next year. They included a former Playboy model named Robbin Young, who claimed to be in contact with Guccifer 2.0, purportedly a lone Romanian hacker (but who was, as US intelligence said, much more likely to be a Russian-backed hacking group). Young said that she and Guccifer 2.0 had long conversations about Seth Rich, and she published the purported chat logs (to which WikiLeaks helpfully tweeted a link). Young did not seem aware that she probably wasn't speaking to who she thought: in an interview with *Vice*, it became clear that her Mr. 2.0 did not speak Romanian, which seems like a real hitch for someone believed to be from Romania. At some point, Young decided she was at the white-hot center of something very dangerous, tweeting that the FBI wanted to talk to her and imploring her followers to avenge her if she died or disappeared.

Alt-right blogger Mike Cernovich got involved, too, as did Jack Posobiec, a slightly lesser-known ideological traveler. Posobiec shot to Twitter mega-stardom when he started working for a group called Citizens for Trump, which brought him into contact with the campaign. He had actively trafficked in hoaxes and disinformation from the election onward, at one point self-investigating Comet Ping Pong, that is, getting kicked out of the restaurant for videotaping himself harassing and interrogating staffers. Posobiec particularly latched onto the Rich case, promoting a fake story that the DC police chief had resigned and taken a job with the NFL as a cushy payoff for covering up the details of Seth's murder. In May 2017, he made it into an Oval Office group photo op and tried to yell a question about the case at Donald Trump.

A conspiracy that Cernovich and Posobiec promote will spread far and fast among their fanbase of alt-righters and Trump Reddit trolls. And the new hucksters joined with the old: the Rich stories were also spread by Roger Stone, who's made political hay for decades out of claiming the Clintons orchestrate the murders of their political opponents. "Clinton body count" is Stone's term, and he's promoted one of the oldest Clinton conspiracies, that White House staffer Vince Foster, who died by suicide in 1993, was killed by the Clintons to cover up a corruption scandal. (These days, Stone's allegation seems to be that Foster killed himself but the Clintons "moved the body.") Thus, Seth Rich's death joined a towering mountain of moldering garbage pushed by some of the worst people ever to open a Twitter account.

IT'S NOT AN ACCIDENT THAT INTEREST IN SETH RICH'S DEATH ACCEL-erated in right-wing news outlets in the spring of 2017. They were spurred by the biggest conspiracy megaphone there is: Fox News, specifically Sean Hannity, the network's biggest Trump defender. We have some reason to believe the White House, or possibly Trump himself, was invested in promoting the Seth Rich murder story, both as an indirect way of rallying his base and to distract from a new problem: in May that year, the Department of Justice appointed former FBI director Robert Mueller to lead a special investigation into "any links and/or coordination between the Russian government and individuals associated with the campaign of President Donald Trump."

Sean Hannity's wholesale fall into Seth Rich trutherism began with Rod Wheeler, another private investigator who briefly worked for the family. (He's also a semifrequent Fox News contributor, who once memorably claimed that gangs of lesbians were stalking the streets, recruiting children.) In a story on Fox 5, a local DC affiliate, Wheeler claimed that he had a source at the FBI who could prove Rich communicated with WikiLeaks. Fox News then ran its own version of the story nationally, which exploded in a spray of bullshit across every right-wing outlet there is.

But Wheeler backtracked almost immediately. He vaguely told Fox 5 there had been a "miscommunication," as it announced on May 17, and that he didn't actually have any such proof. In a defamation and discrimination lawsuit he later filed against Fox, he argued that he never said any of the quotes attributed to him. Fox 5 retracted its story within two days, but it took national Fox News a full week to issue its own weak-kneed retraction, which said only that the story "was not initially subjected to the high degree of editorial scrutiny we require for all our reporting."

In that week, Hannity devoted an increasing amount of time to Rich conspiracies. Fox personalities Laura Ingraham and Lou Dobbs also gave airtime to the Rich case, but Hannity was by far the most fervent. He even announced plans to interview Kim Dotcom, an eccentric Internet maven who lives in New Zealand (and who was resisting extradition to the United States, where he was wanted on charges of fraud and racketeering), after Dotcom dubiously claimed that he had known Rich was the source of the WikiLeaks emails all along. Hannity was giddy. "Stay tuned," he tweeted. "Public invitation Kim Dotcom to be a guest on radio and TV. #GameChanger Buckle up destroy Trump media. Sheep that u all are!!!"

A day after Hannity's invite to Dotcom, Mary and Joel Rich published a raw editorial in the *Washington Post*. "Seth's death has been turned into a political football," they wrote. "Every day we wake up to new headlines, new lies, new factual errors, new people approaching us to take advantage of us and Seth's legacy. It just won't stop."

Why would it not stop? Why the mounting Seth Rich fervor? A possible explanation came via Wheeler's lawsuit against Fox News, in which he said that the White House had encouraged him to push the Seth Rich conspiracy theories to draw attention away from the administration's alleged Russian collusion. Wheeler claimed that he had been paid by a wealthy Trump supporter, Ed Butowsky, who cooked up a plot with the administration and Fox News to "help put to bed speculation that President Trump colluded with Russia in an attempt to influence the outcome of the presidential election."

According to Wheeler's suit, Butowsky had claimed that Trump was eagerly awaiting the Rich story, texting Wheeler, "Not to add any more pressure but the president just read the article," allegedly referring to the Fox News national story. "He wants the article out immediately. It's now all up to you. But don't feel the pressure." The suit noted that Butowsky and Wheeler had met with the press secretary, Sean Spicer, to apprise him of the Rich story. That was, staggeringly, true, confirmed by Spicer, showing a startling level of cooperation between Fox and the White House. Spicer told NPR that Butowsky and Wheeler merely briefed him on the progress of the story: "It had nothing to do with advancing the president's domestic agenda—and there was no agenda." (Butowsky, meanwhile, claimed to NPR that he had been "joking" in his text to Wheeler.)

Other Trump media supporters also weren't particularly interested in the accuracy of Fox 5's report. Between May and June 2017, conservative outlet Breitbart ran at least twelve articles about Rich's death, many of them heavily implying that it was suspicious, and castigated "left-wing media" like CNN and the New York Times for ignoring the story in favor of "conspiracy articles about Russian hacking." That line of thought was echoed by former Speaker of the House and Trump loyalist Newt Gingrich, who attacked the focus on the Russian collusion allegations. "We have this very strange story now of this young man who worked for the Democratic National Committee and who was apparently assassinated at 4 in the morning," Gingrich declared, "having given WikiLeaks 53,000 emails and 17,000 attachments. Nobody is investigating that. And what does that tell you about what was going on? Because, it turns out, it wasn't the Russians. It was this young guy who, I suspect, was disgusted by the corruption of the Democratic National Committee. He's been killed, and apparently nothing serious has been done to investigate his murder."

The Russian embassy in London—another political entity eager to distract from any potential Russian hacking—got in on the action, too. "WikiLeaks informer Seth Rich murdered in US," the embassy's verified Twitter account tweeted. "But MSM was so busy accusing Russian hackers to take notice."

THE REASON THAT TRUMP'S MEDIA SUPPORTERS CLUNG SO TIGHTLY TO the Rich case was not just for its political value, but because it worked on some sector of the public. Outrage over the murder served as a useful focal point to organize a Trump base, a straightforward alternate story that could be picked up and rallied around: a brave truth-teller speaking out against DNC corruption was murdered. We can see the cycle clearly at work: the speculations and insinuations of conspiracy peddlers were amplified until they made their way into the mainstream, first via Julian Assange, then Fox News. That attention gave the conspiracy peddlers more grist for their various mills, which in turn gave the self-investigators already sniffing around the Rich story even more material and motivation to continue.

The effect on the public was visible: as the story spread aloft on the wings of smaller conspiracy sites and Fox, every word was carried further by a pliant mob of followers, who tweeted under the hashtag #WhoKilledSethRich and followed each development on Reddit and other message boards. Those folks were neither swayed or convinced by, or even particularly empathetic to, the Rich family. After all, who could say if they were really the ones pleading for mercy or whether a nefarious entity was working their mouths like they were compliant Muppets?

Caitlin Johnstone, a popular independent writer who mostly releases her work on the self-publishing site Medium, embodied the sentiments of the self-appointed Rich detectives. "Speaking for myself I am not pushing any political agenda at all by reporting on the Seth Rich case," she wrote. "I'm pushing the prevention of a world-ending nuclear holocaust." Johnstone argued that nothing less than the fate of the world depended on the story. "If Rich was the DNC leaker," she added, "the life of every single living organism on earth may depend upon the public gaining access to that knowledge. This is infinitely more important than one family's feelings about American public discourse."

The chaos all this unleashed on the Rich family is indescribable: the dubious tips and offers of "help" soon turned to vitriol when the family didn't behave in the desired way. On his radio show Roger Stone accused Seth Rich's parents of engaging in "suspicious" behavior and told the *Miami New Times* that the family didn't have a right to grieve in private. "Their right to privacy is important, but not as important as the public's right to the truth," he said. "Frankly, at this point, the parents should be charged with obstruction." In July, he tweeted a suggestion that they'd been paid off and didn't want to solve their son's murder.

Cernovich and Stone and Posobiec and even Johnstone, then, were the conspiracy entrepreneurs peddling theories to a receptive audience on Twitter and YouTube and Facebook and Medium. It's an extremely canny publicity tactic, a way for such people to adeptly leap from one issue to another, to whatever happens to be capturing the public's attention at any moment. Right-wing conspiracies helped Cernovich transition away from the no-longer-fashionable world of men's rights and juice peddling; they brought Posobiec out of TV-recap obscurity; and they gave Roger Stone the constant negative attention he requires in order to stay alive.

But the self-investigators are just as important, since these theories would not serve the entrepreneurs' purpose if there were no groups of people who were swayed by them. What really motivates the self-investigators? Not many people set out intending to harass a grieving family or add to their pain. Viewed more charitably, self-investigators seem to find meaning, excitement, and purpose in banding together online to solve tantalizing mysteries and cover-ups. For those reasons, they're the bread and butter of conspiracy entrepreneurs.

"Millions of people . . . are abandoning traditional sources of information, from the government to the institutional media, in favor of a D.I.Y. approach to fact-finding," Jonathan Mahler wrote in the *New York Times*, referring to Pizzagate gunman Edgar Welch. In my travels through the far reaches of conspiracy America I, too, met countless people who told me they had uncovered the truth about Seth Rich or Pizzagate or September 11 by doing their "own research," as virtually every person put it. Tellingly, nobody pointed to Mike Cernovich, YouTube, Reddit, or sites like WhatDoesItMean as their source. Instead they cite "primary documents" or more vaguely "a variety of sources."

Online self-investigation has roots as deep as the Internet. It arguably began as blogs became more popular at the turn of the century—Blogger was created in 1999 and WordPress in 2003—and took off in 2005 with the founding of YouTube. In *Real Enemies*, Kathryn Olmsted points out that a variety of 9/11-oriented websites popped up in 2002, dedicating themselves to questioning the real story and advancing the truth movement.

The purpose of the 9/11 truth movement—and virtually every "research community" that's sprung up since—isn't necessarily to advance a complete, coherent, agreed-upon alternate narrative about what happened. As Olmsted notes, many people simply "contented themselves with pointing out the weaknesses of the official story." *Jet fuel can't melt steel beams*, once again.

That certainly happened with Pizzagate, where the number of alternate theories about what really took place reached a dizzying multitude. The Seth Rich story was slightly more streamlined—most of the online investigators seem to agree that he was killed by someone affiliated with the Clintons—but still had a number of competing factions, each with its own narrative and claims to have done the most exhaustive research. And the DNC and Podesta leaks proved invaluable for aspiring self-investigators, providing an actual third-party source, albeit not one that proved the existence of a global sex ring or the murder of a DNC staffer by a crazed presidential candidate. But that's the thing about self-investigation: it only confirms what the investigator thinks she already knows. It's a closed loop, confined to the Internet and to ideas that the investigator finds believable or plausible from the outset.

Mahler likened the phenomenon to a washing machine: "Proceeding from the assumption that the so-called experts are not to be trusted, self-investigators are pushed and pulled by the churn of memes and social media, an endless loop of echoes, reflections and intentional lies," he wrote. "With only themselves and their appetites as a guide, they bypass any information that doesn't suit their predisposition and worldview. The self-investigator's media diet is like an endless breakfast buffet, only without the guilt: Take what you want, leave what you don't."

This seems like an Internet-specific phenomenon, but not everyone agrees. "I'm generally skeptical of claims that say the Internet has changed conspiracy theorizing," Joseph Uscinski, coauthor of *American Conspiracy Theories*, maintained. "I mean, they were burning women at the stake four hundred years ago, long before the Internet. Facebook didn't tell them to do it." He points out, too, that the number of people who visit conspiracy sites is far lower than those who visit non-conspiratorial, traditional news sites. "There's tons of everything on the Internet," he said. "When I put in the words 'duck confit recipe,' I get half a million recipes. But nobody's racing home to cook duck confit. Just because it's there doesn't mean anyone cares. The things people look at are things they're predisposed to look at."

Uscinski's position doesn't take into account the role of social media, however. Through Twitter, Facebook, and YouTube, more and more people who might not be predisposed to reading about the Clinton body count or pedophiles in the pizza parlor will nevertheless run across that content. More important, Facebook and Twitter have a way of flattening information, making every source look the same or appear equally plausible. And YouTube has been criticized for the way its algorithm promotes conspiracy videos, pushing them into viewers' suggested items to watch next.

That has been a long-standing issue with recent, halfhearted fixes. Facebook rolled out a tag flagging misleading news sources several months after the election and even then only in response to criticism that hoaxes had been allowed to flourish unchecked. YouTube said it would add Wikipedia links to videos touching on "contested" topics, a strangely half-formed proposal that was announced without telling Wikipedia about it. (I have never personally seen a YouTube video with a Wikipedia link attached; by the summer of 2018, though, a few search terms, like "Sandy Hook hoax," would show a link to an encyclopedia article about the shooting at the top of the search page. Other search terms, such as "9/11 inside job," did not trigger a similar result.)

Twitter had no particular mechanism for flagging or questioning fake information. At one point, to widespread outrage, CEO Jack Dorsey suggested that journalists using the site should act as its watchdogs and fact-checkers. Permanent Twitter bans are rare and usually spurred by acts such as inciting virulent harassment mobs or making death threats against celebrities. In the winter of 2017, Twitter started removing verification badges from such people as white nationalists, out of concern that its blue check mark implied endorsement of the author's position; it even deleted a few people's accounts, but this was largely too little, too late. YouTube and Facebook's trending topics and videos continued to feature conspiracy sites and channels, although Facebook eventually killed the trending topics feature entirely.

However, social media sites did turn their focus on one particularly prominent conspiracy peddler: Facebook, iTunes, music-streaming service Spotify, email marketing service MailChimp, Pinterest, and eventually Twitter banned InfoWars content; Facebook also barred Alex Jones's personal profile page. Twitter was slow to take action, finally lowering the boom only after Jones appeared on Capitol Hill during a series of congressional hearings into social media companies' efforts to police their content and filter disinformation. Jones picked a fight with Florida senator Marco Rubio in a hallway ("frat boy" and "go back to your bathhouse" were among the jeers) and separately with CNN journalist Oliver Darcy (a "rat"). Twitter said in a statement that a video InfoWars uploaded of the confrontation with Darcy violated its ban on "abusive behavior."

That's not to say, though, that banning conspiracy peddlers from these services is a long-term fix or one without challenges. Social media sites are private companies and free to ban whomever they like. But where to draw the line? Who decides what constitutes hate speech? And surely, in part, some of these services are hamstrung by a grim, darkly funny logical endpoint: Trump is the best-known political figure on earth to use social media to spread conspiracy theories. Any banning policy would, in the end, have to cover him, too.

SOCIAL MEDIA'S MINOR FIXES ARRIVED TOO LATE FOR THE RICH FAMILY. As they discovered, social sites give enterprising self-investigators access to the subjects of their conspiracies as never before. Investigators can tweet at them, leave hateful messages on their Facebook profiles, and follow their movements. That is what happened to the Riches, who by the spring of 2017 had largely retreated from speaking publicly: every interview was the impetus for another round of vitriol, another chorus of accusations and threats.

Self-investigation is a series of little bonfires, all over the country. With the accelerants of fame, media attention, and politically motivated actors, those bonfires can turn into infernos. The implications of Seth's death kept getting bigger and darker until eventually—perhaps inevitably— they conflated with Pizzagate. The Pizzagate Voat board became engulfed by Seth Rich speculation: Rich's death, once solved, would explain a grand unified theory of diabolical deeds perpetrated by the government, from sex trafficking to murder to global enslavement. "If [his] murder is tied to the DNC and people go down for it I think we'll have a mass awakening to the evil that is our ruling elite," one user opined.

The speculation and anticipatory excitement only continued as every month brought a new and more bizarre Seth Rich development. In June 2017, a group calling itself the Profiling Project announced that its investigation of the primary evidence concluded that Rich's death was the work of either a serial killer or a gun for hire. The volunteers on the Profiling Project were George Washington University forensic psychology graduate students and instructors. One of them, Kevin Doherty, told *Newsweek*, "The fact that this person has gotten away with it shows a level of proficiency." Crucially, the group was wholly funded by Jack Burkman, the Republican lobbyist hell-bent on proving that Russians killed Seth, who pledged that he would never stop his quest, even though the Rich family had long since stopped speaking to him and begged publicly for an end to "partisan narratives."

In the end, the one thing that the Rich family wanted most—to solve the mystery of Seth's death—remained frustratingly out of reach. And while they weren't resistant to hearing theories about what had happened, none of what the self-appointed investigators came up with sounded remotely related to his brother, Aaron told me. "I would be extremely surprised to find out that Seth did any of the things people seem to think he did. I don't think he had the IT skills to do it," he said, referring to the DNC hacking. "I don't think he had the personality to do it." (In interviews, friends and colleagues said that Seth wasn't particularly tech-savvy. He couldn't understand, for example, that companies he would lodge complaints with on Twitter never responded because his account was private.) "You have to point to some proof."

Aaron ultimately sued several people for making what he calls false claims about his brother's role in the DNC email theft, including Ed Butowsky and the *Washington Times*, a right-wing paper that had absurdly blamed Aaron himself for the hacking, writing that it was "well known in intelligence circles that Seth Rich and his brother, Aaron Rich, downloaded the DNC emails and was paid by WikiLeaks for that information." The Rich family also sued Fox News, a lawsuit that was dismissed (for failure to state a claim) at the same time as Rod Wheeler's suit against the media giant was dismissed. And Brad Bauman, the family spokesperson, sued the *Washington Times*, a company called America First Media Group, and America First's founder Matt Couch for defamation. The *Washington Times* settled their case with Rich in October 2018 and issued a retraction and apology. Rich continued to pursue the other parties—Ed Butowsky, Couch, and Couch's media company America First Media—for defamation.

The constant volley of speculation and threats and harassment and misinformation did not only discredit Seth and dishonor his memory. It made it harder for the family to grieve Seth's death and process their loss. "I want to be with my family, but instead we're having to see what's the next article that comes out," Aaron told me. "Because of the claims being made, unfortunately we can't just ignore it, we can't be silent." Instead of mourning, the family was forced to respond to the seeming endless waves of faux investigators. "It's hugely detrimental. It literally is taking—" Aaron stopped and had to take a long breath.

"None of us have any spare emotion," he finished, finally. "And this is taking all the emotion we have instead of it being put into grieving."

6

MEDICAL ODDITIES

THE AIR AROUND ME WAS THICK WITH NOT-QUITE-BOOS. THE SOUND was more like a rising tide of disapproval, a hornet swarm rising above the two dozen or so people staring daggers at me, twisted around in their seats.

"Fake news," someone mumbled.

"Just put the facts down," another hissed, gesturing at my notebook. "Just put down what he said."

"Sit *down*," someone urged, from elsewhere in the darkened room.

This was unpleasant, but it was not a huge surprise. My interactions with the anti-vaccine crowd have always gone badly, and our latest run-in, during a screening of the film *Vaxxed*, was proceeding with only slightly more hostility than I expected. I had questions about this extremely popular anti-vaccine documentary we had just watched, and the audience had questions about who the hell I thought I was.

IN THE PAST FEW YEARS, MEDICAL CONSPIRACIES HAVE UNDERGONE A resurgence like few other alternative beliefs, and they have a unique power to do harm. Anti-vaccine activists have had a direct hand in creating serious outbreaks of the measles, which they have then argued are hoaxes ginned up by the government to sell more vaccines. There's also evidence that this form of suspicion is being manipulated by malicious outside actors. A 2018 study by researchers at George Washington University found evidence that Russian bot accounts that had been dedicated to sowing various kinds of division during the 2016 election were, two years later, tweeting both pro- and anti-vaccine content, seeking to widen and exploit that divide, too.

Medical conspiracy theories are big, profitable business: an uptick in the belief that the government is hiding a cure for cancer has led people back to buying laetrile, a discredited fake drug popular in the 1970s. Fake medicines for cancer and other grave diseases are peddled by players of all sizes, from large importers to individual retailers on websites like Etsy—in spite of the platform's policy of removing products that are illegal or claim to cure or treat serious diseases. People like Alex Jones—but not just Alex Jones—are doing multimillion-dollar sales in supplements and quack cures. According to people I have interviewed who work for his main supplier and other organizations' reporting, some of those supplements are harmless and some of them are capable of turning you permanently blue or causing serious kidney and vision problems.

At the same time, medical conspiracies aren't irrational. They are based on frustration with what is seen as the opacity of the medical and pharmaceutical systems. They have taken root in a country with profoundly expensive and dysfunctional healthcare—some adherents take untested cures because they can't afford the real thing. And there is a long history both in the United States and worldwide of doctors giving their approval to innovations—cigarettes, certain levels of radiation, thalidomide, mercury—that turn out to be anything but safe.

Medical conspiracy theories are startlingly widespread. In a study published in 2014, University of Chicago political scientists Eric Oliver and Thomas Wood surveyed 1,351 American adults and found that 37 percent believe the Food and Drug Administration is "intentionally suppressing natural cures for cancer because of drug company pressure." Meanwhile, 20 percent agreed that corporations are preventing public health officials from releasing data linking cell phones to cancer, and another 20 percent that doctors still want to vaccinate children "even though they know such vaccines to be dangerous." (Though the study didn't get into this, many people who feel that way assume doctors do it because they're in the pockets of Big Vaccine, though vaccines are actually less profitable than many other kinds of medical procedures.) When it came to lesser-known medical conspiracies (the CIA deliberately infecting black people with AIDS, for example) people tended to disagree with them or remain neutral. But the findings were still striking, Wood and Oliver wrote, with 49 percent of Americans believing in at least one medical conspiracy and 18 percent believing in three or more.

Subscribing to those conspiracy theories is linked to specific health behaviors: believers are less likely to get flu shots or wear sunscreen and more likely to seek alternative treatments. (In a more harmless vein, they're also more likely to buy organic vegetables and avoid GMOs.) They are also less inclined to consult a family doctor, relying instead on friends, family, the Internet, or such celebrity television doctors as Dr. Oz or Andrew Weil for health advice.

Statistics give us a broad view, but to understand the profound chaos that medical conspiracy theories can wreak, we need only to look at the long and eventful career of Andrew Wakefield.

Wakefield is tall, with heavy-lidded eyes, a haircut somewhere between a mid-'90s Hugh Grant and an ungainly bowl, an aristocratic British murmur, and an implacable belief that many powerful people are actively working toward his destruction. He's made what some estimates put at millions of dollars and built a following among parents who compare him to Nelson Mandela and Jesus Christ—but that all came later.

The story of Wakefield's public infamy and subcultural rebirth begins in 1998, when he was working as a gastroenterologist and medical researcher at the Royal Free Hospital in London. That year, Wakefield was the lead author on a paper published in the *Lancet* that suggested a link between the measles, mumps, and rubella vaccine (MMR) and the onset of regressive autism. That thin sheaf of paper unleashed a parental panic, and the medical decisions of millions have never been the same.

As it happened, this wasn't Wakefield's first paper proposing a link between vaccines and a serious disease: in 1993 and 1995, he published papers positing that the measles vaccination could be a risk factor for inflammatory bowel disease in general and Crohn's disease specifically. Subsequent research by other scientists failed to confirm his hypothesis, and those papers met with little fanfare. However—and this would become significant—Wakefield filed for two patents, one for a method of diagnosing Crohn's by first detecting the measles virus, and the second for an alternative, "safer" measles vaccine. Wakefield expected that the test for diagnosing Crohn's could bring in €28 million in revenue, according to a prospectus he created for potential investors, much of that income coming from "litigation-driven testing" of patients in the United States and Britain.

The 1998 paper linking the MMR vaccine to autism was based on a study of only twelve children; it noted that eight of them developed what the paper called "behavioral symptoms" after receiving the vaccine. The article itself was cautious, pointing out that there wasn't a definite link, but elsewhere Wakefield didn't hold back. In a press conference, he told journalists that as a "moral issue" he could no longer support the use of the MMR vaccine. "Urgent further research is needed to determine whether MMR may give rise to this complication in a small number of people," he said. What happened next was dubbed a "hysteria": vaccination rates in the United Kingdom plummeted. According to the BBC, parts of England where some 90 percent of toddlers had previously been vaccinated dropped to below 70 percent.

The British media's coverage of the study peaked between 2001 and 2003, and by 2008, the scare had spread to the United States. Actress Jenny McCarthy became the most public face of the American vaccination skeptics. Her son, Evan, has autism, and that year, she and her then-partner Jim Carrey published an editorial on CNN's website blaming a number of factors for his condition, including vaccines. "We believe autism is an environmental illness," the two wrote. "Vaccines are not the only environmental trigger, but we do think they play a major role. If we are going to solve this problem and finally start to reverse the rate of autism, we need to consider changing the vaccine schedule, reducing the number of shots given and removing certain ingredients that could be toxic to some children." McCarthy and Carrey also claimed that a gluten-free, casein-free diet, a "detox of metals," and antifungal medicines were helping Evan "recover."

The effect of parents choosing not to vaccinate was measurable: in 1998, there were just 56 cases of measles in England and Wales. By 2008, there were 1,370. In 2006, the first child in England in more than a decade died from the disease. In 2008, the United States reported 131 cases of measles in the first half of that year alone, more than had been seen at any time in over a decade.

No other research ever succeeded in replicating the link between autism onset and MMR that Wakefield claimed. The British investigative journalist Brian Deer raised even more disturbing concerns in his reporting in the *Sunday Times* beginning in 2004. Deer wrote that some of the costs for Wakefield's research had been paid by lawyers on behalf of parents who wished to sue vaccine makers for damages. (Dr. Paul Offit, a pediatrician and vaccine advocate, has referred to this as "essentially laundering legal claims through a medical journal.") Deer also unearthed the so-called safer measles vaccine Wakefield had patented.

Memorably, Deer found footage of Wakefield joking at a 1999 talk that he had paid children at his son's birthday party five pounds each to give blood samples for research. "Two children fainted, one threw up over his mother," he is seen in the clip telling his audience, who giggled in response. "People said to me, 'you can't do that—children won't come back to your birthday parties.' I said, 'We live in a market economy; next year they'll want ten pounds.'" Wakefield later said he had fabricated the birthday party incident for humor, and he himself launched a series of libel lawsuits against Deer. He claimed that the payments he received from lawyers were for a different study entirely, one that looked for evidence of measles in the intestines of children with autism symptoms.

Still, Wakefield eventually left his job at the Royal Free Hospital after being unable to replicate his 1998 findings. "I have been asked to go because my research results are unpopular," he told the *Telegraph* at the time, in a statement that displayed the particular tone of martyrdom Wakefield tends to affect. "I did not wish to leave, but I have agreed to stand down in the hope that my going will take the political pressure off my colleagues and allow them to get on with the job of looking after the many sick children we have seen."

In 2004 ten of Wakefield's coauthors formally retracted the study that carried their names. Two years later, the British General Medical Council launched an inquiry into Wakefield's alleged misconduct. And finally, four years after that, in February 2010, the *Lancet* article was retracted. Eventually the GMC stripped Wakefield of his medical license.

By then, though, Wakefield was long gone, having moved to Austin, Texas, to set up a center called Thoughtful House to study childhood developmental disorders, although he wasn't licensed to practice medicine in the state. He had also developed a fervent, near-religious following among parents who believed he was the only person with answers to what had caused autism in their children, and he was making a lot of money, earning $270,000 a year and buying a $1.2 million house, the *Austin American-Statesman* reported. He and his wife, Carmel, also purchased three other properties, worth a combined $1 million.

Wakefield subsequently left Thoughtful House and became involved with a series of autism-related foundations and media companies. In some of them, Wakefield's salary made up a huge proportion of the budget. He also regularly spoke to paying audiences, who greeted him with what I can safely characterize as rapture. "To our community, Andrew Wakefield is Nelson Mandela and Jesus Christ rolled up into one," the *New York Times* quoted J. B. Handley, cofounder of Generation Rescue, one of many anti-vaccination parent groups. "He's a symbol of how all of us feel."

The parental fervor did not wane, even after the tides of medicine, law, and the media turned against Wakefield. Between 2010 and 2017, vaccine rates in England and the United States started to tick back up, in response to a sustained public health campaign, though they remained lower than average, several studies showed, in wealthy, white communities, particularly in Southern California. One California study found that vaccine refusal due to personal beliefs doubled from 2007 to 2013, hitting 3.06 percent. In the same time period, more than seventeen thousand children attending more than six thousand schools in California opted for delayed vaccination schedules, which are not recommended by pediatricians and are based in an erroneous belief that "too many" vaccines at once can be harmful.

In 2017, Wakefield scored an enormous public relations coup when he managed to get Robert De Niro interested in *Vaxxed*, an anti-vaccine documentary he had just made. (Its working title was the higher-pitched *Injecting Lies*.) De Niro has a son with autism, and Wakefield somehow managed to persuade him that there were open questions about vaccine safety. The Tribeca Film Festival, which De Niro cofounded, quietly added the film to its schedule, and it became clear in a series of eye-popping TV interviews that De Niro was a vaccine skeptic himself, and one of Wakefield's biggest fans.

"There's a lot of information about things that are happening with the CDC, the pharmaceutical companies, there's a lot of things that are not said," De Niro stated on the *Today* show. "I, as a parent of a child who has autism, I'm concerned. And I want to know the truth. I'm not anti-vaccine. I want safe vaccines." That became the new line for anti-vaccine groups: they merely want the safest possible vaccines, even though decades of rigorous testing have found existing vaccines to be extremely safe. The environmental activist Robert F. Kennedy, Jr., similarly claimed, falsely, that vaccines are full of the kind of mercury that's hazardous to human health, suggesting that appropriate safety studies have not been carried out.

In the case of *Vaxxed*, after an enormous backlash, it was pulled from the Tribeca Film Festival without ever airing. But borne along on a tide of donations, Wakefield and the other filmmaker, a former CBS producer named Del Bigtree, set about airing the film in independent movie theaters across the United States, Canada, Europe, New Zealand, and Australia. The film has been shown at on-demand screenings for years at independent theaters, supported by two different Facebook groups, each with more than eighty-five thousand members. Beyond appearing at *Vaxxed* screenings, however, Wakefield largely receded from the public eye. Meanwhile, Del Bigtree began pledging to push for big legislative changes relating to vaccine safety.

Anti-vaccination activists habitually suggest that there are powerful supporters in the shadows, waiting for the right time to reveal themselves at some future date. Implicit in the promise is a reluctant admission: anti-vaccination beliefs are still radioactive enough that it is wise to avoid admitting to them publicly. Robert F. Kennedy, Jr.'s decades of environmental activism have been overshadowed by his erroneous claims that vaccines contain deadly amounts of mercury and aluminum. Jenny McCarthy's star faded as her name became synonymous with "public health crisis."

The anti-vaccine movement is the most successful medical conspiracy—persistent, lucrative, perpetually able to net new believers in spite of scientific evidence. It is also emblematic of all such conspiracy theories: people get caught up in them through either grief or desperation, exacerbated by the absence of hard answers and suspicion about whether a large and often coldly impersonal medical system is looking out for their best interests. And an army of hucksters stands ready to catch them and make a buck.

THE OPPOSITION TO VACCINES IS ALMOST AS OLD AS THEIR INVENTION. Early forms of inoculation began in the late 1700s, when an English physician, Edward Jenner, built on the recognition that a mild infection with cowpox, a nonlethal disease in humans, could prevent the contraction of smallpox. He tested the safest, most effective way to transmit cowpox, and in 1796 successfully infected an eight-year-old boy. Jenner was able to subsequently expose the child to smallpox without him becoming ill.

With that discovery, widespread, mandatory smallpox vaccinations became common in the early 1800s in England. But even as rates of the disease began to fall, public distrust in vaccinations grew. Vaccine objectors' leagues sprang up, motivated by a mix of forces: suspicions that vaccination went against God's will, distrust of a "cure" that came from an animal, and a lack of understanding of how the disease actually spread. The protest was effective, however: the Vaccination Act of 1898 allowed a provision for conscientious objectors to avoid inoculating their children.

The same process repeated itself in the United States: the two countries have a curious twinship when it comes to vaccine controversies, and what happens across the pond tends to come here not long after. The Anti-Vaccination Society of America was founded in 1879, and in this instance the British influence was clear. The group was created after a visit by a Manchester businessman named William Tebb, who argued in prolific writings and public speeches that mandatory vaccinations were a violation of citizens' rights to bodily autonomy. (Tebb was an unusual guy: a pacifist, he built a monument to the horses killed in the Boer War, and he campaigned against premature burial, which worried him so much that he insisted he be buried only a week after his death, just to be on the safe side.)

To be clear, the history of vaccines has not been without genuine danger and controversy. In the United States, vaccine opponents received sobering confirmation of their fears in 1901, when thirteen children in St. Louis died after receiving a diphtheria antitoxin that had been accidentally contaminated with tetanus. The same year, a contaminated smallpox vaccine killed several children in Camden, New Jersey. Those tragic incidents led Congress to pass the Biologics Control Act, which standardized the vaccination production process and required pharmaceutical firms manufacturing vaccines to be licensed.

That made vaccine formulation significantly safer but did not eradicate resistance to it. In his book, *Suspicious Minds*, Rob Brotherton points to a controversy during the mid-1970s, when parents in England, Asia, and the United States claimed that the DPT vaccine (against diphtheria, pertussis, and tetanus) had made their children sick. It is likely that the vaccine did cause seizures and development delays in some children; like all vaccines, DPT carried a risk of side effects. In 1982 a documentary called *Vaccine Roulette* aired on a Washington, DC, station: it gives equal time to vaccine researchers working for the FDA and to researchers calling the DPT vaccine outdated and insufficiently "pure." It downplays the dangers of serious diseases like whooping cough while presenting the vaccines as irresponsible to give to children. In both the United Kingdom and the United States, vaccination rates dipped in response to the film; as in the case of MMR, they began to increase only after concerted responses from the American Academy of Pediatrics and the CDC, and the British Joint Commission on Vaccination and Immunization.

In 1986, the United States passed the National Childhood Vaccine Injury Act and in 1988 created the National Vaccine Injury Compensation Program, whose very existence has been used as proof by anti-vaccination activists that vaccines are unavoidably unsafe. In fact, though, the program, which is funded through the Department of Health and Human Services, was set up as a response to a wave of DPT-related lawsuits. Parents alleging DPT injuries were awarded huge amounts at jury trials, and soon pharmaceutical companies were no longer producing the DPT vaccine, fearful of litigation. When the last DPT vaccine manufacturer threatened to stop production, the vaccine court was created as a no-fault system for the federal government to award money to the plaintiffs without affecting pharmaceutical companies or burying vaccinations under a tide of lawsuits.

The CDC now uses a tool called the Vaccine Adverse Event Reporting System, which requires doctors to report reactions to vaccinations. The CDC estimates that doctors file about thirty thousand reports each year, about 85 to 90 percent of them describing mild side effects like fever, arm soreness, or "crying and mild irritability." The remaining 10 to 15 percent involve serious adverse events resulting in "permanent disability, hospitalization, life-threatening illness, or death." Even then, the CDC and most public health experts agree that while vaccines can be followed by adverse reactions, they are rarely caused by the vaccine. Nonetheless, there are still vaccine deaths across the world: in June 2017 in South Sudan, fifteen children died after a botched measles vaccination. The vaccine was apparently left unrefrigerated, and one syringe was reused for four days.

For their part, anti-vaxxers tend to downplay the seriousness of disease outbreaks when they do occur. A popular anti-vaccination naturopathic physician, Sherri Tenpenny, has for years claimed that infants "rarely" die from measles. "Why is there such HYSTERIA over measles?" Tenpenny wrote on her medical practice's Facebook page in 2013. "It is a rash, fever and desquamation of skin on hands and soles after 10 days, signaling the end of the infection and the resultant lifetime immunity. Doctors in the 1940s (the last THINKING doctors, IMO) wrote many articles about how important a measles infection was to long term health and vitality. Now, we act like measles somehow equates to DEATH."

In fact, it can. According to the World Health Organization, some 134,000 children worldwide died from measles in 2015. Early that year, a measles outbreak at Disneyland infected 147 people and spread across seven states and into Canada and Mexico. It was the largest outbreak of the disease since 1991, and an analysis in the journal *JAMA Pediatrics* found that it was fueled in part by parents who declined to vaccinate their kids.

The need for everyone to vaccinate their children—except those with legitimate medical reasons—was brutally demonstrated when a sudden measles outbreak in Minnesota revealed that Somali parents there weren't vaccinating their children. Vaccination rates in the area first started to dip in 2008, when Somali parents there noticed, with alarm, that many of their children were enrolled in programs for children on the autism spectrum. They didn't recall having seen autism before coming to the United States. Even though a University of Minnesota study showed that autism rates were virtually the same among white and Somali children, and only somewhat higher than the Latino and African American populations, the findings didn't soothe frightened parents. Oh, and also—between 2008 and 2016, Andrew Wakefield came to speak at Somali community forums at least twice.

In 2016, public health officials found that only about 41 percent of Somali toddlers in Minnesota had received the MMR vaccine, according to the state Department of Health, with many parents in the community apparently following anti-vaccine activists' instructions to either forgo the vaccine entirely or wait till their children were five years old. (The CDC recommends that children get their first dose at twelve to fifteen months old.) The outbreak began in late March 2017; by August, seventy-nine people had become sick and twenty-two were hospitalized. More than eight thousand people in all were estimated to have been exposed to the disease.

In both the cases of Disneyland and Minnesota, anti-vaccination activists attributed the outbreaks to dark machinations. They suggested that at Disneyland the outbreak was either engineered by the government or played up by a compliant media to pass a controversial California state law, SB 277, which requires immunizations for children to attend daycare or public school. Conservative television personality and enthusiastic conspiracist Glenn Beck baldly called the outbreak a "hoax." "Is it possible we have been lied to about the measles, this outbreak?" he pontificated on his show in February 2015. The news reports, he said, were meant to instill a "herd mentality," so that parents would "grab their children and obey the government."

In Minneapolis, health officials told the *Washington Post* they had received word that white women visiting Somali communities across the city had claimed, the *Post* wrote, that "the measles outbreak had been created by the Health Department to persuade Somali parents to vaccinate." The women were never identified. Wakefield, meanwhile, told the *Post* he'd visited the Somali community there only after they became concerned about autism among their children. "The Somalis had decided themselves that they were particularly concerned," he told the paper. "I was responding to that."

As for the outbreak, he added, "I don't feel responsible at all."

THE ARGUMENT THAT THE GOVERNMENT USES MEDICINE TO INSTILL cowlike compliance extends well beyond vaccines. For years, Americans have been terrified of fluoride, which some cities started adding to their water supply in 1945. *Conspiracies and Secret Societies*, a conspiracy-leaning encyclopedia, sums up the most common objection to the practice: the Nazis did it first. "Drinking water containing fluoride was first utilized in Nazi prison camps," the authors, Brad and Sherry Steiger, write. (The couple also cowrote a number of books about UFOs, werewolves, and the paranormal.) "In the 1930s Hitler and Nazi scientists envisioned world dominion through mass medication of water supplies. A report submitted to the German general staff indicated findings that repeated doses of very small amounts of fluoride would gradually decrease people's ability to resist domination, slowly narcotizing a certain region of the brain and rendering the individuals submissive to the will of those who wished to govern them."

That's all very specific (apart from "a certain region of the brain"), but Holocaust historians say there's no evidence whatsoever that the claim is true. Patricia Heberer, who specializes in German medical history, including the hideous Nazi experiments, told *PolitiFact*, "I just can't see it." But, Heberer added, she'd heard similar claims during the Cold War about Communists dumping fluoride in the water to narcotize the populace. The American Dental Association—which, as you'd expect, is sturdily pro-fluoride—points out that historical objections to fluoride tend to shift with the times.

"In the 1950s fluoridation was a Communist plot," according to a surprisingly readable ADA pamphlet on the subject. "With America's growing concern for environmental issues in the 1960s, fluoridation was pollution. After the Vietnam War in the 1970s, the anti-fluoridationists capitalized on the popularity of conspiracy theories by portraying fluoridation as a conspiracy between the U.S. government, the dental-medical establishment and industry. As Americans became more concerned about their health in the 1980s, anti-fluoridationists claimed fluoridation caused AIDS and Alzheimer's disease. In the 1990s, claims of fluoride causing hip fractures and cancer were designed to resonate with aging baby boomers. With the new millennium, overexposure and toxicity, in association with lead and arsenic poisoning, have surfaced as common themes."

Underlying these changing concerns is one constant: fear of the heavy, strangling hand of government control. Mandatory vaccine laws and such measures as putting fluoride in the water are unquestionably good for public health, but they tend to create a noticeable backfire effect, confirming people's beliefs in an overbearing government. Just to complicate things, it is also true that the government has engaged in very real, disturbing medical experimentation on civilians and then covered it up. That includes the widely forgotten yet deeply troubling program of federally funded scientists irradiating thousands of people.

Beginning in 1944 and continuing for the next three decades, in secretive federally backed experiments, thousands of prisoners, terminally ill patients, and disabled children were dosed with radiation, usually derived from plutonium, to test the effects of radioactive contamination. The breadth and cruelty of the program beggar belief: in the late 1940s and early 1950s, a group of children at the Walter Fernald State School in Massachusetts were given both radioactive iron and calcium in their milk and oatmeal, an experiment engineered by the Massachusetts Institute of Technology in partnership with Quaker Oats, who wanted to use radioactive material to prove that the nutrients in its oatmeal "traveled throughout the body," according to the *New York Times*.

In a letter to their parents, the school's superintendent, Malcolm J. Farrell, said the children would be given a "special diet" in order to study the way the body absorbed iron and vitamins. He did not ask for consent to irradiate their children; instead, the boys involved thought they'd been invited to join a special "science club."

The radiation doses were fairly low and none of the former Fernald students—wards of the state who were often inaccurately classified as mentally disabled—are reported to have suffered any significant health effects. But the experiment was still appalling: the boys were talked into participating without any idea what they were ingesting, and it's doubtful they could have refused: until the 1960s, Fernald was known as a brutal place, with meager food and filthy living conditions. One former ward, Fred Boyce, called it "a prison," and told news outlets he was outraged and disgusted when he later learned he'd been one of the children fed radioactive material. In 1996, Boyce organized a class-action lawsuit with about thirty other former Fernald wards, eventually winning a $1.85 million settlement from MIT and Quaker Oats.

In the mid-1960s through the 1970s, prisoners in the states of Oregon and Washington had their testicles irradiated through a project directly funded by the Atomic Energy Commission, part of a study to determine how much radiation astronauts could be exposed to during missions. Participation in the program was supposedly voluntary— as voluntary as anything can be for a prison inmate—but many of the men who participated later said they had not been told of the long-term risks involved. Some told the *Washington Post* decades after that they suffered from rashes, lumps, and irritation on their testicles; one said his testicle became fused to his scrotum after the experiments.

Some cases were so bizarre that survivors were taken to be insane when they discussed them. Such was the sad story of Elmer Allen, an African American train porter who lived in the tiny town of Italy, Texas. He had been diagnosed with bone cancer in his left leg in 1947, and, according to his family, was asked by doctors "whether they could inject him with a radioactive trace element." Allen's leg was injected, but the procedure didn't save it; the leg was amputated and taken by researchers at the University of San Francisco, where he was being treated.

In 1973, Elmer and his wife were offered a free trip to New York, told that doctors there wanted to follow up on the success of the 1947 operation two decades later. But as Fredna and Elmer were on their way to New York, they were pulled off the train in Chicago and taken by limousine to the Argonne National Laboratory. Scientists wanted to run tests to see the effect of the radioactive trace on Elmer's body in the intervening decades. In the process, they found damage in his jawbone that looked like it had been caused by radiation.

In the course of his life, Elmer reportedly struggled with alcoholism and been diagnosed as a paranoid schizophrenic. He would tell his neighbors that he'd been used as a "guinea pig" by the government, but they and, for a time, his family, took that to be the ramblings of a disturbed man.

The mystery was finally solved after Elmer died in 1991, when a reporter, Eileen Welsome, found his name along with those of seventeen other people who had also been injected by government scientists at around the same time at hospitals across the country. The injection turned out to be plutonium, and it had no medical benefit: it was part of the Manhattan Project, the federal research into developing nuclear weapons. The people injected with plutonium were all expected to die soon after receiving the plutonium; scientists were using them to test the body's reaction to exposure to radioactive material.

"The tragic part about Elmer's story," Welsome told Amy Goodman on *Democracy Now!* in 2004, "is that nobody believed him."

Experiments were even carried out on the dead, with bodies being exhumed to test their radiation levels. In those cases, too, families frequently weren't given enough information about what they were being asked to consent to. In one project in the mid-'50s, Project SUNSHINE, the cadavers of dead infants were exhumed from across Australia and Europe and sent to the United States to test whether a particular radioactive isotope was concentrated in their bones. Their next of kin were not informed.

In a particularly ghoulish detail, Willard Libby, a University of Chicago researcher who worked for the Atomic Energy Commission, was quoted in a commission transcript jovially expressing his search for the bodies of dead babies. "I don't know how to get them," Libby said, "but I do say that it is a matter of prime importance to get them and particularly in the young age group. So, human samples are of prime importance, and if anybody knows how to do a good job of body snatching, they will really be serving their country."

In all, about four thousand radiation experiments took place during those three decades, according to an advisory committee created in 1994 by Bill Clinton to examine their grim history. Only a handful of victims or their survivors ever got compensation from the government.

Then there is MKUltra, the series of mind-control experiments conducted by the CIA that would challenge the imagination of the most paranoid of conspiracy theorists. Founded in 1947, the CIA was concerned that the Communists had discovered a mind-control drug, which spurred the agency's efforts to get America into the race. MKUltra was approved in 1953, with a then-enormous budget of $300,000 and a specific mandate to test the efficacy of LSD. Presiding over MKUltra—the umbrella name for one hundred forty-nine bizarre projects designed to test what mind-altering drugs could do for national defense—was Sidney Gottlieb, a chemist and former chief of the CIA's technical services division. (Gottlieb, a very busy man, was also involved in the CIA's "gadget shop," which produced devices aimed at killing Fidel Castro and other inconvenient world leaders.) MKUltra experiments involved testing the drugs on human subjects; in some experiments, the subjects were unaware that they were being drugged. In MKUltra's first year of operation, an FBI agent named Frank Olson, covertly dosed with LSD, died. The LSD had been mixed in a bottle of Cointreau and offered to the unwitting Olson by Gottlieb; after drinking it, Olson suffered a mental break and, nine days later, threw himself from a tenth-story window. But nothing seemed to slow the program's bizarre work for long; even then, MKUltra was only halted temporarily.

Some of the MKUltra experiments straddled the line between science and sadism. In one, the agency set up a controlled safe house, where sex workers were instructed to dose their clients, who were then observed from behind two-way mirrors. The project was dubbed Operation Midnight Climax, which makes it sound as if everyone involved in creating it was having a good time. CIA operatives soon leaped beyond the bounds of the safe house: people were dosed with LSD, marijuana, and other drugs in restaurants and bars and on the beach. A CIA source speaking to author John Marks told him, "If we were scared enough of a drug not to try it out on ourselves, we sent it to San Francisco."

Most of the MKUltra records were deliberately destroyed by the government in 1973. According to a contemporaneous report in the *New York Times*, that was done to hide evidence of possible criminal wrongdoing, including Sidney Gottlieb's personal involvement in the death of Frank Olson. The project only came to public attention in 1975, as a result of two government actions: the Church Committee—a Senate Select Committee assigned to look into spying by the CIA, NSA, and FBI on both foreign leaders and US citizens, which found widespread examples of harassment of political activists, including Martin Luther King, Jr.—and the President's Commission on CIA Activities in the United States, commissioned by Gerald Ford. (Even then, it took investigative stories by Seymour Hersh at the *New York Times* and other journalists to expose the worst of the outrages, as well as the destruction of records.) The CIA called MKUltra a shameful chapter in its history, never to be repeated, but its shadow was not easily dispelled. Concerns about government mind control are so entrenched as to be the subject of jokes; the original idea of a tinfoil hat, after all, is to keep the government from beaming its rays of influence into one's brain.

Gottlieb, meanwhile, never faced any consequences for his work with the CIA—why would he?—and upon retiring, moved to India for eighteen months with his wife to run a leper colony, according to a *New York Times* obituary. From there, he bought a cabin in Virginia, tried unsuccessfully to start a commune, and focused his time on folk dancing and herding goats along with, as the *Times* put it dryly, "consciousness-raising and fighting lawsuits from survivors of his secret tests." He died at eighty. Secretive to the last, his wife declined to disclose his cause of death.

The army, too, experimented with the effects of psychedelic drugs, hoping they could be used during interrogations. Its experiments also sometimes involved unwitting human subjects. One of the more notorious episodes came to light after the death of Harold Blauer, a renowned tennis player, who was receiving inpatient treatment for depression at the New York Psychiatric Institute. The institute had an agreement with the Army Chemical Corps to secretly administer drugs to patients to study their effects. Blauer was given five doses of mescaline derivatives intravenously over a period of several weeks. On January 8, 1953, after he received his fifth and final injection, according to notes from the experiment, Blauer started to sweat profusely and flail his arms. His body stiffened as he began frothing at the mouth; within two hours, he'd lapsed into a coma. Not long after, he was dead.

The true nature of Blauer's death only came to light in the 1970s, when an unrelated congressional inquiry turned up records about the mescaline injections, and Blauer's family was notified. His oldest daughter sued the federal government and in 1987 she and her sister were awarded $700,000. In his ruling, the judge called Blauer a "guinea pig" and noted that his medical records were falsified to disguise the cause of his death, attributing it to a weak heart. Indeed, the army, in cooperation with the state of New York and the federal government, covered up the experiments at the Psychiatric Institute for twenty-two years. The investigation and subsequent lawsuits also revealed that the same day Blauer died, a twenty-one-year-old woman at the institute had been injected with the same drug and had a violent negative reaction, though she didn't die.

In most of these historical cases, the human rights abuses committed weren't acknowledged by the government until its hand was forced—by activists, journalists, or lawsuits. Even then, such agencies as the FBI and politicians tend to insist that the incidents were a regrettable oversight, a surprising breach of an otherwise ethical system. "When the government does wrong, we have a moral responsibility to admit it," Bill Clinton said in a 1995 speech, apologizing to victims of radiation experiments. "The duty we owe to one another to tell the truth and to protect our fellow citizens from excesses like these is one we can never walk away from." Yet we have managed to walk away from it, repeatedly.

THE—SOMETIMES JUSTIFIABLE—PARANOIA ABOUT GOVERNMENT CONTROL in medicine has also led to the conviction that the government has deliberately suppressed or withheld real cures for disease. Nowhere is that more evident than in the history of laetrile, a quack cancer cure making a startling comeback.

There is a centuries-long saga of curious cures claiming to beat cancer: a 1914 medical text called *The Cancer Problem* lists some of them,
including green frogs attached to the body like leeches, the liver of a
tortoise "laid on the cancer continuously," and a horrid-sounding con-
coction made of "crow's feet, dog fennel, sulphur, and arsenic." Turpen-
tine and kerosene were both used in the 1950s, and so was a discredited
drug called krebiozen, which subsequent analyses showed contained
only a common amino acid called creatine mixed with mineral oil.

None of those products took hold quite like laetrile, however, which
was originally developed in the early 1920s and patented in the 1940s
by Ernst Krebs, Sr., a California physician, and his son, Ernst Krebs, Jr.
The two claimed that amygdalin, a chemical compound found in apricot
seeds, had anticancer properties (a claim that scientists and researchers
had periodically been making since the mid-1800s). Amygdalin is also
found in bitter almond, apple, and plum seeds, and Krebs Sr. reportedly
discovered its miraculous properties while tinkering at home, trying to
find "a method for improving the taste of bootleg whiskey," according to
Dr. Irving Lerner, who in the 1980s wrote a history of laetrile's use. (Laetrile was the trade name for the chemical compound they created.)

There was one small drawback. The other thing those pits contain
is cyanide. That means laetrile, as several studies would later discover,
can have side effects that mimic cyanide poisoning. Those include liver
damage, nausea, vomiting, blue skin due to lack of oxygen in the blood,
low blood pressure, fever, coma, and death.

Krebs Sr. began selling laetrile as a remedy for cancer, for which he
was arrested in 1962 and then in 1966 and fined $4,000. He died in
1970, but his son carried on his work, crucially refining the message
about what exactly laetrile did. Krebs Jr. came to claim that cancer was,
contrary to all established science, a vitamin deficiency and that amygdalin, in laetrile, supplied the missing vitamin, which he called "vitamin
B17." (He also dubbed himself a doctor and a biochemist, despite having
no medical degree.) There is no such thing as vitamin B17, but Krebs Jr.
made his claims at a felicitous time. As Lerner points out, it was during
the Watergate crisis, and suspicions of government were at their height.
The trend in favor of natural foods, healing crystals, and astrology
was just taking off. And, crucially, calling amygdalin a vitamin rather

than a drug took advantage of the new public interest in vitamins and meant that Krebs didn't need to seek approval from the Food and Drug Administration.

In 1972, Krebs Jr. set up clinics in Mexico and West Germany peddling laetrile. Patients touted a wonder drug that shrank their tumors. And Dr. John Richardson, a friend of his and a member of the John Birch Society, began prescribing it out of his US office, to disastrous effect: his practice was raided that year, and he was arrested, charged, and stripped of his medical license. His prosecution was the spark that formed the Committee for Freedom of Choice in Cancer Therapy, set up by a group of Birchers in defense of medical freedom (Maureen Kennedy Salaman and her husband Frank, who figured prominently in the committee, also happened to be mother and stepfather to Sean David Morton, the UFO expert turned redemption theorist and fellow traveler on the Conspira-Sea cruise).

Soon after, a number of the committee members, including Frank Salaman and Richardson, were caught attempting to smuggle laetrile into the United States; they were each convicted and ordered to pay thousands in fines. Undaunted, the group pushed for state-by-state legalization of laetrile, and pressured the National Cancer Institute to authorize tests of its efficacy. The job of testing fell to Dr. Kanematsu Sugiura, a biochemist at the Memorial Sloan-Kettering Cancer Center, who found a startling result: in preliminary tests on mice, laetrile did seem to inhibit metastases of lung cancer.

Sloan-Kettering, according to a *New York Times* report, found the data interesting but hardly persuasive and asked for more testing. However, someone surreptitiously released Sugiura's tests to a laetrile activist, who sent them on to the Committee for Freedom of Choice. They published the findings, claiming a drastic and nefarious governmental cover-up. In the group's self-published newsletter, *The Choice*, they blasted the vicious "Fedstapo" and its war against cancer patients.

Additional studies failed to replicate Sugiura's exciting results; there is, to date, no proof that laetrile works any better than a placebo. Thousands of people took the pill anyway, including actor Steve McQueen, who ventured to Mexico to acquire it from a border clinic the year he died of mesothelioma. Meanwhile, as federal law banned the import of laetrile and made it illegal to ship it across state lines, twelve states voted to legalize it for use within their borders.

Despite the inconclusive results, people desperately wanted to be able to take the drug without having to leave the country. In 1976, a terminal cancer patient from Oklahoma, Glen Rutherford, filed suit against the FDA, arguing that if he waited for the agency to test laetrile, he might be dead by the time it finished. Rutherford's suit, in effect, demanded that terminal patients be allowed access to unproven drugs and last-ditch treatments, and it worked: a federal judge ruled in his favor.

In 1977, as the controversy raged, the Senate Subcommittee on Health and Scientific Research called a hearing on laetrile, chaired by Senator Edward M. Kennedy. Representatives from the FDA, the National Cancer Institute, and the American Cancer Society all declared, again, that there was no evidence that laetrile worked. Representatives from the prosecutor's office in San Francisco also testified, pointing out that laetrile proponents were making a lot of money from the drug, particularly in California. One California doctor submitted affidavits on nineteen of his patients who he said had died after they chose laetrile against his medical advice.

Then it was the laetrilists' turn, who managed to turn the hearing into a large, showy, and successful display of the power of a grassroots organization against the evil medical establishment. "With a *j'accuse* flair," the *New York Times* reported, "they spoke of a government 'conspiracy' to hold back a 'valid' anticancer substance from the public; they condemned the Establishment for arrogantly denying cancer victims the right to freely choose their mode of treatment; they argued that Laetrile is harmless and that in many cases it might do some good when taken as part of a total dietary and vitamin program." The laetrile supporters claimed that the drug gave them relief from pain and even remission in the disease, and they waved affidavits to prove it. "One speaker went so far as to compare the advent of Laetrile in the cancer field to the Copernican revolution," the *Times* added, "which changed man's view of his role in the universe."

The FDA maintained its federal ban on transporting laetrile across state lines, but by 1977, twenty-seven states had legalized its use. And vitamin B17 also got a renewed boost in 1978, when G. Edward Griffin, the most important conspiracy theorist you've never heard of, dubbed it a miracle cure.

Griffin is the author of *The Creature from Jekyll Island*, an influential doorstop of a book that accuses the Federal Reserve of being a globalist tool used to enslave US citizens. He also authored the popular *World Without Cancer*, which spread the story of the so-called Sloan-Kettering cover-up and baldly accused the government and mainstream medicine of suppressing laetrile out of greed. Their desire to keep treating cancer forever with costly and profit-driving drugs was greater than their desire for a healthy world, he argued.

Griffin was careful not to accuse the medico-political cabal of outright genocide, though, writing, "Men of finance and politics do not have to be members of a global cabal to decide to oppose Laetrile or vitamin therapy; and it is certain that they do not consciously seek to commit genocide by thwarting a line of research that they know will lead to life-saving discoveries." Instead, he added, "What has happened in this field is the result of forces and policies previously set in motion in the quest of economic and political goals. Their organizations and institutions react reflexively against any obstacle to profits. The result is a scientific quagmire which now is claiming millions of lives each year."

By the late 1970s, the Committee for Freedom of Choice claimed to have thirty-five thousand members, including two thousand doctors who were allowed to prescribe laetrile to patients who got a referral from the group. The FDA subsequently declared laetrile not just illegal to transport across state lines, but flat-out illegal, a decision that was fought by several states but ultimately upheld in federal court.

Laetrile use began to die off in 1981, when a federally funded clinical trial found, once again, that it was worthless. Of the one hundred seventy-eight patients studied, one hundred five died. A few reported feeling better seven months after completing their treatment, but follow-ups found that cancers had continued growing in all those patients who were still alive at that point. The study also found that several patients showed "symptoms of cyanide toxicity" or "blood cyanide levels approaching the lethal range," the authors wrote. In response, the Committee for Freedom of Choice contended that the doctors had used the wrong kind of amygdalin.

Clinics in Mexico that prescribe laetrile and other discredited or untested cures are still open. A long-running group called the Cancer Control Society leads tours there at least three times a year. And in 2017, both Buzzfeed and ABC ran stories noting that laetrile had made a startling resurgence. Buzzfeed reporter Stephanie M. Lee found dozens of online vendors selling apricot seeds, although they were careful to avoid claiming powers of treatment or cure for any disease. The customers make those claims, writing such testimonials as, "Raw Apricot Kernels help to stop Cancer in its tracks."

The sale of these products continues in spite of the FDA ban because the Dietary Supplement Health and Education Act, passed in 1994, specifically exempts vitamins and supplements from the kind of scrutiny to which the FDA subjects drugs before they're put on the market. The FDA can warn the public about dangerous products and it sends aggressive warning letters to companies claiming that amygdalin, B17, or laetrile are cancer treatments, but that's about all it can do: most websites selling the products just change the name or the descriptions to make them sufficiently vague.

To this day, popular natural-health websites feed into the conspiratorial claims about laetrile not being approved for cancer treatment in the United States. Joseph Mercola, an osteopathic physician and vaccine "skeptic," writes that it's all part of the greedy medical-industrial complex, and that in fact "science" itself is suspect. "Our current medical system," he wrote, "has been masterfully orchestrated by the drug companies to create a system that gives the perception of science-based medicine when it is really a heavily manipulated process designed to boost their profits, and more accurately labeled science-biased medicine."

The FDA has its hands full combating such claims, because the problem does not stop with laetrile. In April 2017, the agency released a public warning about a whopping sixty-five different bogus cancer drugs being sold online, many of them making explicit claims such as "miraculously kills cancer cells in tumors," "more effective than chemotherapy," and "treats all forms of cancer." The products are frequently touted as "natural" and therefore appear to be safe. Some of the more recognizable ingredients are powdered vitamin C, milk thistle, and "Siberian Chaga Mushroom Extract."

There is also a particularly pernicious skin cancer "treatment" called Indian Black Salve that is advertised on natural-health websites: it's a thick black paste that burns the skin away, leaving ropey black scars. It is aggressively promoted as being alluringly "natural," a Native American remedy, redolent with the wisdom of the ages. One company selling the salve calls itself Two Feathers, and it writes lovingly about how this "unique formula" is "a time capsule sent to us from a distant past when knowledge was more of the Spirit than of the intellect." The product is purportedly produced in "the original Native American manner," cured in smoke ovens, and mixed in wooden (never metal) bowls, none of which equips it to fight cancer, but which must sound reassuring to people desperate for hope.

A great many people are making money off these bogus cures— thousands of small operators and fly-by-night companies, which, when confronted by the FDA, change their names, shift their marketing language ever so slightly, and begin again. The big business of bullshit cure- alls targets customers on every side of the political spectrum.

THE KING OF DUBIOUS HEALTH CLAIMS IS ALEX JONES, WHOSE INFOWARS Life Health Store sells a variety of supplements ranging from the harm- less to the profoundly dodgy. Most of Jones's products come from a Houston-based company called the Global Healing Center and are rela- beled with the InfoWars logo. Global Healing Center's CEO, Dr. Edward Group, is also Jones's go-to health expert, appearing regularly on the program to opine about vaccines (he thinks they're bad) and fungus (the root of all evil—luckily, one of the supplements that Jones and Group sell helps banish it from the body).

Group isn't a medical doctor but a chiropractor, although his web- site claims a string of other credentials, like degrees from MIT and Har- vard, where he attended continuing education programs that are virtually impossible to fail provided you pay the bill on time. Until a few years ago, Group also claimed to have a medical degree from the Joseph LaFortune School of Medicine. The LaFortune School is based in Haiti and is not accredited. That one is no longer on his CV.

Several disgruntled Global Healing Center staff members spoke to me for a 2017 Jezebel story about Group and Jones's relationship, claiming that the company earns millions a year while toeing an extremely fine line in making claims for its products. "Global Healing Center pretends to care about FDA and FTC regulation but at the end of the day, GHC says a lot of things that are completely fabricated, flat-out incorrect, totally circumstantial, or based on incomplete evidence," one employee said.

Nowhere is that clearer than in the claims that Jones and Group make about colloidal silver, which Jones sells as Silver Bullet. Colloidal silver is a popular New Age health product, touted as a miraculous antibacterial and antimicrobial agent that is dabbed on the skin. But Group and Jones advocate drinking the stuff. In 2014, Group told the InfoWars audience that he's been doing so for years. "I've drank half a gallon of silver, done a ten parts per million silver, for probably ten or fifteen days," Group said reassuringly.

Group also claims that the FDA "raided" his office to steal his colloidal silver, because it is too powerful. "It was one of the things that was targeted by the FDA because it was a threat to the pharmaceutical companies and a threat for doctor's visits because it worked so good in the body."

Colloidal silver doesn't, in fact, work so good in the body; you're not supposed to put it there. The Mayo Clinic says silver has "no known purpose in the body" and drinking colloidal silver can cause argyria, a condition that can permanently turn skin, eyes, and internal organs an ashen bluish color. (Jones and Group acknowledge on InfoWars that this can happen, but only when people are using silver incorrectly.)

Of all the conspiracy medical sites, Natural News is the most conspiracy-minded and far-reaching, with an audience that, according to the web analytics site Alexa, may be larger than Gwyneth Paltrow's New Age lifestyle site Goop (web traffic is proprietary information, but Alexa shows that Natural News has a higher global ranking than Goop, an indicator of their relative popularity). Natural News was founded and run by Mike Adams, the self-appointed Health Ranger, who boasts more than one hundred thousand Twitter followers. Adams was born in Kansas and says that he cured himself of various maladies using natural remedies and a raw-food diet. His site is an overlap of anti-government paranoia and bogus health claims, espousing conspiracies about the disappearance of Malaysia Airlines flight 370, September 11, Sandy Hook, and Hillary Clinton's health in between dispensing intensely, feverishly false health advice.

Echoing G. Edward Griffin decades before him, Adams has claimed, for example, that chemotherapy "actually causes cancer to spread throughout the body," but that our medical overlords are covering this up: "The medical industrial complex can't sustain their billion-dollar-a-year cancer business if they blame the real culprit," by which he meant chemo itself. (He recommends preventing cancer by drinking baking soda daily, along with regular ingestions of hemp oil, cinnamon, and garlic supplements. He also warns against tap water, saying that fluoride causes cancer.)

Jones, Adams, and their ilk complain that they are under attack by the media, the government, and some shadowy third entities for telling truths too powerful to ignore. In the summer of 2017, Adams said that someone had subjected his website to a "massive, well-funded, multination DDoS attack" in response to a petition he began to "end legal immunity" for vaccine manufacturers; he blamed the CDC, which he called "a known criminal organization and pillar of the deep state that functions as the vaccine propaganda branch of the pharmaceutical industry."

Unusually, medical conspiracy thinking is not solely the province of the far-right or the Libertarian bluish-from-too-much-silver fringe. The bourgeois hippie left participates, too. The website Quartz published an astonishing story showing that many of the products sold by Jones are identical to those peddled by Goop. And there's David "Avocado" Wolfe, another New Age lifestyle vlogger, who has called vaccine manufacturers "criminal and Satanic" and said that chemtrails are real and toxic. ("Chemtrails" are actually contrails, or water vapor from airplanes, which people in the deep end of the conspiracy pool think are clouds of poison gas being showered on the populace to, once again, make us docile and weak.)

It is only fair to note, however, that every one of these people—Jones,

Paltrow, the Avocado man—have been made prominent by the Internet, but they are also rigorously fact-checked because of it. Alex Jones has been subjected to a very thorough investigation of his claims, particularly since the 2016 election, when his friendship with Donald Trump gave him an enormous boost in public attention. Goop is regularly skewered by doctors, including Dr. Jen Gunter, a gynecologist who takes great joy in wryly puncturing the site's weirder assertions about vaginal health, such as the benefits of jade "yoni" eggs for vaginal toning. (That particular claim also cost Goop money: in September 2018, the Orange County, California, District Attorney's office said that two types of vaginal eggs offered by the website, as well as an essential oil blend, had all been sold using unproven and unfounded claims. Goop agreed to settle for $145,000 and give refunds to anyone who purchased an egg or the oil blend.)

But it's difficult to figure out whether the two sides balance each other out, whether the scrutiny bestowed by the Internet is equal to the new set of consumers it potentially introduces to Goop or InfoWars products. And when people follow the advice of Alex Jones or the Health Ranger or Paltrow's Goop, it may not only be their wasted money at risk. In October 2017, a nonprofit watchdog group, the Center for Environmental Health, independently tested two InfoWars supplements—Caveman True Paleo Formula and Myco-ZX—and found high levels of lead in both. Myco-ZX is meant to rid the body of "harmful organisms," and it is one of InfoWars' most heavily marketed products.

"It is not only ironic, but tragic, when we find lead in dietary supplements, since consumers are ingesting the toxic chemical with every sip and swallow," CEH CEO Michael Green said in a press release. "These products are supposed to enhance human health and performance," Green added, "not lead to increased risk of heart attacks and sperm damage."

7

A NATURAL MAN

THE FEDERAL COURTHOUSE IN DOWNTOWN LOS ANGELES IS A towering cube of spotless glass and mile-high white walls, designed to instill awe and good behavior. On the tenth floor, sunlight sends tiger-stripe shadows across the walls. Birds manage to enter the building periodically and fly around the rafters, making confused circles. Sitting alone on a cool, ash-blond bench outside the courtrooms is like waiting in Heaven's administrative wing.

Sean David Morton was out of his element. Whenever I had seen him in the past, he was always among his people, greeting his adoring fans or getting his cheek pinched by the delighted ladies at the Conscious Life Expo. Hustling through the courthouse halls in a tan blazer with an unidentifiable crest on the pocket, wearing thick tan orthopedic shoes, he looked shabby, befuddled. His wife, Melissa, leaned heavily on a cane, her blond hair pulled into a low ponytail and secured with a headband. A few months later, one of them would be a fugitive on the run and the other angrily selling off his beloved comic-book collection.

It was April 2017, and the Mortons were going to trial for conspiracy to defraud the government, filing false claims, and creating "fictitious financial instruments." In English: they were accused of falsifying their tax returns and submitting fake bonds to credit card companies and the federal government to pay off various debts, taxes, and fines. Sean faces a whopping maximum of six hundred fifty years in prison, while Melissa faces six hundred twenty-five.

The things the Mortons were accused of doing were a direct result of their conspiratorial beliefs and also, according to them, their friendship with a man named Brandon Adams, who was himself, at the time of their trial, serving a substantial prison sentence. Their story is a window into a tiny corner of conspiracy culture, one that has resisted every attempt by the federal government to strangle it with fines and jail time. Until the feds put a stop to it, the couple were practitioners of redemption theory, a set of beliefs according to which the government is hoarding secret money, there are secret loopholes for accessing that money, and a canny citizen using the right combination of words and little-known tax maneuvers can find it. Redemption theory rests on three peculiarly American things: a desire not to pay taxes, the conviction that the government doesn't have the right to boss you around, and a willingness to spend vast amounts of time in court to back up those beliefs.

Redemption theorists are a subset of the sovereign citizen movement, which, according to estimates by the Southern Poverty Law Center, has some three hundred thousand adherents, one hundred thousand of whom are described as "hard-core." The SPLC admits that's a very rough number, since sovereigns, as they are called, mostly prefer to hide from view—until they get arrested. Broadly, sovereign citizens believe they are not subject to federal law and that swaths of the federal government are acting illegally, in ways the framers of the Constitution never intended.

Sovereigns have been known to create their own driver's licenses, form their own police force, attempt to carry out citizens' arrests, and, more optimistically, try to prise their members out of jail with the use of pseudo-legal reasoning. Sovereigns have also tried using their anti-federal stance to evade paying child support or reclaim their children from foster care—this one by filing pseudo-legal documents claiming their children as private property, illegally seized by the state. Their best-known and most recent moment in the spotlight was the occupation of the Malheur National Wildlife Refuge in 2016, seized by Ammon Bundy with the help of homegrown militias and various ragtag sovereign groups, who contested the federal government's right to own land and argued they had a legal obligation to turn it over to the states.

Redemption theorists will sometimes deny that they are sovereign citizens and express contempt for them, but the two groups indisputably share some DNA. At its core, sovereignty is about trying to do an end run around the more unpleasant aspects of living under state control. But the Mortons aren't violent or dangerous. They're not armed occupiers holed up in a bird refuge. And their quest against taxation is part of a long American tradition.

There have been tax protesters in the United States since our founders angrily dumped tea into a harbor, but the tax denier movement really took hold in the 1950s. In 1951, a Kansas building contractor named Arthur Julius Porth sued the federal government to return his taxes of $135, claiming they were taken from him illegally. Porth held that the Sixteenth Amendment, which gives the United States the power to levy an income tax, subjected him to "involuntary servitude." He even got specific about who was doing the enslaving, claiming that the Sixteenth Amendment "put Americans into economic bondage to the international bankers," which is, as the SPLC points out, a classic, barely disguised anti-Semitic trope.

Porth's demand for his money was not a success, but he kept his one-man protest going throughout the 1950s and 1960s, eventually pleading the Fifth Amendment (by writing "I plead the Fifth") on a blank tax return; he also refused to deduct taxes from his employees' paychecks. After a prolonged court battle, in 1967 he was sentenced to five years in prison and ordered to undergo psychiatric evaluation.

Despite its lack of success—a recurring theme with redemption theory's star players—Porth's crusade won him a number of ardent fans. After serving his sentence, he spent much of his life speaking against taxes, distributing a book called *A Manual for Those Who Think That They Must Pay an Income Tax*. He even attempted—also unsuccessfully—to issue arrest warrants against government employees who he believed were violating the Constitution.

One of Porth's biggest fans was William Potter Gale, the founder of the racist and anti-Semitic Ministry of Christ Church, itself a part of the (racist and anti-Semitic) Christian Identity movement, which teaches that Europeans are descended from the Lost Tribes of Israel. Everyone else is a vile mud person, worthy of destruction. Jews in particular are described as the literal children of Satan. In 1971, Gale created Posse Comitatus, the earliest modern sovereign movement in the United States. Its members pioneered a lot of the tactics used by sovereign citizens today, like refusing to get a driver's license, declaring themselves exempt from federal citizenship, and filing liens against individual employees of the IRS, claiming ownership of their homes or cars or other property as payment for nonexistent debts (and as a form of revenge for those IRS employees trying to collect their taxes: the liens aren't legal and don't stand up in court, but they are a serious nuisance). One Posse Comitatus member, Gordon Kahl, managed to fuse some early tax-protester ideas with his own special brand of hatred, calling his tax dollars "tithes to the synagogue of Satan." In 1983, Kahl killed two federal marshals before going fugitive for four months, eventually dying in a shootout with the FBI.

Posse Comitatus started to fragment in the early 1980s, but an Ohio man named Roger Elvick was on hand to help Gale found the Committee of the States, another white supremacist organization in which tax denial and sovereign citizenry fused with overwhelming anti-government hostility. The Committee of the States was quite explicitly focused on the overthrow of the US government; at a 1987 meeting, the organization's founders drew up an "indictment" of Congress for "malfeasance in office," directing those lawmakers to be replaced by the committee. Somehow, that didn't work. Instead, Gale and other committee members were convicted of sending threats to IRS agents and their families.

Elvick, meanwhile, set down his own impossibly strange yet determined path. He focused his fight against the federal government on another front, creating the concept of redemption theory.

After the United States stopped using the gold standard in 1933, the government, according to Elvick, secretly began using a different form of insurance to back our currency: human lives. His theory holds that with the birth of each new citizen and the issue of each birth certificate, the federal government deposits $630,000 into a secret bank account. That action, he claims, creates a "strawman" persona, used by the government as collateral to back our monetary system the way gold used to do.

In Elvick's conception, each citizen is little more than a slave to a tyrannical currency system, the financial equivalent of unconscious fetal beings floating in vats in the vast lab in the famous scene from *The Matrix*. But he believed that, by using little-known aspects of the Uniform Commercial Code—the laws governing commercial transactions—US citizens could "reclaim" their straw-man persona, access their secret bank account, and start spending that $630,000.

While still acting as spokesperson for the Committee of the States, Elvick began advising aspiring redemption theorists across the country, selling a booklet called *The Redemption Package*. The SPLC says he focused on people such as "desperate farmers" trying to keep their land, but the ideas were aimed at anyone with money problems.

The track record of success for those ideas was, to put it mildly, feeble: in 1990, a federal judge in North Dakota convicted Elvick and two other men of conspiracy to impede justice by filing false tax documents. He ended up serving time in prison and was, like Porth, ordered to undergo psychiatric testing. Elvick was charged with conspiracy again even while incarcerated, and after his release promptly began peddling redemption ideas in his home state of Ohio; new forgery, extortion, and corruption convictions followed. As of 2017, he was a free man, but did not respond to attempts to contact him. (In fairness, I may have been calling old numbers: Elvick has a dizzying number of past and possible addresses across the Midwest.)

Of course, suspicion of the IRS is not limited to conspiracy theorists or sovereign citizens, and many of the claims of redemption theorists are echoed by mainstream right-wing media. Conservative groups argued that the Obama administration's IRS audited them unfairly because of their political leanings; talk show host Rush Limbaugh, too, claimed to have been audited twelve years in a row, implicitly tying that to his status as a brave, shouty truth teller. (In a legal settlement in 2017, under conservative Attorney General Jeff Sessions, the Justice Department apologized for auditing conservative groups, saying, "There is no excuse for this conduct. Hundreds of organizations were affected by these actions, and they deserve an apology from the IRS. We hope that today's settlement makes clear that this abuse of power will not be tolerated.")

———

THESE DAYS, REDEMPTION THEORY HAS FRAGMENTED: IT'S NO LONGER just about reclaiming your straw man, but a thousand other far-fetched legal and financial ideas, peddled by just as many would-be redemption experts. It's become a tidy little cottage industry, despite an irritable statement from the IRS rebutting "the notion of secret accounts assigned to each citizen" as "pure fantasy" (to redemption theorists, though, the IRS *would* say that, to throw everyone off the truth).

Redemption theory is all but invisible if you don't know where to look. Yet once you start to see it, the signs are easy to spot: there are redemption theory explainers on YouTube ("Reclaim your straw man!" chirps a perky black-and-white cartoon) and online experts selling DVDs and booklets and seminars full of guaranteed get-out-of-debt-quick information. The style is fairly uniform: the designs often look antiquated, the material dotted with incongruously happy clip-art people, and the text full of abstruse, close-typed legalistic nonsense.

In fact, an eccentric use of language is one of the biggest flags for both sovereign citizens in general and redemption theory in particular. Court filings submitted by sovereigns, such as homemade habeas corpus petitions or demands claiming that the IRS owes them $2 million, tend to contain some common grammatical elements. To redemption theorists, a name typed all in upper case indicates the straw-man persona, whereas the name in lower case refers to the real, flesh-and-blood person, or "natural man." Sometimes hyphenation or creative colons and semicolons are used to distinguish the true self from their government-made golem. The labels vary: one of the Malheur occupiers, Ryan Bundy, when awaiting trial on conspiracy and firearms charges, described himself as "an idiot," writing in a filing: "I, ryan c, man, am an idiot of the 'Legal Society'; and; am an idiot (layman, outsider) of the 'Bar Association'; and; i am incompetent; and; am not required by any law to be competent." (Bundy and his brother Ammon were both acquitted, along with several other occupiers.)

The SPLC points out that redemption theory, like sovereign citizenry, has proved very popular in prison, particularly with people who think that accessing their straw man will help them get out of the clink. There are also numerous black nationalist sovereign groups and redemption theorists, despite the movement's explicit roots as a white supremacist enterprise. The Moorish Nation includes black sovereign citizens, who distinguish themselves from the population as Moors and use the last name el-Bey; as noted, the Washitaw Nation in Louisiana, also a branch of sovereign citizens, describes itself as a Native American tribe to bolster its claim to sovereignty and gain tribal rights.

Unsurprisingly, the court system seems to be even more impatient with black sovereigns. The SPLC recounts the fate of one man, Frederick R. James of East St. Louis, Missouri, who went by Nkosi Niyahuman-Dey and was charged in the early 2000s with selling marijuana. James claimed to be a member of the Cahokia Great Seal Moors and refused to answer questions in court; he denied that he was subject to the court's jurisdiction and sent the judge a bill for $151 million—"half a million for each time the judge mentioned his name, which James said was copyrighted," according to the SPLC. James's tactic was also unsuccessful: he was convicted on drug charges, with two counts of contempt of court piled on for his trouble.

TO HIS ETERNAL MISFORTUNE AND THAT OF HIS CLIENTS, SEAN DAVID Morton became deeply involved in redemption theory sometime around 2006. For much of his life, Morton had focused on celestial matters: his switch to the earthly came with a heavy cost. His story neatly illustrates the nature of the redemption movement and the point where conspiracy theories meet New Age ideas; it also pinpoints the line where the federal government stops ignoring conspiracy theorists and comes down on them with all its might.

As I've heard it told, Morton's origin story goes like this: He was born on October 1, 1959, in Texas but spent much of his life in California. His parents, like him, were colorful crusaders for unusual ideas: his mother, Maureen Kennedy Salaman—the same Maureen Kennedy Salaman who fought to make laetrile available to all—was a well-known natural-health author in the 1970s and 1980s, a time when those ideas were less acceptable in the mainstream.

In old photos, Maureen Salaman has the glossy, tightly updoed beauty of Nancy Reagan. Morton's younger sister, Colleen Morton Anderson (estranged from her brother "probably since birth, in a way," she said in an interview), describes growing up with their mother as "the strangest childhood ever." Both Maureen and the siblings' stepfather, Frank, were devoted members of the John Birch Society. In Colleen's telling, they were militantly prepared for showdowns with Russians, the feds, or both. "We went to John Birch camp," she remembers. "And apparently there was a property my dad bought in Marysville that had a bomb shelter." At home, she says, "We had Uzis and hand grenades and food stores, and the government was out to get us."

All of this seemed unremarkable at the time. "For me, it seemed normal to have an Uzi in the house." In the den, she says, Frank positioned a skeleton with a bullet hole through its head, claiming he'd brought it back as a spoil from fighting in the Japanese theater in World War II.

Communists loomed large. "The Russians were taking over," Colleen explains. At the same time, the family "didn't have to abide by the law." If it wasn't the Russians, then the government was going to take over, becoming a totalitarian state, and, as she puts it, in either case, "you needed to arm yourself, you needed to stock up food." She pauses. "Yet my mom went shopping every day. If we're going to become a Communist country, what do you need the clothes for? It was an interesting philosophy."

Though he was deeply shaped by his parents' conservative views, their devout Christianity, and their attitude toward the federal government, Morton took a different path, shaped by his psychic abilities. "I started developing them when I was very young," he told me in an interview. "My grandmother was Irish and could see around a few corners, as they say. Also, I worked very hard to open myself." Morton became fascinated with the paranormal in 1985, when he traveled to England and Ireland and discovered the "Green Stone saga," as he called it, a mystic jewel supposedly set into a sword belonging to King Arthur, held by the Knights Templar, and owned by Mary, Queen of Scots. True believers claim that the stone is hidden somewhere in a country manor in the Scottish highlands, and Morton said that he was part of the quest to find it. (One website claims the stone was discovered in 2005, but it's unclear where it's gone to since.)

Morton says that after his travels through England and Ireland, he went to India and met the Dalai Lama. From there, he holed up in a Nepalese Buddhist monastery, where monks taught him the secrets of time travel and a particular type of extrasensory perception known as remote viewing. "Viewers" are able to use their ESP abilities to gain images and impressions of faraway objects and situations. Morton wasn't the only one intrigued by remote viewing: in the mid-1990s, declassified government documents revealed that the United States spent $20 million or so funding Project Stargate, in which the armed forces and later the CIA tried to determine whether remote viewing had any military applications (and whether it was real, which all available scientific evidence shows it's not).

When she finished laughing, Colleen offered her version of Morton's biography: "He was a DJ at Houlihan's," she said.

Whatever version of his background is accurate, Morton did spend much of the 1990s making documentaries about UFOs and extraterrestrial experiences, including one called *UFO Contactees*. He said that he worked for Paramount, had been a producer for the TV news show *Hard Copy*, and, in his words, was "a freelance producer and pitching stuff and working behind the scenes on *Unsolved Mysteries*," a deliciously creepy show that was popular in the mid-1990s.

Morton's greatest supposed claim to fame is that he is the person who shone a national spotlight on Area 51, a remote and restricted Air Force base in Nevada that conspiracists believe to be a hub of extraterrestrial activity. "I . . . found the hilltop that looked down on the base and put it on the front page of the *L.A. Times*," he said. "And that turned Area 51 into a global phenomenon. It was already locally known in Las Vegas, and that made it a national deal."

There are plenty of UFO buffs who would dispute that history, but there's no doubting Morton's passion. He became fascinated with Dulce Base, a purported hidden military base inside a mesa in northeastern New Mexico. UFO researchers believe it has subterranean levels occupied by workaday aliens running their own sort of parallel military bureaucracy. Morton says he led a research expedition to Dulce, where an "ultrasound of the mesa" proved that the lower layers are really there. (Morton felt sorry for me when I told him that even though I'm from New Mexico, the subterranean alien base somehow escaped me. "Talk to the Jicarilla Apaches," he said. "They talk about fighting the ant people.")

For a time, the UFO world contented Morton. He led reporters from the *Los Angeles Times* and the *Orange County Register* on wild UFO-hunting expeditions. One *OC Register* story from May 1993 captures him driving very fast toward Area 51 while explaining that the aliens there were from the planet Krondac. "They're actually bluish-gray and a little bigger than most people think. They're 3 to 4 feet tall." During that era, Morton was a regular guest on the beloved UFO-oriented radio program *Coast to Coast AM*, back when it was hosted by founder Art Bell. (His relationship soured with the current host, George Noory, and he eventually stopped appearing.)

It was then that he met Melissa Thomson, who was originally from Utah. According to Colleen, Melissa (who tends to avoid giving interviews) came from a large and tight-knit Mormon family that disapproved of Sean and their relationship. (In one email Colleen received from Melissa's brother, he described Sean as "a mental midget" and expressed a desire to kick his ass.)

At their trial, Morton said that the two met in 1998 at a New Age conference in Las Vegas. "Melissa had heard me on the radio and came to the conference for us to meet," Morton told the jury, smiling. "It was love at first sight." She moved to Hermosa Beach in California in the summer of 1999 and the couple has been together ever since.

Everything seemed to be rosy in the Mortons' world for about a decade, until Sean decided to turn his psychic abilities into a profit center. He had started a mailer a few years earlier, in 1993, called Delphi Associates Newsletter, where he offered financial and political predictions and began referring to himself, ambitiously, as "America's Prophet." But now he made the leap from an observer of the stock market to a player, founding the Delphi Associates Investment Group, run out of the couple's home. Delphi claimed a special advantage: Morton's psychic abilities, which guided him to make smart and profitable investments. He marketed himself to the New Age community as one of their own, someone they could trust. In a long-winded letter to investors in 2010, Morton said he'd seen too many scams and Ponzi schemes targeting his fellow spiritual seekers.

"I am putting my faith, energy, spirit and reputation on the line to do the very best that I can for all of you," he wrote. "I am not willing to risk my immortal soul or spiritual path by ripping anyone off. I am a public figure. I speak regularly at expos and conventions. I am not hard to find, not hard to contact, have lived in the same house for 23 years, driven the same CAR since 1983, and published my Delphi Associates Newsletter for the last 14 years. I'm not going anywhere."

The Securities and Exchange Commission had other ideas. That same year, the SEC sued Morton for fraud, claiming he'd bilked investors out of $6 million and disputing the legality of selling one's psychic abilities as an advantage. The SEC also maintained that not all of the money he'd collected from investors had even made it into the stock market; instead the Mortons had dumped it into various shell corporations, including the nonprofit Prophecy Research Institute, a religious entity.

Morton argued two things: the SEC charges were bunk, initiated by a disgruntled investor; and they were part of a broader pattern of government harassment, spurred by the fact that he knew too much. "Because I'm on the cutting edge, I'm obviously hated by some force in the government," he said in an interview. "When I started messing around with Area 51, I was told, 'They are going to come after you.' I had a five-star general say, 'You're too funny to kill.' Some agent told me that the fact that I'm psychic makes me easy to discredit by the media and 'that's why they're not putting a bullet in your head.'"

Morton knew he was being investigated by the SEC as early as 2007, Delphi newsletters show, and in 2009 he attempted to sue the agency, arguing that its agents were harassing him and Melissa so that they could go on taxpayer-funded trips to California where, he charged, they alternated between bullying the couple, visiting Disneyland, and making runs to In-N-Out Burger. The lawsuit was dismissed and the Mortons lost their SEC case as well. In February 2013, they were ordered to pay $11.5 million to the SEC within fourteen days.

They didn't pay. Instead, Morton essentially wrote the government an IOU for $50 million, instructing them to withdraw the money from the Federal Reserve, another tactic favored by redemption theorists. He insisted that had taken care of the matter and successfully shaken the feds off his back. Life seemed to return to normal. He started hosting an Internet-based radio show every afternoon called *Strange Universe*, ruminating on taxes and UFOs with equal verve.

Meanwhile, Morton had dipped a toe into redemption theory and was heading deeper into those waters. The turning point was a lecture given by Brandon Adams at a New Age bookstore and event space in Los Angeles called the Living Temple where Morton heard about some novel methods for getting out of debt. Adams and his business partner, Gordon Hall, a brash, Trumpish real estate developer and gym impresario, had set up a company called Creditors In Commerce that drew up fake money orders for their clients to send to the IRS.

Adams comes from a family of redemption theorists, very prolific ones: they advanced far beyond Roger Elvick's basic ideas of how to reclaim one's straw man and started experimenting with their own ideas about how to eke money out of the federal government and avoid paying taxes. At one time, his father, Alexander, his brother, Garrett, and he were all in the business of preparing falsified tax returns using phony money orders. Then, through Creditors In Commerce, Adams and Hall sent the IRS fake payments amounting to a whopping $93 million. The money orders did not actually discharge anyone's debt—surprise—and Hall, who already had previous fraud and racketeering convictions dating from financial entanglements with the mob, was sentenced to ninety-six months in prison while Brandon was given a forty-month sentence. In a press release, the Justice Department said the men had met at "various seminars associated with the sovereign citizen movement."

You would think that seeing Adams troop off to prison would act as a deterrent, but it didn't seem to work that way for Morton. He began to use a system to evade debt that relies on something called a 1099 OID form. OID stands for "original issue discount," and a 1099 OID form is used to report to the IRS the interest expected on bonds or other financial instruments that won't mature for at least a year. Redemption theorists believe that OID forms function something like an IOU from the government. If a person sends one to a creditor, such as a bank or a credit card company, in the amount that's owed, the creditor can then reclaim the money from the Treasury. Redemption theorists also believe that a 1099 OID can provide direct access to a person's straw-man account—by reporting huge expected earnings from future interest, a person filing taxes can claim a sizable tax refund from the IRS.

In the Mortons' case, they had reported various kinds of income on 1099 OID forms, according to the IRS. In documents filed with the court, it looks as if they simply reported their credit card debt as income. They also reported large withholdings from income that they hadn't earned to claim a refund from the IRS.

At least once, these schemes worked: in 2008, the IRS mistakenly issued Sean a refund of $480,323. According to the Justice Department, "the couple took immediate steps to conceal the money" on the same day the refund was deposited into their joint account, which involved "opening two new accounts, transferring over $360,000 to the two new accounts, and withdrawing $70,000 in cash."

The Justice Department claimed that when the IRS tried to take back the mistaken refund "the Mortons began a campaign to thwart the government's collection efforts." Melissa, for example, claimed that the joint account was hers alone. (At various points, she also listed herself on Facebook as single; perhaps part of a plan or simply some unrelated marital tension.) The IRS was also reportedly presented with "various 'coupons' and 'bonds' that purported to pay off [the Mortons'] debt." In essence, Morton did what he'd done years before with the SEC: instructed the government to pull money out of the Treasury to pay what he owed. And he sold the same bond scheme to others who owed money to the IRS, the state of California, or credit card or mortgage companies, filing paperwork on their behalf that the FBI described as "useless."

Morton, for his part, says he was just fighting gross injustice. "There's a huge inequity in society," he told me. "People are just being raped by the banks. If you really want to know why I got into it, I wanted to help kids with student loans." And that the charges are all made up. "It's all inchoate offenses. It's all imaginary," he insisted. "They will not be able to produce a single original piece of evidence," he said confidently. "Nor will they be able to produce a single person that we've harmed." He was fairly sure the case would never actually go to trial.

IN THIS, MORTON'S PREDICTION WAS WRONG. THE TRIAL BEGAN ON AN unremarkable sunny April day in Los Angeles in Judge Stephen V. Wilson's courtroom. The Mortons silently took a seat at a long table with Melissa's attorney, Steve Brody. Sean had chosen to represent himself, filing dozens of motions before the trial began that the judge called "utterly devoid of merit" and "frivolous." He refused to attend a pretrial conference or call any witnesses in his own defense, and on day one he also objected to the jury hearing the full indictment against him and his wife.

"It would be prejudicial for them to hear that many lies all at once," he told the judge. Morton chuckled. No one else did.

Over the course of the trial, Morton looked cocky, exasperated, infuriated, and, by the end, in a state of shock and close to panic. Watching him was a surreal experience: it took him, in my view, a startlingly long time to realize how much trouble he was in. He was in weirdly good spirits, singing "King of Pain" by the Police as he took the stand until he was reprimanded by a bailiff. At various points he laughed as he watched himself in YouTube videos shown to the jury. Melissa appeared blandly pleasant and impassive. In fact, she was mild and near-silent most of the time. In contrast to her husband's colorful peacock persona, Melissa reminded me of a Sunday school teacher or, frankly, a sister-wife in a sunny fundamentalist fantasy. In their free time, I know from social media, the two of them raised show cats, pampered longhaired creatures with their own bedroom, which the IRS raided in an attempt to find various tax documents.

One morning, as the trial was getting under way, Melissa stopped in front of me, resplendent in a puffy pink sweater. I looked up in surprise. "You do not have permission to use my name or likeness," she said very sweetly, in an even tone. "And no comment." As she walked away, I called after her with something like "Ms. Morton, that's not how it works!" She didn't turn around.

Melissa remained a mystery to the judge and jury, too. The prosecution focused most of its case on Sean, but noted that Melissa had certainly participated, sending out paperwork and talking to clients by phone. Brody, her lawyer, wanted to separate Melissa's actions as much as possible from her husband's. It seemed difficult to do. "Is your argument that she was the dutiful wife and he was the decision-maker?"

Judge Wilson asked him at one point, outside the presence of the jury. During his testimony, Morton let drop that Melissa previously worked for a bank, which would—you would think—mean that she knew just how foolhardy the OID form scheme was. Brody moved for a mistrial at that moment, arguing that the tidbit was impossibly prejudicial to the jury, but Wilson denied it.

Over five days of testimony, a string of witnesses—bank and credit card company employees, mostly—explained that the Mortons, on behalf of themselves and their clients, tried filing 1099 OID forms as well as exotic financial instruments they weren't permitted to use, like Treasury offset forms. Also testifying was Ted Lepkojus, a retired IRS agent whose job is pursuing what he gently terms "unpaid tax cases," who also admitted that he and other IRS agents use aliases to investigate people like the Mortons. (The IRS declined to answer questions about that. For years, much of Morton's income was derived from giving workshops, first in ESP, and later in straw man and redemption theory tactics. I'd been present at a few of his seminars, and while the information presented ranged from nonsense to flatly illegal, they were usually full of people busily taking notes. After the trial concluded, it occurred to me that some of them might have been undercover agents from the IRS.)

The agents' use of an alias only reinforces the redemption theorists' sense of taxes as an illicit enterprise. Although redemption theory targets desperate people, it also takes advantage of two facts: the tax code is impossibly, impenetrably hard to understand; and there is always someone, somewhere who has found a way to beat it. Anyone who knows that corporations and millionaires often end up paying very little in taxes is primed to find that argument persuasive. In court, Morton himself tried to tap into Americans' fundamental distrust of financial institutions. "We're swimming in debt," he told the courtroom. "All of us. We're being crushed by two organizations. Look who we're going up against today: it's the banks and their surrogates, the Internal Revenue Service." He described the banking system and the IRS as "two of the most malicious and pernicious organizations on the planet," which is not, honestly, an unreasonable or unsympathetic argument.

Morton's logic was persuasive: Barbara Lavender, a victim of his scheme, had paid the Mortons $2,500 to help get her out of debt.

Lavender and her husband had debts amounting to $48,000 when she was laid off from work; the amount ballooned to $70,000, and they were getting desperate. Her husband saw Morton speak at a conference and came home with one last-ditch idea. Lavender didn't think what she was doing was illegal: "I thought the bank would accept [the OID form] as a method of payment."

"Did it seem strange to you that you could get rid of $70,000 in debt by paying $2,500?" a prosecutor asked Lavender. "I suppose when you put it that way, it does," she said, sounding a little abashed. "But I honestly thought he'd found a loophole. You hear it all the time, that wealthy people have their tax loopholes. I was heading into retirement, and I was willing to give it a try."

As his own lawyer, Morton got to question and cross-examine witnesses, a task he clearly relished. At one point, he was face-to-face with Luke Yoo, an IRS agent who had raided his home. The IRS seized computers, tax documents, and the Mortons' marriage license. Sean maintained that they kicked in the couple's door, entered with guns drawn, and dragged Melissa, recovering from knee surgery, out of bed. (The IRS says they knocked.)

"How many on your team were dressed like jackbooted Nazis?" he asked Yoo, raising his voice. "Did you witness them assault my wife, take her wheelchair, and throw it across the room? Did you photograph the physical assault on my wife?" (Yoo responded that he'd been covering the operation from outside and hadn't witnessed anything in particular.)

When it was his turn to testify in his own defense, Morton took the stand with tiny glasses perched on his nose and a thick sheaf of notes and delivered a long monologue—his version of the magic words—meant to stop the trial in its tracks. "Be seated and answer questions," Judge Wilson ordered him, cutting through Morton's declamations of "in good faith I do move" and "in violation of rights." Reluctantly, Morton sat.

Crucially, the trial sought to determine whether the Mortons knowingly broke the law, whether they genuinely believed that OID forms could be used in the way that they tried, and whether Morton chose selectively to avail himself of US citizenship, which would undercut the sincerity of his positions.

As Judge Wilson told the jury, "ultimately, one of the things you'll have to decide is whether or not [Morton] had a good faith belief in what he did. Crimes require a specific intent and bad faith, a bad motive. Good faith is a defense. So, I'm not going to allow him to tell you what the law is or how the banking system works because he hasn't established—at least in my view—his qualifications to do that. But he can, if he wishes, tell you what he believes the system involved and what the law was when he did the things he did."

And Morton did. He knew nothing about the 1099 OID process before meeting Adams, he testified. "I was a spiritual guy who was writing spiritual newsletters." He truly believed that Adams's system was "a legitimate process under the law." He added, "I never, ever, ever in any of this thought that I was breaking the law. I thought this was the law. I thought everything we were doing was absolutely legal."

But Morton's own picture of himself shifted, from insisting he knew nothing—a spiritual, naive innocent—to painting himself as nothing less than a financial freedom fighter. "I still firmly believe," he told the jury, "even though I have all this evidence to the contrary, that there's hope for us. There's got to be some kind of system to offset the crushing debt that the banks put us all under—that there's some way to stand up to them and be a hero."

It got worse for Morton when Assistant United States Attorney Valerie Makarewicz started to ask her questions. Makarewicz, who was in the Tax Division of the Southern District of California, was personally sued in civil court by Morton before the criminal trial began, along with another government attorney, James Hughes. The two were accused of a battery of very strange things: fraud was the most legible accusation, followed by "malicious legal processes." A few other things were thrown into a voluminous thirty-nine-page complaint: accusations that the attorneys acted as foreign agents, that they failed to post photographs of their bar cards as required by law, and probably ten or twenty other items I missed. Every paragraph is a logical and grammatical and punctuational adventure. Morton identifies himself and Melissa as "of the Morton hacienda," and every page was inscribed with the words "In the Name of Our Heavenly Father."

Makarewicz intended, as quickly as possible, to get Morton to admit that he behaved like a citizen of this country when it suited him.

"Are you a citizen of the United States?" she asked him directly.

"That's a hard question to answer," he told her placidly. "Under the Fourteenth Amendment, I consider myself a citizen of California and an American national."

The Fourteenth Amendment is the one that says anyone born or naturalized in the United States is a citizen of the United States and the state where they reside. It holds a special place in the cosmology of sovereign citizens: many believe they can formally renounce the first part, that which makes them a federal citizen, while keeping their state allegiance intact.

The jury didn't know of any of this: they just watched, brows furrowed, as Morton declined to respond to something that probably looked simple.

"Your honor," Makarewicz said, a little exasperated. "Please ask the witness to answer the question."

"Again, I'm a citizen of the state of California, the sovereign people of California and an American national," Morton said.

"Do you reside in the United States, sir?" Makarewicz asked icily.

"There's different definitions," Morton said, smiling faintly. "Can you define the United States for me?"

Makarewicz looked at Judge Wilson, who verbally shrugged back at her. "I can't go any further," he said. "You've asked the question and he's given the answer."

Makarewicz got Morton to admit that he hasn't filed a California state tax return since 2000. She also tried to get him to admit that he enjoyed the "benefits of being a US citizen," as she put it.

"You enjoy the benefits of the US military, don't you?" she asked.

"California has a national guard and local police," Morton shot back. "I don't know that I've ever been protected by the US military."

Makarewicz got Morton to admit that he drove to court on a public road, that he used state water and sewer systems, and that he's used the state court system.

"You sued me," she reminded him.

"I did, because you wouldn't answer my questions about what's the jurisdiction you have under the Sixth Amendment," Morton informed her. "And how come I'm not facing a plaintiff here today."

Makarewicz also asked if Morton had a passport, an answer that perhaps gave her more than she anticipated.

"I've had diplomatic passports from countries and nation states that we're attempting to start," he told her. (One of them was called the Republic of New Lemuria; starting ersatz countries is another sovereign practice.) "As an ambassador I was immune from filling out tax ID numbers," he added. Makarewicz almost imperceptibly shook her head, as if to get a gnat out of her ear.

Makarewicz came to the trial seemingly irate at Morton for having sued her, but in truth she and her co-prosecutor could have had it much worse than a tiny, easily swattable lawsuit in civil court. As noted, sovereigns and redemption theorists regularly file liens against court officers and law enforcement officials as a method of retaliation. In 2013, for example, a Minneapolis couple named Thomas and Lisa Eilertson filed a whopping $250 billion in liens against various government employees, an act of revenge after their home had been foreclosed in 2009. Their targets included the local sheriff, the county registrar, various court employees, and attorneys for the county. "It affects your credit rating, it affected my wife, it affected my children," Sheriff Richard Stanek told the *New York Times*, referring to the liens. "We spent countless hours trying to undo it."

The tactic is referred to as "paper terrorism" (and Morton himself has jocularly referred to himself as a "paper terrorist"). It takes advantage of the fact that anyone at all can file a lien under the Uniform Commercial Code. Though invalid liens can be cleared up, it can take a very long time. Some states have made it a felony to file fraudulent documents to retaliate against government officials, and some places give secretaries of state more discretion in whether to accept a lien filing, but the system remains pretty piecemeal.

Even though Morton didn't file a lien, suing the attorneys who are prosecuting you seems like a good way to earn a specially heaping portion of their ire. But it also illustrates something fairly central about redemption theorists: they recognize the legitimacy of some institutions—like the court system—when it suits them, and try to use it to their advantage.

Morton can elicit fury and disgust for promoting a misleading set of promises to desperate and broke customers. Indeed, during her questioning, Makarewicz noted that at least twice, Morton had charged families $2,500 to get their loved ones out of prison using some version of his bond scheme. Both times he failed, and both prisoners were still very much locked up. Redemption theory can feel like a thin legitimation for greed and a desire to live outside the law, an unwillingness to follow rules the rest of us have agreed to live by. It's not like I *enjoy* paying my taxes.

At the same time, though, Morton's crimes are a tiny droplet in the vast, dark ocean that is American economic Darwinism and financial cruelty. Morton was correct that the system is stacked against ordinary Americans: the subprime mortgage crisis forced millions from their homes while the banks were assiduously bailed out; millionaires were allowed to flee from the mess they created with the sturdiest of golden parachutes. Our state protections are so weak, our safety net so threadbare, that it is hard to condemn people who seek a way out, even an illegal one.

Indeed, some people do believe in the redemption system: one witness stepped forward, Carol Lee Meyer, who insisted that Morton's plan worked, that he saved her home from foreclosure. (Makarewicz gently pointed out that the bank was still trying to seize her home and that she had to file for bankruptcy. Morton's bond process might have slowed and tangled the process, the way that phony filings sometimes do, but Meyer was almost certainly going to lose her house.)

And Sean Morton, especially, belongs to a long and colorful tradition of American hucksters, seekers, and strivers, a traveling salesman with a paper blend of snake oil. When I looked at him, I could lower my blood pressure by thinking of medicine shows and quack cures as forms of national eccentricity. He was often hard to demonize, with his weird blazers and their pocket crests, his obvious joy when he talks about aliens (at other times, when I heard him make xenophobic jokes about Muslims, or used rape as a metaphor for what the courts were doing to him, he was far less sympathetic).

By the last day of his trial—when reality finally appeared to take hold—there was little but pity. Before closing arguments, Morton sat outside the courtroom, rocking gently, a sad Humpty Dumpty.

"Sit down," he invited me, without preamble. "It's so hard," he said, looking at the ceiling. "Especially when all I set down to do is help people." He seemed short of breath. "It all boils down to intentions, doesn't it? We were following the letter of the law. We studied and studied. But they're spending ten million dollars on this case. They want to give us jail time in amounts like Nazi war criminals or Jeffrey Dahmer." When he was in the monastery in Nepal for eight months, he took a sacred vow to work for the enlightenment of all beings, he said. And now his rights were being violated because of his choice to shun corrupt systems.

"This is all about freedom," he claimed. "We're fighting the IRS and their mangled bastard child, the banks. People voted for Trump because they wanted to tear down the IRS."

Jury deliberations took just two hours. Upon hearing the guilty verdict, Melissa reportedly collapsed to the floor and had to be revived by paramedics.

THE JUDGE SET A SENTENCING DATE FOR SEAN IN JUNE 2017, BUT HE failed to show up. He filed a nonsense motion that same morning, directing that his case be moved to the Supreme Court. He also missed the taping of *Strange Universe*, his radio show, calling his cohosts from what sounded like a car on the highway.

"I'm fine," he said, not quite convincingly. "I'm out and about here somewhere. It's okay as far as everything goes." He insisted that the case was indeed "with the Supreme Court" now.

In the days that followed, while still a fugitive, Morton created a GoFundMe fund-raiser titled "Future for Melissa," asking for money to help her move. Where she planned to go, it wasn't clear, given that she was facing her own sentencing date. ("I think she'll get all the assistance she needs relocating to a bunk bed at FCI Dublin," one Twitter follower said dryly.) The GoFundMe soon disappeared.

For her part, Melissa signed a presentencing agreement committing to avoid contact with Sean. "Does anyone know how to sell a whole lot of comic books that isn't too time consuming?" she posted on social media one day. Another time she posted, "I'm not afraid to admit when

I make mistakes—like the one time I got married!" But love isn't the most rational of forces, and in August the Mortons were arrested together, at a hotel in Desert Hot Springs, California. According to the government, they'd checked in to watch the solar eclipse.

AT THEIR SENTENCING, MORTON TRIED TO CHANGE HIS PLEA TO DECLARE himself a Fourteenth Amendment citizen. Judge Wilson denied every one of his proposed motions, saying only, "Too late, Mr. Morton." He was sentenced to seventy-two months in prison and five years' probation and ordered to reimburse the $480,000 owed to the IRS, as well as a fine of $2,900, to be paid in quarterly increments of $25 from prison. He was also barred from working in any business related to debt relief.

At Melissa's sentencing, according to the website UFO Watchdog, she entered the courtroom in a wheelchair and read an emotional letter of apology: she was taking responsibility for her actions, the experience had "kicked her in the behind" and "set her on the right path." She added, "This would have never happened had I not met Mr. Morton." Judge Wilson believed she had come under "some kind of Svengali-type influence" from her husband: she was sentenced to twenty-four months in prison and five years of probation, and fined $2,800.

The government was eager to set an example for other would-be redemption theorists. To Melissa's sentencing memorandum, the prosecution added that the case presented a powerful need and opportunity for the court "to deter similar 'sovereign citizen' fraudsters," as they put it. "Members of the tax-defier movement will take note of whatever sentences the Court imposes upon defendant in this case."

But the sentence served only to strengthen Morton's inherent belief that the American financial system is a stacked deck, impenetrable, unfair, a Minotaur's lair built to ensnare people who enter into it without the proper weapons.

"The courts and the bar association are all protecting the banks," he had said, months before his disastrous day in court. "Redemption *should* work, *does* work, *legally* works." He looked troubled, as though he were getting a psychic twinge of what was to come. "But they just refuse to do any of it."

8

WHITE NATIONALIST COOKOUT

"The white majority are fed up with all of these lying, cheating, thieving, war-mongering, child-molesting, political pimps and whores," Arthur "Art" Jones roared. "Of this corrupt and decadent two-party, Jew-party, queer-party system!" He was gesturing wildly, waving liver-spotted hands. At his throat, his tie quivered, bedecked with a two-headed enamel pin: an American flag and a red flag with a black swastika, fused together.

It was a glorious, soft late April evening in 2017, and a coalition of white supremacists were gathered high in the lush green foothills of southeastern Kentucky. Their meeting place was a grassy, lumpy field on private land, overtaken with trucks and dotted with a few tents and a duo of Porta-Potties. A very pale, very male crowd, laughing and smoking, was lingering among the cars as the sun set. A guy who looked to be barely out of his teens bounced by, wearing a T-shirt for the Daily Stormer, a website popular with neo-Nazi Internet trolls. A bald man with a neat, professorial beard and round silver glasses stopped in front of me and the photographer I was traveling with.

"Do y'all have any unscented lotion?" he inquired, gesturing at the new tattoo on his leg, scabbed over and looking itchy. We didn't, but I made a show of looking in my purse anyway, to be friendly, I guess. The purpose of the evening, after all, was to make new friends, to try to bring together disparate racist groups into a harmonious whole, to denounce the vicious Jewish cabal enslaving the country and the world, and to prepare for possible war the following day.

For Matthew Heimbach, this meeting of the different groups was a moment he'd been waiting for his whole young life. Heimbach was the founder and most recognizable face of the Traditionalist Worker Party, and at this moment in Kentucky, he was busy capitalizing on two things: increasingly open rage and disaffection from white voters, and Donald Trump's shameless pandering to those feelings a few months into his presidency.

The TWP is described by the Southern Poverty Law Center as "a neo-Nazi group that advocates for racially pure nations and communities and blames Jews for many of the world's problems." Put more simply, the TWP was Heimbach's baby, the conduit for all his white nationalist ambitions.

Personally, I couldn't help thinking of Heimbach and his cadres as the Social Justice Racists. At the time of the rally, Heimbach was barely twenty-five, chubby and beaming, with a beard creeping up his face and down his neck. He lived in a trailer in Indiana with a wife, a baby son, and another one on the way. He often mentioned his family when he was getting floridly poetic about his determination to organize in defense of the downtrodden white man.

Heimbach's focus on his family would seem quite ironic in a little over a year, when he was humiliated and the TWP fell apart after it was revealed that he was accused of domestic abuse and had had an affair with the wife of his father-in-law, Matthew Parrot, cofounder of the TWP. Meanwhile, though, his popularity was at its peak, due to his affable demeanor, his ability to forge alliances, and his surprising set of policy positions. Heimbach's TWP was against climate change but supported better drinking water and healthcare in poor, heavily white regions of the country. He talked a lot about Appalachian children's teeth and the safety net that failed their parents. The TWP also fulminated against "mass immigration" and promised that under the glorious white ethno-state it hoped to build, only "white Caucasians who are descendants of indigenous Europeans" would be allowed to immigrate, and would, moreover, have to assimilate "to the dominant culture for the sake of national unity."

Slightly more quietly, Heimbach wanted to see white supremacist groups organize in a concerted way against their common enemy, world Jewry, which was the purpose of the evening in Kentucky: the rebranding and relaunch of a white nationalist coalition, uniting several groups—the TWP, the National Socialist Movement, Vanguard America, and League of the South—to be called the Nationalist Front. This was, in fact, the second try at forming such a coalition: the first was launched by the NSM in Georgia in April 2016 and called the Aryan Nationalist Alliance. The TWP joined several months later. The coalition had decided to re-form around November 2016, with the Southern Poverty Law Center speculating that the NSM was, at Heimbach's encouragement, trying to lightly veil its appreciation for Hitler.

In early 2017, the TWP announced that it would hold a rally and conference for the white nationalist groups near Pikeville, Kentucky, a small town in a region that was hard hit by the collapse of the coal industry. Between 2010 and 2015, the county lost 5 percent of its population, driven elsewhere to look for work. Pike County is an overwhelmingly white area, and about 80 percent of its registered voters went for Trump. "We didn't vote for Trump because we're racist," Chase Goodman, who'd lived in Pikeville most of his life, explained to me. "We just want our fuckin' coal jobs back."

Heimbach hoped to tap into the thick, ropey veins of anger and despair over those lost jobs; he was also hoping to be there when the anger turned on the new president. Just before the rally, he told me that he felt the common man's inevitable disappointment with Trump would work to his advantage. "I knew he wasn't one of us," he said. "I never thought he was a closet white nationalist. I was just hoping he would buy us more time and further polarize politics, which he has done."

In time, he said, the white working class would reject Trump and the Republican Party more generally: "They'll lose any hope they had in conservatism. They're not going to become Democrats. And if you like Trumpism, maybe fascism is something you'll like. Where else can they go?"

The "conference" portion of the event was held on private land after the neo-Nazis were unable to get a permit to hold it in a state park. To get there, the photographer and I joined a convoy of cars proceeding out of a Walmart parking lot in the town of Whitesburg. A few young guys in black T-shirts wandered the lot carrying semiautomatic rifles, looking chipper.

From Whitesburg, the convoy followed a narrow, winding road through a landscape dotted with billboards for personal injury attorneys, the US Army, organ donation. As the towns got smaller, the billboards gave way to campaign signs tacked onto trees: GIBSON FOR CONSTABLE, one announced. Another: TRUMP DIGS COAL! The towns themselves turned into vanishing tiny pinpoints with alluring names: Rowdy, Dwarf, and finally Democrat, marked by a hand-lettered sign, permanent marker on plywood, stuck with an American flag in the corner. Trees crowded the road. Little girls played ball in the front yard of a house with a sagging wooden porch cluttered with stuff. They waved sweetly at the convoy of cars; the white supremacists waved back.

THE SLIMIEST, DANKEST POOL OF THE OVERLAPPING CONSPIRACY PONDS is extremism, and, particularly in the United States, white supremacist-based hatred. Hate groups all over the world are fueled by terrified, wild conjectures about the people they hate, from globalist Jew bankers pulling the global strings to Islamists spreading Sharia law across America. One Klan group, the Original Knights of America, Knights of the Ku Klux Klan, posts dire warnings on its website about the secret plots of moderate Muslims: the Common Core curriculum is, they advise, an attempt to promote "Islamic Supremacism" in schools. Supermarkets are even selling halal meat without noting that it's halal (tricking non-Muslims into eating halal meat is, I suppose, part of some other dreadful plot).

For many of these groups, it is the Jews, above all, who are the hidden, rotten core of every evil, the most powerful foe, the hooked nose behind everything wrong in America. There are detours—white supremacists also make the vilest claims against black and Latinx people—but after many years and new flavors of hatred, the extremists have maintained one steady and consistent focus. Conspiracy theories about Jews are some of the oldest in history: depending on who you talk to, Jews have poisoned wells, stolen children for blood rituals, or formed a many-headed hydra to run the world's governments and financial systems. Their power is legendary: "The Jew *never* sleeps," said Brian Culpepper of the National Socialist Movement, addressing the crowd in Pikeville. "He works 24 hours a day, 365 days a year to eradicate us."

The history of racist extremism in America is heavily larded with conspiracy theorism: neo-Nazism is premised on secret Jewish control, of course, as well as a generous dose of Holocaust denial. The Christian Identity movement, some of whose proponents became the earliest sovereign citizens, relies on the concept that only European whites are part of the Lost Tribes of Israel, while Jews and nonwhites are those mud people plotting to enslave the world. That's just one aspect of American hatred, which is a much longer, blood-drenched book. We've never been free from hate groups, whether it's the Klan's emergence just after the Civil War, its resurgence during the 1920s, or the birth in the early 1970s of the frequently racist far-right militia movement, beginning with the loosely organized Posse Comitatus.

A big preoccupation for conspiracy theorists on the far right, as discussed, is an imminent one-world government takeover, an army of shock troops who plan to put the country under the savage thumb of tyrannical control. (The anti-globalization movement on the so-called radical left isn't really the same: anarchist demonstrators in Seattle in 1999 protesting the World Trade Organization, for instance, weren't concerned with "one world government," per se, so much as the human rights and environmental issues they saw as an endemic part of corporate-backed globalization.) Right-wing militia groups took the one-world government fear to particular lengths: they identified the New World Order as the main threat of the 1990s, and were thrown in an intense tizzy about it when they heard George H. W. Bush echo the term in a speech. Other, more Nazi-oriented folks, referred to the threat as the Zionist Occupation Government—the ZOG—a term that's been kicking around since the mid-1970s.

Vanquishing the ZOG is a central theme in the seminal *The Turner*

Diaries, a 1978 novel by William Luther Pierce, founder of the National Alliance, a white supremacist group. It centers on the Order, a cell of brave white men who orchestrate a violent guerrilla war against the System, a Jewish-controlled government that has snatched everyone's guns and made it a hate crime for white people to defend themselves against the savage hordes. Taking its name from *The Turner Diaries*, an actual group called the Order also borrowed its most gruesome tactics, assassinating a Jewish radio host named Alan Berg in Denver in 1984 for the crime of mocking them on-air. Oklahoma City bomber Timothy McVeigh was also a big fan of the book; he justified his attack by calling it a counterstrike in a war against an oppressive government system. Photocopies of pages from *The Turner Diaries* were found in the car driven by McVeigh just after the attack.

New World Order fears and anti-Semitism are evident even in one of the oddest conspiracy theories ever constructed, which holds that many world leaders are secretly twelve-foot-tall evil human-lizard hybrids. That pioneering concept was popularized by David Icke, a one-time sports presenter in Great Britain. In 1991, Icke disappeared for a few months, reappeared in all-turquoise garb, and declared himself the "Son of the Godhead." He also announced that the world would end in 1997.

When that didn't pan out, Icke tried again. His new theory, which he began advancing around 1998, is that the world is ruled by the Babylonian Brotherhood, a group of "reptilians" disguised as human world leaders, among them Queen Elizabeth, Henry Kissinger, the Clintons, and a large number of Hollywood celebrities.

Icke warned that the reptilians, which he also called by their proper name, the Anunnaki, were propelling us all toward a fascist system of one-world government. He was barred from speaking in Canada in 1999, after many organizations took his talk of lizard domination to be a reference to Jews. "HOW FUNNY!" Icke wrote, in caps for some reason, in a release about being unable to enter the country. "SINCE I BEGAN TALKING ABOUT THE REPTILIAN CONNECTION, THE OPPOSITION HAS BEEN INCREASED SUBSTANTIALLY." In the same missive, he called the allegations of anti-Semitism "a fiction," while referring to the Anti-Defamation League as an "Illuminati front."

While he might have at first meant human-lizard hybrids, in subsequent years Icke's theories shifted toward a scenario in which the Earth is, in fact, controlled by a global cabal with Israel at its center. It's not blatantly anti-Semitic—more like blatantly anti-Zionist—but Icke does argue that what he calls "Rothschild Zionists" are lurking among the vast masses of ordinary Jews, plotting all manner of dark deeds. "Rothschild Zionism is an elite secret society at its rotten core," he wrote in 2015. "And the people I am naming here and so many more are not agents of Jewish people as a whole, but agents of the secret society that has mercilessly manipulated the Jewish population for centuries to advance its goals." He's also made frequent reference to the *Protocols of the Learned Elders of Zion*, the anti-Semitic forgery, making his claims that he's only talking about *some* Jews significantly less believable.

Icke's heyday was in the 1990s, around the same era that proved to be an especially fruitful time for the more serious hate groups in the United States. Extremist organizations have tended to wax and wane, and although a few died out or changed form (specifically the last of the Posse Comitatus crowd, whose main organizers faded away), there was also a resurgence of public neo-Nazi and skinhead groups, beginning in the late 1980s and taking off in 1998. The militia movement, a heavily armed, better organized offshoot of the earlier Patriot group, was an indisputable heir to Posse Comitatus ideas.

Neo-Nazism tends to be an ugly, distorted reflection of what is happening in the broader culture at any given moment, and the early 1990s saw a potent wave of anti-immigrant feeling, tied to an economic recession, which, though it lasted less than a year, gave rise to a disproportionate sense of scarcity. As tends to happen, a corresponding fear developed of undocumented immigrants "taking" dwindling public resources. A raft of anti-immigrant legislation was adopted, most infamously California's Proposition 187, in 1994. Known as the Save Our State provision, it barred undocumented people from using virtually any public services in the state. It passed overwhelmingly through a voter referendum before being struck down in a court challenge five years later.

Another factor in the growth and shocking violence of the neo-Nazi movement at this time was a concept called "leaderless resistance," popularized by former Klansman Louis Beam. He encouraged far-right hate advocates to organize in small groups and protect themselves against prying law enforcement and government eyes as they were plotting their acts. Their violence continued, and even heightened: in 1991 the Church of the Creator—founded in 1973—lauded its members for killing a black sailor named Harold Mansfield in a parking lot.

At the same time, as these groups were becoming bolder, they were also sowing the seeds of their own destruction. The Mansfield killing prompted the Southern Poverty Law Center to sue the Church of the Creator on behalf of Mansfield's mother, Connie, seeking damages for both the pain and suffering caused by his death as well as a host of other minor crimes committed against the family in the commission of the murder, like illegal transport of firearms across state lines. The lawsuit managed to bankrupt the church into nonexistence, although a new leader, Matthew Hale, quickly emerged to restart the church. (It eventually became the World Church of the Creator and continued as a potent force until Hale's arrest in 2003. It exists today as the "Creativity Movement.")

Lawsuits are a tactic that has been useful several other times in defanging hate groups. In 1993, the Ku Klux Klan received a serious blow when the Invisible Empire, Knights of the Ku Klux Klan lost a lawsuit brought by the SPLC for a 1987 attack on civil rights activists marching to observe Dr. Martin Luther King, Jr.'s birthday. After a protracted court battle, the Invisible Empire was forced to hand over its membership list and pay $37,500 to some of the civil rights marchers.

A new strain of anti-Semitic conspiracy thinking followed the September 11 attacks when various fringe websites started claiming that Jews and/or Israelis who worked in the World Trade Center were told to stay home. (Poet Amiri Baraka infamously cited the Israeli aspect of that conspiracy theory in a work called "Somebody Blew Up America.") And the attack of course kick-started a virulent anti-Arab, anti-Islam paranoia that never dissipated: during his campaign, Trump falsely claimed to have seen crowds of Arab-looking people celebrating after the Twin Towers fell. "There were people over in New Jersey that were watching it, a heavy Arab population, that were cheering as the buildings came down," he told ABC *This Week* host George Stephanopoulos. "Not good."

In the decade after September 11, the now-familiar menu of far-right fears and conspiracies entered deep into the mainstream: gun confiscation by the federal government, the imposition of martial law, an invasion by the UN to take all our guns, and 9/11 as an inside job (which was just as popular on the left). But in 2010, the SPLC noted a new flurry of activity on the "extreme right" of the conspiracy culture, triggered by the election of Barack Obama, who was seen by "Patriots" as a Manchurian candidate sent to usher in the New World Order. Journalist Alexander Zaitchik, writing for the SPLC, noted what he called "an anti-Semitic flavor." Regardless of the subtle historical tides washing in and out, the persistent paranoias clung to the shore: Jews and Muslims are infiltrators. Jews want to take control through powerful institutions like the financial system and Muslims want to force everyone to convert and implement Sharia law.

The Jew banker–world control paranoia was echoed by Donald Trump during his presidential campaign, when he attacked what he called "the Clinton Machine" for meeting secretly with moneyed donors. "We've seen this firsthand in the WikiLeaks documents," he thundered in one characteristic speech. "In which Hillary Clinton meets in secret with international banks to plot the destruction of US sovereignty in order to enrich these global financial powers, her special-interest friends, and her donors." At one point, Trump released a meme on Twitter that showed Clinton smirking against a backdrop of stacks of cash. Next to her was a red six-pointed star, which read "Most Corrupt Candidate Ever!" He later insisted it was meant to be a "sheriff's star," not a Star of David.

Not coincidentally, the 2016 election saw the meteoric rise of the so-called alt-right, a group that will cop to being nationalists but has different reactions to being called racist, ranging from indignant denial to shrugging acceptance (the Proud Boys, for instance, are a nationalist men's group who rather dubiously insist they have no racist overtones—and threaten to sue news outlets who report otherwise—but will cheerfully acknowledge being Islamophobic). The best-known

US figure is Richard Spencer, who is an open racist interested in forming a white ethno-state. (Spencer's views on Jewish people are somewhat veiled: he's been explicit that he considers Jews a race unto themselves, and has tweeted dismissively about the "Holocaust industry" after Trump cut millions from the budget for the Holocaust Museum in Washington, DC.)

Spencer was made famous by an ocean of not-mean-enough profiles by mainstream media outlets, many of them marveling that he had a discernible chin, a passable haircut, and owned a suit. He popularized the term "alternative right" in 2011 when he first took over the National Policy Institute, a dusty academic racist organization that he managed to turn into his personal vehicle for stardom. Seeking political power and public acceptability, Spencer's goal was to keep a careful distance from unabashed racists like those who gathered in Kentucky (though he did, at various times, have a respectful working relationship with Heimbach).

To that end he effectively built relationships with alt-right types across Europe, working toward a global movement. Spencer created a company, Altright Corporation, with the leaders of Arktos Media, a Swedish bookseller, which claims to be the leading (and probably only) publisher of the alt-right, as well as with a European white supremacist YouTube channel called Red Ice. The goal of the new partnership, Spencer told Buzzfeed News when it was first announced, was to extend connections with his fellow European ideologues to help "displace the conservative movement."

Patrik Hermansson, an activist from Sweden in the group Hope Not Hate, infiltrated the alt-right movement both in the United States and abroad and spent several months among its leaders. Given their glorification of Norse culture, he was welcomed with open arms. What he discovered was a world that looked remarkably like standard-issue neo-Nazism, one of "extreme racism, antisemitism, Holocaust denial, esoteric Nazi rituals, and wild conspiracy theories . . . a movement that sometimes glorifies Nazi Germany, openly supports genocidal ideas and is unrelentingly racist, sexist, and homophobic."

———

THAT EVENING IN THE FIELD IN KENTUCKY THE UNAPOLOGETIC, UNGEN-
teel variant of hatred was blasted at top volume by Art Jones, the elderly
anti-Semite from Illinois with a surprisingly strong set of lungs. "Now
President Trump, he has surrounded himself with hordes of Jews," he
yelled, not entirely accurately. "Including a Jew in his own family!" His
audience, seated at long wooden tables under a white tent, muttered in
disgusted agreement, save for two little girls who were coloring oblivi-
ously. "I'm sorry I voted for the son of a bitch," he shouted some more.
A woman bounced a fretful baby; a squat little man in a tan shirt and
a swastika armband poked around behind Jones at the lectern, looking
for another beer.

Ostensibly, poor whites from Kentucky were the reason the racists
had trekked out to Pikeville. But the actual townspeople of Pikeville
weren't present at the gathering. A local man donated his land for the
white nationalists to use—his sympathies were unclear—but almost
every one of the attendees was from out of state.

The forces of whiteness were a varied bunch: some of them were
young racists and some were slightly older. The National Socialist Movement was there, a neo-Nazi party whose leader, "Commander" Jeff
Schoep, lives in Detroit. (The NSM's use of military titles is part of a
pretension to military rigor that's common among white supremacist
groups.) The Global Crusaders: Order of the Ku Klux Klan were there,
an arm of the KKK that seemed especially young: most of them were
from Alabama, skinny, acne-pocked, chicken-necked. A few representatives from the Original Knight Riders Knights of the Ku Klux Klan
were beside them, older guys in paramilitary black; one went by the
name Sky Soldier and bore an unsettling resemblance to Willie Nelson.
He shyly handed me his card when I asked for an interview. SOLDIERS
OF GOD, it read, MILITANT CHRISTIANS SINCE 1118 A.D.

Vanguard America was there, too, a younger, hipster-looking white
nationalist group that seemed to make everyone else a bit uncomfortable, although its members' sentiments were indistinguishable from the
party line: a separate country for whites, Muslims out, beware the Jew.
("Know your enemy," one of their flyers read, over a sagging, eyeless
visage of George Soros wearing a red Star of David on his lapel. "He
knows you.)"

And Brian "Sonny" Thomas was there, a white nationalist from Ohio with a graying mullet and a love for classic rock. He made headlines in 2010 for tweeting about wanting to shoot Latinos ("Illegals everywhere today! So many spicks makes me feel like a speck. Grr. Where's my gun?"), despite having had a child with a Latina woman. He ran an online radio show and periodically popped up in the local news for doing things like unfurling Confederate flags during school board meetings; a state politician got in trouble not long before the conference for appearing on his show to promote a ban on sanctuary cities.

I wandered over to Thomas to chat. "Are you gonna be fair?" he demanded.

"I hope so," I replied. He grinned and genially lapsed into a long near-monologue on a variety of subjects: Donald Trump ("He's totally surrounded by cucks and Jews," he says, using the derisive supremacist term for a conservative sellout or a weakling of any kind); the president's recent bombing of Syria (an outrage, we agreed, for different reasons); Venezuela; states' rights; fathers' rights; the gold standard; Charleston mass shooter Dylann Roof (a false-flag attack, Thomas thought, or maybe simply a victim of MKUltra or similar mind control). He was also concerned about child molestation: "Deep within the upper echelons of power, there's a lot of pedophilia," Thomas explained. "It's arrogance. These people think they can't be touched." Pizzagate had made inroads here, too, although nobody used that name for it.

Thomas blamed most of the world's problems on the globalists, people like CNN founder Ted Turner and Bill Gates, but placed America's moral decline firmly at the feet of the Jews: "The whole media is owned by six companies, which are all owned by Jews." But he could feel a new and encouraging shift, he added: "I can talk to people like you at a gas pump and we're not talking in hushed tones, you know? Communication is the first step."

"I'm Jewish," I told him. His face registered several different shades of polite surprise.

"That's fine!" he said at last, reassuringly. "You might think I'm full of shit. And that's fine."

Art Jones, the yelling elderly anti-Semite, hailed from the Chicago suburbs and was the head of the America First Committee, a group of which he seemed to be the sole member. He'd been generating head-lines since the 1970s for making outrageously bigoted statements, like calling the Holocaust "a big international extortion plot that was greatly exaggerated." He also ran repeatedly, unsuccessfully, for Congress. His wife came along, too, wordless and frail-looking, wearing a tragic wig and blocky glasses. An old *Chicago Reader* profile of Jones from 1994 includes a revealing, heartbreaking anecdote: Jones's father, a World War II veteran, was outraged to see American neo-Nazis goose-stepping down the street. He ran out from the pub where he was drinking, fists up, ready to kick the ass of the man leading the Nazis. When he saw that it was his own son, he collapsed in tears and walked away.

There were only a few women present, and four or five children. Otherwise, the crowd was male. As I was pondering that, I noticed Mike Enoch wandering among them, a white supremacist cohost for a show called *The Daily Shoah* on a site he ran called The Right Stuff. Back in January, Enoch temporarily vanished in disgrace when it was revealed by anti-fascists who doxxed him (published his real name and other personal information) that his wife had Jewish heritage. Enoch's cohosts said he was temporarily unavailable to host the show because he was in the process of separating from her.

Meanwhile, Heimbach and a few TWP helpers were focused on cor-ralling a small group of reporters, whom the crowd was eyeing warily.

"Can the *Lugenpresse* please come forward?" Heimbach boomed cheerfully, using the Nazi term for the lying press. We walked over as the crowd giggled.

"No media past the Porta-Potties this way," he said, gesturing. "That's for everyone who wants privacy."

"I'm in a fuckin' union job," one guy cracked. He was wearing a T-shirt that read MY BOSS IS AN AUSTRIAN PAINTER. "I don't give a shit." The white supremacists chortled. This friendly, convivial evening was unusual. For a very long time, white supremacist groups were riven by disagreements and factionalism and infighting. "There was bad blood," Thomas explained. "Things were said. Girlfriends were stolen." It was more than that: a lot of racist groups in the United States fall apart almost as quickly as they are formed, either because their members murder one another or because they end up in prison. But in the age of

Trump, racists were hoping to usher in a new era of cooperation and an advancement for the white, Jew-less, Muslim-less, Latino-less country of which they all dreamed.

"It's not about the uniform you wear or the colors you fly," "Commander" Schoep of the NSM told the audience. He was wearing a pinstripe suit, for some reason, which looked out of place in the context of his being in a grassy field with men in pseudomilitary outfits. "It's about the color of our skin. Our enemies have thrived on our infighting, but nationalism is rising in the United States."

Still, the turnout was a little disappointing: in the end, this mass meeting of the champions of whiteness amounted to about one hundred people, quietly eating fried chicken and biscuits out of Styrofoam containers as speaker after speaker droned on at a rickety podium. As the speakers wound down, they turned to their anxieties about the following afternoon, when a rally was planned in downtown Pikeville. They expected anti-fascist counterprotesters to show up, and both sides had been talking a big game online: after recent violent clashes at Auburn University and UC Berkeley, they thought that Pikeville might be the next explosive battleground. "If I see anybody running or breaking ranks, you better hope the Reds catch you," Schoep told the crowd. "You better hope the antifa catch you."

They needed to make a good impression on the townspeople, too, "Major" Mike Schloar of the NSM sternly reminded everyone. "I told people at a rally in Harrisburg last month, 'Don't use foul language or racial slurs,'" he commanded the audience, irate. "Apparently people had their ears closed. We're going to be in front of a lot of media. Keep it clean. Don't use any foul language: spic, spook, kike, gook—do I have to go through a whole list?" The crowd tittered. "If you say something at some hoodrat ghetto thug, they'll think you're no better."

THE BIG QUESTION IS ALWAYS WHETHER RACIST IDEAS ARE SPREADING. How much damage can they do? How does the rank contagion of their prejudice affect the rest of us? The contagion certainly isn't spreading very far or fast: in an August 2017 poll by ABC News and the *Washington Post*, just 9 percent of those surveyed said it was "acceptable" to hold neo-Nazi or white supremacist views. Ten percent said they supported the alt-right movement, while 50 percent said they opposed it (the remaining 40 percent had no opinion, indicating they weren't familiar with the meaning of the terms).

There was wide division of opinion about whether the alt-right held white supremacist views: one 40-percent segment of those surveyed said it did, while another 40-percent segment said it did not. A more recent study by a University of Alabama researcher found that though people might not use the term "alt-right," plenty of white Americans are willing to say they agree with those beliefs. "Roughly 5.64 percent of America's 198 million non-Hispanic whites have beliefs consistent with the alt-right's worldview," the author George Hawley wrote, or about eleven million Americans.

Whatever the figure, barely veiled racist ideas drew closer to the mainstream after 2016 than they had been for a while or should ever be. Trump, after all, ran on a platform of xenophobic populism that proved attractive to a lot of people: he continued to use the slogan "America First" long after groups like the Anti-Defamation League pointed out its controversial (and conspiratorial) history. The original America First Committee opposed the United States' entering World War II for reasons both isolationist and anti-Semitic. In 1941, Charles Lindbergh, a spokesperson for the group, blamed American Jewish leaders for rushing the country into conflict: "I am not attacking either the Jewish or the British people," he said. "Both races, I admire. But I am saying that the leaders of both the British and the Jewish races, for reasons which are as understandable from their viewpoint as they are inadvisable from ours, for reasons which are not American, wish to involve us in the war."

Moreover, much of the TWP's specific rhetoric on immigration—its fretting about "mass migration" from non-white countries—is about two steps away from actual policy of the Republican Party and the White House. Trump launched his presidential campaign with an infamous speech about Mexican "rapists" and "criminals" crossing the border. Former Breitbart chairman and White House advisor Steve Bannon made the ills of legal immigration and accepting refugees a cornerstone of his politics, and racist rhetoric existed on Breitbart for years, tagging some stories as "Black Crime." The alt-right figure Jason Reza Jorjani

186 REPUBLIC OF LIES

claimed to have had "connections" with the Trump White House, although these ended when Michael Flynn and Steve Bannon were ousted, he said.

No small number of marginal anti-immigrant groups have also made their way into the mainstream. The far-right Federation for American Immigration Reform was, in the early 1980s, a fringe organization, fear-mongering about immigrants sneaking across the border, filling the country with garbage, and stealing jobs. Today, FAIR and such related groups as the Center for Immigration Studies have wide support in the Republican Party. All of them advocate for a drastic reduction in legal immigration, and, not that far under the surface, there is the implication that nonwhite immigrants mean to do us harm. The Trump administra-tion listened, dedicating itself to mass deportations, tightened immigra-tion rules, and a brutal new chapter of increased power for Immigration and Customs Enforcement; Trump himself also frequently used crimes committed by undocumented immigrants, particularly murders, as talk-ing points in his stump speeches and on Twitter.

FAIR's specific allies inside the White House presumably included advisors Kellyanne Conway, who publicly defended policies such as separating migrant children from their parents, and immigration hard-liner Stephen Miller; Conway also did polling for years on behalf of the anti-Muslim Center for Security Policy, a group led by Frank Gaffney, who claimed that Obama was a secret Muslim and that the govern-ment was overrun by secret members of the Muslim Brotherhood. Gaff-ney, whose center distributed pamphlets urging people to oppose mosques opening in their communities, was praised by Bannon as "one of the senior thought leaders and men of action in this whole war against Islamic radical jihad." He was even reportedly brought on at one point to advise the Trump campaign.

Another former White House defense advisor, Sebastian Gorka, also had a reported history of associating with far-right and anti-Semitic groups in Hungary, where he spent much of his adult life. He denied being anti-Semitic, but Gorka and his wife, Katharine, built their careers as self-identified experts in radical Islamic terrorism and what he calls "global jihadism." In NPR interviews Gorka declined to say whether the Trump administration considers Islam a religion, and counterterrorism experts told the *Washington Post* that his ideas about Islam and terror are "dangerously oversimplified." The Council on American-Islamic Relations has a simpler descriptor for the Gorkas: "Islamophobes." After Gorka left the White House, he landed as a bloviator on Fox News.

Beyond the Trump White House, 2017 and 2018 also saw an uptick in the number of white supremacists running for office. Paul Nehlen, an unapologetic anti-Semite with a maliciously, gleefully provocative Internet presence—he was eventually banned from Twitter—ran to replace House Speaker Paul Ryan in Wisconsin. James Allsup, a twenty-two-year-old affiliated with the hate group Identity Evropa, won a Republican precinct committee officer position in Washington State. A man named Steve Smith, associated with the Pennsylvania skinhead group Keystone United, had won a similar position there in 2012 and was reelected in 2016. Corey Stewart, a candidate whose main issue involved preserving the Confederate flag, won the Republican primary in a Virginia district, even after being pictured in a grinning buddy clinch with Jason Kessler, an infamous "pro-white" blogger who went on to organize the Unite the Right rally in Charlottesville. And Art Jones, the Pikeville speaker, became a semi-successful candidate by winning his Republican primary race in Illinois after no one else bothered to run, given that the district was heavily Democratic. "I snookered them," he exulted to Politico. "I played by the rules, what can I say?"

MATTHEW HEIMBACH WAS CHEERED, CERTAINLY, BY THE RISE OF TRUMP-ism, by the more open discussion of white supremacist ideas in the public square, by various kinds of fellow travelers making their way into electoral races. But his vision for America was one that would preferably see it fracturing into little pieces. A realist of sorts, he liked the idea of forming separate nation states within the United States, even, he assured me, leaving space for the deluded souls who still believe in diversity.

"My hope is that we can agree that this was cute and a nice experiment but it didn't work," he said, referring to the republic of fifty states united as one. "If there are areas that want to be multicultural, they can do that. We just kind of want to opt out. If there are other people who want to be more progressive and multicultural, you should be able to do that. And if Idaho, Kentucky, and Tennessee want to opt out and be a white ethno-state, they should be allowed to do that. If the black belt in Alabama and Mississippi and Georgia wants to be self-determined like the Black Panthers, I don't see why they shouldn't, or Chicanos in the American Southwest." In the end, he said, "I don't want to force anyone to live in a way they don't want to. I don't want anyone to force me to live in a way I don't want to."

Heimbach also outlined what sounded like a reasonable set of immediate policy proposals, designed, it seemed to me, to appeal to a liberal reporter's sympathies. The events in eastern Kentucky were planned there "because it's a place where the war on poverty was launched. Democrats and Republicans alike have abandoned it. In the last ten years dental care for children has actually gotten *worse* after a slight improvement," he said. "Some of these problems that have been worked on for decades are compounding each other: income inequality, long-term wage stagnation, the opioid epidemic. There's a lot of problems."

Heimbach also pointed to a host of environmental issues that have devastated Appalachia, like mountaintop removal mining. Especially when he spoke to reporters, he often talked about the dangers of climate change. "Donald Trump has abandoned the people when it comes to clean air and water," he told me. "We're coming to an area that doesn't have any advocates and hasn't historically. We want to be able to step in as a third-party alternative." The sole goal of Heimbach's proposed Nationalist Front, he concluded, was to act as a voice for the forgotten white American. "Our mission for the Nationalist Front is to have groups come together to advocate for our people."

"Your politics must be . . . confusing for a lot of people," I said, searching for the precise term.

"Whiteness is part of our policy," he replied. "Advocating for white people. But I also really want to be able to have jobs and justice and smash capitalism and Wall Street. People usually don't see those things intersect. Our big mission in bringing those pro-white groups together is being an anti-capitalist, anti-imperialist force."

Heimbach was good at staying on-message and being blandly pleasant a lot of the time—and he was very good at not talking about the

World Jewry part when speaking to journalists, focusing instead on the kinds of story lines that proved so irresistible through the 2016 election cycle: angry white voters and how they got that way. But on the Daily Stormer, Heimbach took a different tone. "We are winning this war," he wrote in a guest post.

> Around America and the entire European world, we see that nationalism is on the rise, and young men are taking to the streets to fight for their people. No longer will the Jewish minions and their lying media hacks be allowed to dominate the public sphere; our time is now. There is no option to sit on the sidelines any longer, we must push forward in order to secure the future we so desperately desire for our families.

The final sentence is a clear echo of the white supremacist slogan coined by a man named David Lane, the so-called fourteen words: "We must secure the existence of our people and a future for white children." (Lane had spearheaded the Order and died in prison, sentenced to one hundred ninety years for his involvement in the murder of Alan Berg.)

Heimbach added to his post, referring to the gathering in Kentucky:

> With all of the fun and festivities it is also important to remember what we are up against. Dr. Joseph Goebbels once wrote *"If someone is attacked by the Jews, that is a sure sign of his virtue. He who is not persecuted by the Jews, or who is praised by them, is useless and dangerous."* In the American context, the Jews like to hide behind their various minions whenever possible: the degenerate left and their "cuckservative" controlled opposition.
>
> The System is agitating all of its forces against us, and when the forces of Organized Jewry are set on the warpath, it means that you are onto something.

Heimbach has occasionally lost his hold on his reasonable affability at public events, too. At a 2016 Trump rally, he reportedly shoved a black woman protester and was charged with misdemeanor harassment. The woman, Kashiya Nwanguma, sued him in civil court. In a characteristically interesting twist, Heimbach argued in court filings that Trump himself encouraged him to shove protesters when the candidate shouted, from the stage, "Get 'em out of here." In his response to the lawsuit, Heimbach wrote that he "acted pursuant to the directives and requests of Donald J Trump" and that "any liability must be shifted to one or both of them."

"In many ways, and some people disagree with me on this, Heimbach is David Duke 2.0," Ryan Lenz said, referring to the infamous white supremacist and former member of the Louisiana House of Representatives, who was, for a while, making inroads into American public life to a surprising and unsettling degree. Lenz, a senior investigative reporter at the Southern Poverty Law Center, had been talking to Heimbach for years in a sort of curious not-friendship where, as Lenz put it dryly, "he always picks up the phone when I call, for some reason."

Heimbach "knows how to package the ideas in a way that he feels will lead to real political power in this current era," Lenz said. "He's smarter than Schoep and much more of a politician." He knows "what faces to put on to make the audience that he's talking to happy with what he says. I sometimes call him the consummate glad-hander of the radical right."

Heimbach also took advantage of the broader cultural conversations that have occurred about why people voted a racist into office and the public resurgence of white supremacists. The temptation of journalists and pundits has been to blame white supremacist conspiracy thinking on a loss of economic status: people have lost so much and they need someone to blame. Certainly that explanation—that Trump tapped into economic anxiety and frustration—was offered to explain his popularity among conservative voters.

But Chip Berlet, a left-leaning researcher who focuses on right-wing extremism and conspiracy thinking, found that to be an overly simplistic, ahistorical framework to explain how hatred takes root. "How come the KKK grew in the boom cycle in the twenties?" he asked in a phone interview. "As many as five million or more joined. If you go back and you read the newspapers being put out by the Klan, that newspaper was obsessed with the Jews taking over America and destroying the country. It wasn't economic. Most people were doing *well*. It was the fear of falling, as Barbara Ehrenreich puts it. The middle class is always afraid of falling down the economic, social or cultural ladder." Or, perhaps, the fear of losing one's place on a narrow ledge to someone seen as inferior.

THE DINNER IN KENTUCKY ENDED QUIETLY, WITH THE WHITE SUPREM-acists trooping back to their cars at around 10 p.m. (or, in a few cases, weaving unsteadily, reeking of beer). A campfire was dying down; the owner of the property, a paunchy local guy who looked to be in his midfifties, stood mournfully by the fire, playing a trumpet, staring into the embers.

The following morning, the antifa forces beat the white suprema-cists, by several hours, to downtown Pikeville; they were mostly young, with many more women, and seemed woefully unprepared to deal with angry racists with guns. Nonetheless, they traded jeers with the League of the South, a neo-Confederate secessionist group. The League hadn't been at the previous night's party, but they were out that day, standing alone in a large barricaded-in area in front of Pikeville's courthouse, in the area designated for protesters.

The counterprotesters stood behind barricades on the other side of the street. State and local police were placed in between, looking grim.

"Why don't you have any women with you?" one counterprotester yelled.

"Our women are mothers!" a League of the South guy yelled back, indignant. "They have no business with us here today!" That prompted a chorus of laughter, boos, and something I didn't catch from a woman on the antifa side.

"We can't understand you because we don't speak nigger!" a League member shot back, although the woman he was screaming at was white. I heard a chorus of gasps. A moment later, a backup group of antifa arrived, seventy or so, carrying a banner that read ANTIFASCISTS WORLD-WIDE UNITED. A couple were banging drums or hooting into vuvuzelas.

"Every nation, every race! Punch a Nazi in the face!" they chanted. "From the Midwest to the South, punch a Nazi in the mouth!"

Michael Hill was watching all of this in disgust. He founded the League of the South back in 1994, after, ironically, working for decades as a history professor at Stillman College, a historically black university in Tuscaloosa, Alabama. (Hill resigned in 1998; in subsequent years, according to the SPLC, he's done things like send the names of some of his former students to a racist email list as a bit of comic relief.)

Hill, too, was worried about the Jews. "We're always concerned about people with dual citizenship," he said amiably. "And most American Jews have dual citizenship. A lot of problems, from the Southern perspective, come from the Jews. The Jew has been no friend to the South. They're behind every left-wing organization that wants to take down our monuments, you know. Where we can oppose them, we will."

He stopped to curl his lip at the counterprotesters. "Look at that crowd," he muttered, more to himself than to me. "Cheering on their own destruction."

It was hours before Heimbach and the rest of the white brigade arrived (according to the *Guardian*, one leader blamed their lateness on car trouble). They took up their place in the designated area to lots of booing from the other side of the barricades.

Then, despite all their posturing, for the next several hours everyone just stayed put: the police, the protesters on their respective sides, and a gaggle of local folks, looking on in dismay.

"These people aren't from here," a man in a Johnny Cash T-shirt complained. (He declined to tell me his name: "I work for the government. I'm not giving you my name.") "Neither side. They've singled us out for some unknown reason. This is pathetic. This entire fiasco. Please don't portray the locals like we're part of this. None of us were involved."

He looked back and forth between the two sides, getting heated. "Do they even realize there are *black* coal miners?" he asked, shaking his head. He pointed out that Pikeville—a university town—also has a hospital with an excellent medical school. "We have a large Islamic population here now. I owe my life to a doctor from Palestine.

"I'm not naive," he said, before walking away. He knew that Pikeville has its racists. "But we're not all dumb hillbillies."

They might have all stayed put, but they didn't keep quiet. "You're on the side of the Jews who own the banks!" a League of the South protester yelled energetically across the street. The NSM guys chimed in, leading a rousing chant of "Race traitor cucks! Race traitor cucks!"

"Shut the fuck up!" the antifa side of the street chanted back cheerfully.

I walked around the back of the white supremacist pen to chat with the current leader of Vanguard America, who was standing guard, holding a very large German military assault rifle. "Commander Dillon," as he called himself, was a young a former marine (his real name is Dillon Hopper, I later learned, changed from Dillon Irizarry). After a few minutes of pained conversation I managed to elicit that he was from New Mexico.

"Me too!" I said delightedly. I told him that as a child, my family split time between Santa Fe, where I mostly grew up, and a ranch that my dad and uncle ran in southern New Mexico, in a town so small Dillon had never heard of it.

"That's weird," he muttered.

We got to talking about the Jews. Like Michael Hill, he was pretty sure we all have dual citizenship, and he'd like us to go "back to Israel" under his preferred form of nation-state.

"What about me?" I asked. "I'm not from Israel. I'm from where you are."

Dillon looked at me thoughtfully. "Well, it's complicated," he said at last.

After hours in the broiling sun listening to antifa yelling and Nazi droning, it was over: a column of state police in riot gear appeared out of nowhere and led the white supremacists out of their pen, back to their cars. The antifa and other counterprotesters followed, still staying safely across the street. An NSM member posed next to his ratty Toyota Corolla for a photographer. A guy in a muscle tank top reading DONALD PUMP and with a 'roided-out image of the president stood in the back of a pickup truck, yelling insults. Some of the youngest neo-Nazis piled into a sagging Honda together and sarcastically waved at me as they pulled away. I smirked at them and waved back, although I wasn't sure what I meant by doing so.

What is it that I spent the day looking at? From one angle, it all seemed like a shabby, threadbare showing by a bunch of hateful shitheads with no real money or power behind them: sweaty white guys in ridiculous uniforms perspiring under a merciless sun, while the locals they came to save wished they'd all just go away.

But I knew that there are more people like them who didn't make an appearance. And what worried me, particularly, was the youth of the ones who did show up. I was thinking about the readers of the Daily Stormer, which promoted the rally. Andrew Anglin, the site's founder, was in his early thirties, Ohio-born, shave-headed, and in photographs, slightly bug-eyed; in 2012 he launched a website called Total Fascism. That one wasn't very popular, but his audience grew: the Daily Stormer is believed to reach about 220,000 readers in the United States every month, according to Quantcast data.

That's less than a needle in the haystack of Internet traffic; more of a pinprick on the face of the sun. Nonetheless, it can have a real impact. In the spring of 2017, Anglin was sued by the SPLC for inciting what it called a "troll storm" against a Jewish real estate agent in Montana named Tanya Gersh. Richard Spencer's mother, Sherry Spencer, accused Gersh of trying to pressure her into selling her property in Montana. And in support, Anglin rallied his readers to send vile threats and harassment to Gersh, her family, and her twelve-year-old son, much of it Holocaust-themed. After the SPLC lawsuit, Anglin's readers raised about $150,000 dollars for his legal defense fund. Anglin didn't attend the Kentucky rally in person, though—he seemed to be hiding at the time (rumored to be in Germany or the Philippines or a remote part of Russia, though I personally believe he was in a relative's basement in Ohio somewhere). But his readers were there, people willing to get off the computer and spill into the street.

Even then, it was hard to envision most of these men ever getting or maintaining real political power, given that some of the leaders were too scared to show up, and given how damp-browed and maladjusted and just plain at a loss they are in dealing with the larger world. They even seemed unnerved by little old me: I stayed at a Holiday Inn in Pikeville alongside a bunch of League of the South guys and a few scattered white supremacist types from the East Coast. To my great delight, they meekly fled the breakfast bar every time I entered the room, a sort of one-woman reverse invasion of Poland.

Still, the rally had some of its intended effect: a show of force, however small, and the media attention that went along with it. Heimbach beamed the whole day, basking in the glow of a dozen television interviews, being chased by a perspiring blond documentarian who had been filming him throughout the weekend in Kentucky. "I'm very happy," he told a camera.

Sonny Thomas, the mulleted racist from Ohio, came by to chat as the rally wound down. He was wearing a bright-red WHITE PRIDE T-shirt, and he seemed happy, too. "Went pretty good," he said, and wandered off.

A minute later, he returned. "I know you're a Jew and all," he said, not quite looking at me. "But you're a *beautiful* woman." He grabbed my hand and kissed it, then walked away without looking back.

THE RELATIVE PEACE AT PIKEVILLE TURNED OUT TO BE MISLEADING. A few months later, in the fall of 2017, at a rally in Charlottesville, Virginia, given the name Unite the Right, the peace imploded. Most of the same groups showed up again: Heimbach and the TWP, Vanguard America, some KKK affiliates. Marching with Vanguard, wearing their polo-and-khakis uniform, was James Alex Fields, Jr., a twenty-year-old from Ohio. A few hours later, in front of a horrified crowd and dozens of cameras, he drove his Dodge Charger directly into marching counterprotesters as they turned up a narrow side street, killing thirty-two-year-old Heather Heyer and wounding dozens of others.

Beyond Heyer's horrific death, the event was marred by countless other acts of white supremacist violence: a black man named DeAndre Harris was beaten nearly to death in a parking garage by a group of white men. (He was arrested on a felony charge of "unlawful wounding" while most of the people who attacked him initially remained free. The man who filed charges against Harris, Harold Ray Crews, described himself as a "Southern Nationalist.") A man in a bulletproof vest fired a gun at the ground near a group of counterprotesters while shouting racial slurs (after initially pointing the gun directly at one of them, a guy holding a flamethrower). Unlike the police in Pikeville, who kept the two sides apart, the Charlottesville police were quite absent, standing aside until they decided to disperse both sides.

Commander Dillon of Vanguard said he hadn't been in Charlottesville and denied that Fields was a member of his organization. He
claimed Fields had been photographed with them due to "poor leadership and uncoordination" at the event. "This was a major disaster, with
a life taken, this is reprehensible behavior that I personally would never
tolerate in my ranks," he wrote to me. Fields had been photographed in
their uniform, holding one of their shields because, Dillon said, "Our
dress code is public knowledge. A simple white polo shirt and brown
slacks is all one would need to blend in. At past events other groups,
including ours have worn the same attire to appear larger in number
and not isolate ourselves via clothing. I do not know what this man's
intentions were but I can only assume they were nothing more than vile
and disturbing."

In a *Vice* documentary about Charlottesville, Chris Cantwell, another
racist media personality who'd also been in Kentucky, unpacked a small
arsenal onto his hotel bed.

"We're not nonviolent," he assured reporter Elle Reeve. "We'll fucking kill these people if we have to."

I realized that my preoccupation with the size of the racist right, the
number of supporters, was not exactly relevant. The movement didn't
have to be big. It didn't have to have mainstream support or the ear
of the White House. All it took was one person with immovable beliefs
and a willingness to do what his fellow travelers publicly insisted was
unacceptable or unthinkable.

Even then, a new and particularly vile conspiracy theory was taking
form: alt-right trolls and neo-Nazis, including Anglin himself, claimed
that Heather Heyer died from a heart attack, not because she was run
down by a car. They implied that she was out of shape and bleeding-
heart liberals were trying to pin her death on the Charlottesville march-
ers to vilify them. A medical examiner's report released two months
later showed clearly that she died from blunt force trauma to the chest.

Not surprisingly, the man who filmed Fields driving his car into the
crowd became implicated in another bizarre conspiracy web. Brennan
Gilmore, a Virginia native, took part in the counterprotest; he is also a
former State Department employee, which struck some people as *very
suspicious*. Gilmore released the footage of the collision because, from

his vantage point, he believed it was indisputably intentional, that Fields had rammed the crowd on purpose, careening down an empty street to do so. Gilmore gave several media interviews making that point, and then the predictable happened: Nazis and the online detectives and the online Nazi detectives started trying to figure out who he truly worked for.

"They wrote that I was a CIA operative, funded by (choose your own adventure) George Soros, Hillary Clinton, Barack Obama, the IMF/World Bank, and/or a global Jewish mafia to orchestrate the Charlottesville attack in order to turn the general public against the alt-right," he wrote in Politico. "I had staged the attack and then worked with MSNBC and other outlets controlled by the left to spread propaganda. They claimed my ultimate goal was to start a race war that would undermine and then overthrow Donald Trump on behalf of the 'Deep State.'"

In the aftermath of Charlottesville, eleven people sued the Unite the Right organizers, including Heimbach, Spencer, and Jason Kessler. The League of the South was also named as a defendant, as were two KKK groups—the Loyal White Knights of the Ku Klux Klan and the East Coast Knights of the Ku Klux Klan—and Vanguard America, putting all of the newly formed Nationalist Front in danger of being sued out of existence. When Kessler tried to hold a follow-up Unite the Right rally a year later, only about two dozen participants showed up, drowned out by thousands and thousands of people who flooded into Washington, DC, to oppose them.

A few months before the flopped Unite the Right 2, the Traditionalist Worker Party fell apart when Matt Parrott, who was also Heimbach's father-in-law, found out that Heimbach was having an affair with his wife. In the melee that ensued, police said, Heimbach physically assaulted his own wife and Parrott. The Heimbachs divorced, and in September 2018, per the SPLC, Heimbach pleaded guilty to assaulting Parrott. Soon after entering his guilty plea, Heimbach began working as "community outreach director" for the National Socialist Movement.

As these white supremacist movements and their leaders flamed out, collapsing under the weight of sordid affairs and major lawsuits, other groups were gaining steam. A tiny paramilitary neo-Nazi cell called the

Atomwaffen Division, first founded in 2015, started to show up more
and more frequently in the news. It bore a disturbing similarity to the
Order, which had murdered Jewish radio host Alan Berg; its materials
called for acts of violence to destroy "the System," and they were engaged
in active weapons training. The group was linked to five murders across
the United States, including the knifing death of Blaze Bernstein, a gay
Jewish college student stabbed more than twenty times. Atomwaffen
were believed to be recruiting through literature they distributed on
college campuses.

9

THE POLITICS OF UFOS

Corey Goode was barely in grade school when he was classified as "an anomaly."

"Apparently, I was identified as being on the intuitive empath spectrum," he told a rapt audience one hot summer morning in 2017. "They thought that would be useful," he said, referring to the people who would become his secret government handlers. "And they can enhance it through genetic manipulation."

Goode claims that he was soon placed in alternative classes. His parents, he says, gave permission for that. But what they didn't know was that he'd been tapped to take part in a military program: Every morning he'd wait outside with his lunchbox to be picked up by a white van, which would drive him out to Carswell Air Force Base in Texas, a little ways northwest of Fort Worth. From there, they'd go through a back gate, across two runways, through another security gate and into a motor pool hangar, down a cargo elevator into a secret underground facility, where nine to fifteen other children would be waiting.

The training ran the gamut, Goode claims: "Sensory deprivation, VR stimulation, pharmaceutical enhancement, trauma bonding. They would subject you usually in VR to trauma along with your team and force you to bond with them or with an adult." Beyond that, the children were trained in use of traditional firearms, hand-to-hand combat "similar to judo," map reading, radio protocols, and, of course, "acclimation to non-terrestrials"—that is, aliens.

According to Goode, the non-terrestrial beings started showing up at trainings early on. "Most of us had weird memories or dreams," Goode says, prior dreams of pirate ships coming to pick the children up and taking them away to a strange place. "It turns out we were being introduced before the program to non-terrestrials." In the VR simulations, Goode says, they would see gray aliens, sitting quietly at a table.

"There were also hybrid children present at Carswell," he adds, meaning part-human, part-alien. At night, he would be taken to meet with "cells," as he puts it, of ninety to one hundred twenty other children, to continue their training in dark, closed indoor malls.

At the end of all this, in around 1986, Goode says he was drafted into the Secret Space Program, a purported hidden government entity doing clandestine research and fighting secret wars with extraterrestrials in outer space. He was not yet seventeen. Specifically, he claims to have been part of a Navy program called Solar Warden, which since merged with another program whose name he doesn't know. The duties of the recruits were both heady and mundane, he says: "Protecting the solar system, going to other solar systems to do surveillance and recon." The mission of the research vessel where he was stationed "was similar to the *Men in Black* program. Except they"—meaning the other enlisted Solar Warden officers—"were doing mainly interrogation of these beings—finding out who they were and why they were here."

The work was urgent, given that non-terrestrials are all around us, and some of them are quite unfriendly. "They're working in high-rise buildings, blending in with us." The military was routinely arresting them, Goode says. His own missions involved lots of contact with alien races, some of them hostile. "They didn't care about human life at all."

There's plenty more to Goode's story, but a little of this goes a long way. Corey Goode's self-stated biography is an obvious mash-up of pop culture alien lore that many of us have been primed to recognize. In some ways, it is a classic hero's journey, set on a galactic scale: a child

THE POLITICS OF UFOS

is plucked from home as special; as a man he sets out to save the galaxy. Goode has told his account at many places, but I heard it at the annual meeting of the Mutual UFO Network, known as MUFON. It is the oldest UFO research group in the United States, active since 1969, and it presents itself as a scientific organization, seeking hard evidence of the UFO phenomenon and pursuing that evidence wherever it might lead.

Most of the year, state MUFON chapters investigate tips of UFO sightings, hundreds of which pour into their email and voicemail each month. But on a blazing summer day in Summerlin, a wealthy suburb in northwest Las Vegas, the MUFON members were all together, and things were tense.

Outside, there was the kind of dry desert heat and intense klieg-light sun that gave our surroundings a sense of the surreal. Speakers took the stage one after another in the dim, ice-cold ballroom of a casino resort hung with bulbous chandeliers and lined with the same carpet I'd seen at every conspiracy conference I had been to that year. (Sometimes I felt as though I'd been sitting in the same ballroom for months, with different people cycling through it yelling dubious facts at me.) When I walked outside for a lunch break, I marched through the heat, past a gasping fountain and into the casino, through a light haze of cigarette smoke and down a pulsating, blinking, whirring row of slot machines.

MUFON often feels like a family reunion. But people were unusually on edge, because earlier another well-respected speaker, Richard Dolan, called Corey Goode a liar and quite possibly a plant. "I'm not accusing anybody of anything," Dolan said delicately at the start of his talk, in the manner of someone about to accuse someone of something. "But it's absolutely a fact of US history that there's been government interference in many organizations. Many of you have heard of COINTELPRO. And that goes on to this day."

UFO culture is an unsettling yet embedded part of us, the type of conspiracy road that has become so well trodden we pound it under our feet without noticing that we walk on it every day. Although broad discussion of UFOs has been eclipsed in the general culture by fresher, shinier conspiratorial ideas—birtherism, false flags, pedophile rings—a

remarkably high number of Americans believe in the existence of extraterrestrial life. The poll numbers can vary wildly and frustratingly. In
1997, a CNN/*Time* poll showed that a whopping 80 percent of the adult
population believed the government was hiding "knowledge of the existence of extraterrestrial life forms." In 2015, a YouGov survey found
that 54 percent of the adult population believed that alien life exists,
while 30 percent were convinced, in their words, that "extra-terrestrial
intelligent life has already contacted us but the government has covered
it up." According to the Chapman University Survey of American Fears
that same year, 42.6 percent of respondents thought the government was
concealing what it knows about alien encounters. The Chapman survey noted that more Americans believe in UFOs than believe in natural
selection or that the earth is 4.5 billion years old.

The belief is strong, but, as with so many research communities, it's
not uniform or unaffected by controversy. In the last few years the UFO
world has been afflicted by the kinds of conspiratorial cracks that have
appeared throughout American culture: Who can be trusted? What is
true? What constitutes an acceptable standard of proof? Who is a spy,
a plant, an agent? Is the government engaged in covert actions to disrupt communities it deems dangerous?

Dolan has been a respected UFO researcher for a long time, which
means the same thing here that it means in a lot of conspiracy subcultures: you might not know who he is, but he's indisputably a giant in
his field. At MUFON he had the look of a man who'd recently come
into good fortune but didn't quite have the time to enjoy it. He recently
became engaged to a beautiful woman named Tracy; he was wearing a
nice suit and had freshly cut salt-and-pepper curls. As I watched, though,
Dolan was visibly irritated, lobbing verbal bombs at an audience full
of his fellow UFO researchers.

He is far from the first of his kind to suggest that the government
has planted misleading information to throw the field into chaos.
And MUFON itself is frequently accused of pursuing and promoting
pseudo-science. The Center for Skeptical Inquiry wrote in 2013 that
local MUFON chapters were following "decidedly unscientific" ave-
nues of inquiry, scheduling "talks on alien abduction, conspiracy theories, human-ET hybrids, hypnotic regression, and repressed memories."

But MUFON does maintain a public commitment to science, at least, which is why some of the most dedicated members stayed away in 2017, why a few resigned in protest, and why a wave of newcomers came in their place. The year's conference wasn't particularly scientific—it was dedicated to the Secret Space Program, the supposedly hidden government agency Goode claims took over much of his early life. One last thing about that: Goode says that when his space military service came to an end, he returned to Earth, where his government handlers performed an "age regression." He awoke as a child again, in his bedroom at home, with his mother unaware that he'd ever been gone.

"There are a few very conservative people who want to just talk about the nuts and bolts of the crafts," MUFON's executive director Jan Harzan told me, referring to spacecraft. "But this is what people are interested in: the whistleblowers. They want to know what's really going on." The whistleblowers, as Harzan and others call them, are the men in the UFO world, Goode among them, who make colorful and eye-popping claims about the roles they played in the government's secret space programs. The week's other notable speaker was Andrew Basiago, who said that he went on a series of missions to Mars with a young Barack Obama, then known, he says, as Barry Soetoro. (That is also the name birthers sometimes claim Obama used as a "foreign student" in college.) The story of how he *got* to Mars is even better: the "chrononauts," as he called his group, were transported via a very high-tech elevator that's located in El Segundo, California, and operated by the CIA.

"Yes, Obama was involved," Basiago said in his talk, impatiently. "His service was no more distinguished than mine or any others." He asked, rhetorically, why he would choose to make up such an outlandish fact. (It did seem like a good question.)

In conspiracy subcultures, "whistleblowing" is a common phenomenon. For every government plot and dark scheme, someone will eventually show up claiming to have been part of it. That happened during the 1980s Satanic panic, it began to occur in Pizzagate, and in the mid-2000s the newest crop arrived in the UFO world, when Basiago started talking of his travels with the then-president (he seems to have first claimed that he journeyed to Mars with Obama in a talk in Hawaii in 2011). In 2014, Goode appeared on the scene. A year later, the two of them were joined by another man, Randy Kramer, who claims to be a former marine who served on Mars for seventeen years and on a secret spaceship for three more.

Among earlier generations of UFO whistleblowers, the most famous was Bob Lazar, who maintained that he worked as a scientist at a subsidiary facility of Area 51 called S-4. His task was to "reverse-engineer" alien spaceships to figure out how they worked. But the new whistleblowers are in a league of their own, having apparently been to reaches of space that humans have never touched before, having had repeated and direct interaction with aliens, and, if I understand Basiago's assertions correctly, having been chased around by dinosaurs on Mars. (I admit to leaving his lecture early due to a sudden inexplicable headache.)

Author and lecturer Michael Salla—he studies "exopolitics," which is, basically, the all-too-human politics around extraterrestrial life—has written about Goode, Kramer, and Basiago and promoted their accounts, Goode's in particular. Salla believes that many of the world's governments are engaged in a long-range, ongoing, and large-scale UFO cover-up, and the debate over extraterrestrials is a source of tension and intrigue thrumming beneath international politics. Salla has stuck with Goode no matter how far-out his claims have become: in 2017, according to Goode, US Special Forces began arresting members of a "Satanic pedophile group," all of whom were government officials in the United States and European Union. It was a clear echo of Pizzagate, and, more to the point, you'd think those arrests would be newsworthy. But Salla doesn't seem bothered by the fact that there's no evidence: no names, no mug shots, no press release from the Justice Department.

Goode has an unusual skill—the ability to make outlandish claims but to weave them together with common and popular UFO positions. Among the more fantastical threads that he manages to pull in: the engineers who work on secret space technologies are part of "secret societies and occult rituals"; and Goode maintains contact (through his organization the Sphere-Being Alliance) with benevolent aliens called Blue Avians, who have chosen him to "deliver important messages to humanity." But he also peddles the more traditional beliefs: the government isn't just hiding what it knows about aliens and UFOs, but also the advanced technologies that aliens have revealed to humans. Those include "healing and anti-aging technologies" and "zero-point energy" or free energy, which some UFO researchers believe has been secretly available since Nikola Tesla's time. And some basic conspiracist tropes are in the mix, too. There's "lots of human and child trafficking going on with these corporate types," Goode says. "I won't go into it because it's very disturbing."

Chase Kloetzke, MUFON's deputy director of investigations, calls Goode's more extravagant claims "extraordinary." She adds: "Our mind-set at MUFON has always been that extraordinary claims require extraordinary investigation and fact-finding." But she's willing to cut Goode quite a bit of slack. "The type of information he's bringing forward, it's difficult to do that," she explains. "Not so much because he's made it all up, but because of the secrecy and the technology that's tucked away." Her embrace of Goode, who has a popular television show on the New Age network Gaia, might have something to do with the fact that he commands some of the most intense applause I've ever heard.

MUFON CONFERENCE-GOERS WERE, AT LEAST THE YEAR I WAS THERE, mostly older and overwhelmingly white; every one of the speakers was also white, and all but one was male. (I spotted two middle-aged Japanese men in the audience as well as one black woman, who seemed to be there with her husband; she spent the weekend crocheting with ferocious concentration). Several men were in baseball caps that identified them as Vietnam vets, and I overheard some poignant conversations: "It was *hovering*," one old gentleman said to another. Nearby, a woman to her companion: "I grew up knowing we're not supposed to talk about these things . . ." Throughout the conference, I was treated to the charming and unexpected sight of old ladies with haloes of snowy hair carefully taking notes while they listened to presentations about Nazis flying experimental spacecraft over DC.

But the whiteness and maleness and elderliness of the room was misleading, because alien belief is a profoundly ingrained part of American life across the country, one that cuts across lines of race, class, and age: we all seem to enjoy thinking about aliens. Our enthusiasm is to some extent most likely rooted in the fact that pivotal events in the received history of purported human-UFO contact happened here. Alongside the doubts about JFK's assassination, the oldest, most stable conspiratorial idea in the United States is that the government has concealed what it knows. It's not just Americans, of course: the intensity, depth, and breadth of the conversation about aliens throughout the world says something profound about human hopes, about our desire to not be alone in the universe, and our wish for some wise and mysterious force out there in the farthest reaches of space that is ready to show us the way. UFO enthusiasm coexists with a certain degree of New Age spirituality: there's a sense that extraterrestrials don't just exist, but that they will someday reveal to us both those miraculous technologies and a better way to live, a higher state of being.

The most successful UFO speakers know how to align their message with those sentiments, blending just enough uplift into an otherwise unsettling narrative. Goode talks up the benign aliens along with the hostile kind. The good ones, he said, strive rather selflessly to teach us all to live better lives. "Since the 1950s, non-terrestrials have had a consistent message," he told the quiet, reverent MUFON crowd. "They tell us we need to raise our consciousness, become more spiritual, and demand the release of suppressed technologies."

The alien world wasn't always that exalted. Alien mythology was born, as many people know, in Roswell, New Mexico, in 1947, when *something* . . . crashed. That summer had already been a strange one: Across the Southwest, people had reported sightings of strange flying disks. Then one morning a ranch foreman named William "Mac" Brazel, working close to Roswell, found something bizarre while walking the property. It was what Kathryn Olmsted in *Real Enemies* describes as "a pile of sticks, tinfoil thick paper, and smoky-gray rubber, all stuck together with scotch tape."

Brazel called Roswell's sheriff, George Wilcox, who sent out two deputies and then phoned the Roswell Army Air Force Base, wondering if it was something of theirs. Then something very strange happened, in a way that has echoed for decades. The base's public information officer announced that a "flying disc" had been recovered. By the next day, the story had changed: the region's commanding general reported that what had actually been recovered was a "high altitude weather balloon."

Public interest in the story quickly faded. But a full three decades later, in 1978, alien researchers started to suspect there had been a cover-up at Roswell and began interviewing dozens of people who claimed to have seen the object crash or had some involvement in the ensuing Air Force statement. In 1980, the first conspiracy book on the crash, *The Roswell Incident*, posited that what had actually been recovered on that ranch was an alien spaceship that had been monitoring the US military's atomic research. The authors, who'd previously written a tome on the Bermuda Triangle, claimed that the alien craft had been downed after it was struck by lightning, and that the government concealed the accident so it could study alien technology. (To make things stranger, one of them said at a 1989 MUFON conference that he was a paid agent for the government, assigned to spread ridiculous alien stories on purpose, to create uncertainty and spread disinformation, keeping people away from the truth.)

Around 1991, Glenn Dennis, a new self-proclaimed eyewitness, came forward, saying that he had worked at a Roswell funeral home at the time, and that the military had requested "child-sized caskets" for tiny alien bodies. He also added that he had met a nurse who was present at an autopsy of the downed dead aliens. It's unclear why the military would go through the formality of burying the aliens in teeny tiny caskets, but Dennis's version of the story took off, transforming into the Roswell story as we all commonly know it, the one where the military has little gray bodies stacked knee-high in a freezer. In later years, popular imagination moved the location of the little gray bodies, iced over like mysterious pearlescent fish sticks, to Area 51.

In 1994, a genuine conspiracy came to light: an Air Force report commissioned by the federal General Accounting Office revealed that the downed balloon was probably debris from a top-secret surveillance program known as Project MOGUL, which sought to record audio evidence of Soviet atomic tests. And in 1997, a second report found a possible explanation for the witnesses who reported seeing alien bodies pulled from the wreckage: the crash-test dummies routinely dropped during other military test operations involving high-altitude balloons.

Most mainstream news sources presented the reports as evidence that there were definitively no UFOs and nothing strange about the matter whatsoever. "No bodies. No bulbous heads," wrote William J. Broad of the *New York Times* News Service in 1997. "No secret autopsies. No spaceship. No crash. No extraterrestrials or alien artifacts of any sort. And most emphatically of all, no Government cover-up."

But the 1994 report did provide proof that the Air Force had lied about a top-secret program, blaming a weather balloon and a rancher's distorting eyes, which fed certainty among UFO researchers that there were other cover-ups yet to be discovered. Similarly, the CIA fueled distrust by only officially acknowledging the existence of Area 51 as late as 2013, after taking eight years to respond to a FOIA request on the development there of the U-2 spy plane.

For UFO researchers, such belated admissions confirmed their belief in the legitimacy of supposedly top-secret documents that had surfaced in 1987, which revealed the existence of a program called Operation Majestic-12 (MJ-12). According to the documents, MJ-12 was formed by President Harry Truman in 1947 to recover an alien spacecraft, examine it, and conceal the whole thing from an unsuspecting public. When the FBI received copies of the MJ-12 report, the agency quickly deemed it bogus. But some UFO enthusiasts still insist MJ-12 is real, covered up just as Project MOGUL was before it.

Thus the history of UFOs is a perfect illustration of the way in which genuine government secrecy feeds citizen paranoia. The disclosure of hidden Air Force programs made just about anything seem possible, and over the next few decades, it was joined by wave after wave of revelations, some of them real and some imagined, until the field of ufology became a morass of competing claims and high suspicion that everyone is a government agent and no one is to be trusted.

The number of UFO-related conspiracy theories is dizzying and too numerous for us to explore each one. Aliens have been linked to everything from the JFK assassination to cattle mutilations (extraterrestrials perform bizarre, bloodless surgeries on livestock, generally taking, for some arcane purpose, their eyes, tongues, and anal cavities). The point is that none of these assertions can ever be settled: there is no evidence the government can produce that will satisfy UFO buffs, and UFO researchers have no evidence to prove any of their claims definitively to a skeptical public. The CIA and the FBI have both supplied documents that outline their full involvement in the alien question, they argue. In 2013, the British government declassified files on its own UFO unit, which was shuttered in 2009 (a report recommended that move because the unit "is consuming increasing resources but produces no valuable defence output").

The CIA concludes its website's capsule history of the subject on a bit of a resigned note: "Like the JFK assassination conspiracy theories, the UFO issue probably will not go away soon, no matter what the Agency does or says. The belief that we are not alone in the universe is too emotionally appealing and the distrust of our government is too pervasive to make the issue amenable to traditional scientific studies of rational explanation and evidence."

RICHARD DOLAN, THE UFO RESEARCHER, IS CONCERNED WITH WHAT he calls falsifiability. Accepting the claims of someone like Goode feels more like religious faith to him, and it makes him nervous. Dolan, who's also a self-styled historian, laid out his own theories in dozens of articles: that the national security state is concerned about "real objects with extraordinary capabilities," as he put it in a 2002 piece, and that there's also evidence that the UFOs, as described by witnesses, do things that human technology isn't capable of doing. He and other more traditional ufologists try to back up their claims with declassified government memos, eyewitness photos of purported UFOs, interviews with ex-military personnel: much of it more closely echoes traditional scholarship, although the results are eclectic.

"I do think some of these self-described whistleblowers aren't particularly credible," Dolan said, rather grimly, standing in a hallway of the hotel in Summerlin and making no particular effort to keep his voice down. "Believing such stories without genuine evidence takes us down a dangerous road within an already treacherous field," Dolan wrote in a Facebook post in 2017, one "that is constantly in the crosshairs of a skeptical establishment." His fear of foul play—government infiltration meant to discredit and confuse the UFO disclosure movement—is grounded in the past. "In US history, we're replete with provocateurs and disinformation coming from US government channels."

Dolan isn't being paranoid entirely without reason. He points to Cass Sunstein, who worked in the White House under President Obama. In a 2008 paper, "Conspiracy Theories," Sunstein and coauthor Adrian Vermeule suggest that "false conspiracy theories" about the government should be countered with "cognitive infiltration": paid agents who plant correct information among antigovernment and conspiratorial groups. There's no evidence that the idea was ever executed, but the proposition was enough to make various "truth communities" very nervous.

Dolan's suspicions echo those of earlier UFO researchers. In his 1991 book *Revelations: Alien Contact and Human Deception*, famed UFO researcher and computer scientist Jacques Vallée wrote that he had come to believe many UFO events were hoaxes, engineered sometimes by delusional private citizens and sometimes by government agencies with bigger aims in mind. "This bears emphasizing," he wrote. "Some UFO sightings are covert experiments in the manipulation of the belief systems of the public. And some cases simply did not happen. The stories about them, numerous rumors of crashed saucers and burned aliens, were not so much the result of delusions as the product of deception: rumors deliberately planted in the eager minds of gullible believers to hide more real facts about which it was felt that the public and the scientific community had no 'need to know.'"

The idea that some UFO sightings are fabricated to draw people away from the real truth still holds some sway. Lorin Cutts is another UFO researcher I've come to know, someone who believes in the existence of alien beings even as he doubts and detests almost every facet of modern UFO theorizing. He takes a complex middle ground on the UFO issue, siding with neither Dolan nor Goode. "Extra-terrestrials almost certainly exist," he told me in an email exchange. "What they have to do with the phenomenon of UFOs is questionable and largely a cultural and mythological construct—I don't believe that we can know for certain right now."

I think any serious student of the UFO subject would do well to put these alleged whistleblowers, secret space program aficionados and the click-bait vultures that promote them to one side. Sure, people will always listen and be entertained by them, but let's call it what it is— ufotainment. I'm always amused when people hold up one whistle-blower as credible, simply because of apparently corroborating stories, whilst the next is deemed laughable. Almost none of them have provided any credible evidence as to what they are supposedly revealing. In that respect they are all even. The fact that two or more stories may apparently corroborate one another is not corroboration of anything. How easy would it be for individuals—or the intelligence community— to fabricate such a set up?

In a way, the suspicions felt by Cutts—an apparently levelheaded person—reveal the profound and continuing legacy of the US government's tactics of disinformation. COINTELPRO was, after all, a disinformation campaign created by the FBI to disrupt and discredit American activist groups. The fact that UFO researchers—and Pizzagaters, and every other conspiracy community—are so paranoid about plants and saboteurs in their ranks shows just how well that program worked to destabilize many different kinds of dialogue and research.

So what will bring all of this arguing and debating and finger-pointing to an end? UFO researchers call it "disclosure," the time when the world's governments will finally reveal everything they know about UFOs, extraterrestrials, and alien technology. It is a day that they yearn for and urgently seek: their talk about it echoes the language of end-times preachers who describe a coming climactic battle, a grand revelation, a final decisive moment when humanity will be divided into the drowned and the saved.

John Podesta, Hillary Clinton's campaign chairman, has been a vocal advocate for disclosure. When he served as Bill Clinton's chief of staff, he told CNN, he asked the president to disclose "some information about some of these things, and in particular, some information about what was going on at Area 51." Asked if he believes in aliens, he responded, "There are a lot of planets out there. The American people can handle the truth."

Podesta promised that if he became Hillary Clinton's chief of staff, he would renew his efforts to declassify government records on Area 51.

And even Clinton herself signaled a willingness to entertain disclosure, telling one radio interviewer, "I want to open the files as much as we can." When she was asked if she believed in UFOs, she responded, "I don't know. I want to see what the information shows." But, she added, "There's enough stories out there that I don't think everybody is just sitting in their kitchen making them up." Coming from a careful, centrist politician, Clinton's position signals just how far alien belief has gained acceptability.

Beyond the campy, Bigfootish novelty of aliens and UFOs, even the most amateur and outlandish researchers pose questions that are important and relevant—about government secrecy and wasteful military spending, and about the real challenges of compelling transparency when it comes to things like defense programs and military innovations.

SOMETIMES, OUT OF NOWHERE, WE HAVE HAD STUNNING AND SERIOUS proof that the government continued to investigate UFOs and has seen some things it can't quite explain. In December 2017, the *New York Times* published a story revealing that from 2007 to 2012 (at least), the Department of Defense carefully buried a secret, $22-million-a-year program in the budget called the Advanced Aerospace Threat Identification Program. It was devoted to investigating sightings of unidentified aircraft, created at the behest of Nevada Democrat Harry Reid, the former Senate majority leader. A Pentagon spokesperson insisted to the *Times* that the program ended entirely in 2012, while a former administrator, Luis Elizondo, claimed that it continued in partnership with officials from the navy and the CIA. (Elizondo went on to work for Tom DeLonge, a guitarist with the band Blink-182 who became a UFO activist.)

Together with its story, the *Times* ran a remarkable video, released by the Defense Department in response to a FOIA request: a 2004 encounter between two navy fighter jets and a whitish object, one that was moving very, very fast. "Look at that thing!" one pilot exclaimed. "It's *rotating*." Intriguingly, the *Times* report claimed that a Las Vegas warehouse was storing a collection of "metal alloys and other materials" that were said to be recovered from "unidentified aerial phenom- ena." As part of the program, the paper added, "Researchers also studied people who said they had experienced physical effects from encounters with the objects and examined them for any physiological changes."

The idea that the government was storing alien alloys in a Vegas warehouse was, well, mind-boggling. "Someone explain to me the alien alloys before I fucking explode," Tom Ley at the sports website Dead- spin wrote, speaking for a lot of people. Strangely, though, the *Times* story didn't make a big splash in the UFO world, likely because it revealed what UFO researchers would have said they already knew. Instead, there was a sort of quiet satisfaction, a sense that here, at last, disclosure was perhaps upon us. (For Dolan and a few other research- ers, there was also skepticism. He specifically charged that the paper has "a history of cooperation with the U.S.-military intelligence community," which is a reasonable point. He suspected that the government, feeling unable to ignore this particular UFO story any longer, cooperated with the *Times* as "an exercise in damage control.")

The *Times* story did uncover some potential lines of inquiry about questionable government spending. Most of the program's funding went to just one contractor: Bigelow Airspace, founded by Robert Bigelow, a friend of Reid's, which was supposedly keeping watch over the alien alloys. And it confirmed that the government was, until very recently, interested in investigating craft sightings, viewing it as an urgent national security priority.

"This is about science and national security," Reid tweeted in response to the *Times* story. "If America doesn't take the lead in answer- ing these questions, others will."

Goode's not holding his breath. "True disclosure can only come from the people," he told his MUFON audience. "If we sit back and wait for someone to walk to a podium and make an announcement, I think we're just going to keep waiting." A core part of Goode's message has always been that disclosure is nearly upon us. He and other UFO researchers have long claimed that shows like *Star Trek* are part of Hollywood trying to soften us up for the big reveal (Hollywood is, of course, in on the whole thing). "Recently Hollywood has decided we're ready, because they've made us ready," Goode told his audience six months before the *Times* story appeared. "But people finding out about crimes against humanity is really going to flip a lot of people out."

NEXT TO THE LECTURE HALL WHERE THE TALKS TOOK PLACE, THERE WAS a big room filled with tables and merchandise: DVDs, books, and a set of lumpy handmade alien pendants and figurines. In the next room, a UFO art show with creatively shaped interpretations of planets kept me occupied for far too long.

As I walked among the misshapen ceramic aliens and chatted with the vendors, I felt genuinely glad to be at MUFON after weeks spent in the more stressful company of Nazis and Pizzagaters and Sandy Hook truthers. It occurred to me that UFO lore might represent conspiracy culture at its best: our interest in the hidden, the unknown, the ineffable, the magic of what's hidden and yet to be revealed. "The UFO mystery holds a mirror to our own fantasies," Vallée once wrote. "It expresses our secret longings for a wisdom that might come down from the stars in new, improved, easy to-use packaging, to reveal the secrets of life and tell us, at long last, who we are."

Except that the world of UFO researchers is not quite so innocent or depoliticized since they too believe they're being watched, surveilled, and deceived by the government. We know that the government does do this to targeted groups, but I was bothered by the suspicions of the UFO enthusiasts as I slowly drifted into hypothermia in that air-conditioned ballroom. I kept thinking rather persistently about Black Lives Matter, a group that has been met with forceful government repression, and about the Native activists at Standing Rock, who were subject to real surveillance and infiltration: recall the firm Energy Transfer Partners, which retained the company TigerSwan to surveil activists with drones and actual spies, who in turn fed their information to local and federal law enforcement.

There is—at the risk of being unkind—something indulgent and self-absorbed about a group of people engaged in a voluntary recreational subculture declaring that they are government targets. COINTELPRO aimed at wrecking the lives, families, and psyches of activists. It takes a profound level of self-importance to claim without evidence that the feds are after you.

Along with self-absorption, MUFON's leadership has also demonstrated some abhorrent racial politics, right in step with the Trump era. In May 2017, John Ventre, the state MUFON director for Pennsylvania and Delaware, was furious about a Netflix show called *Dear White People*—about a group of black college students navigating the often racially obtuse world of Ivy League universities—writing on Facebook, "I don't find this funny. The last thing blacks want is for white males to organize and that's not too far away!" Ventre went on to fulminate that white males are an "absolute target of the government" with "illegal affirmative action," as well as a target of the media, since there are interracial couples on television and because white men are "portrayed as incompetent."

Ventre concluded by inferring that black people are genetically predisposed to violence ("Google serotonin by race") and also stupid: "Everything in this world was created by Europeans and Americans," he wrote, incorrectly. "F'ing blacks didn't even have a calendar, a wheel or a numbering system until the Brits showed up."

The reaction was widespread outrage by UFO researchers and demands for Ventre's ouster. But Jan Harzan, the organization's director, responded defensively, writing in a now-deleted post, "Who is worse, the person posting, or the haters hating? If you need further evidence of this just watch the nightly news where depending on which channel you watch people line up behind one side of an issue, or the other, and then begin yelling at each other." Harzan also added, "Finally, it is okay to disagree with others, but let's challenge ourselves to dialogue with that person to first understand their rationale for the opinion they are stating, and then begin a discussion with them on the subject. For only through dialogue and discussion do we advance as a civilization."

If that was a reference to Ventre's posts, it sounded like a challenge to consider his opinion that the "f'ing blacks" didn't have wheels until Europeans showed up to help them out. There's being insular, and then there's being toxically out of touch and willing to tolerate absurdly hateful commentary from your leadership.

Two MUFON investigators resigned in the wake of Ventre's comments; one of them, James Clarkson, called them a last straw in his increasing disaffection with the group and said Harzan's lack of response made remaining in the organization "morally unacceptable." Both Clarkson and the other investigator who left, Rich Hoffman, also expressed unease that MUFON had been infiltrated at a high level by what Clarkson called "mysterious people." They were specifically referring to a Washington State New Age teacher named J. Z. Knight, who has been called a "cult leader" and who claims to channel a supernatural entity named Ramtha, a "35,000-year-old warrior spirit." Knight is a member of MUFON's Inner Circle, an advisory board open to anyone who's donated more than $5,000 to the organization.

In the end, the stakes in any MUFON controversy are questionable. The UFO world is concerned with its own dramas, villains, and celebrities, and these do not often leak out beyond that world, barring genuinely newsworthy developments. UFO researchers pull data points from the wider society when it suits them, and entirely retreat otherwise, and seem largely incapable of doing harm: its adherents do not harass people, and the questions they raise about official secrecy are truly interesting. The call for the government to simply and directly tell everything it knows is of value to us all, and there is something both sad and a little heroic about the UFO-curious as they devotedly await the truth.

Take Gary McKinnon, who, in 2002, got tired of waiting. Someone was going to force the government to come clean, he decided, and that someone would evidently have to be him. A Scottish-born man with Asperger's syndrome, McKinnon did what seemed reasonable to him at the time: he hacked into army, navy, air force, and NASA computers to rummage through their files. He also left a note on a military website reading, "Your security is crap." On another, he referred to himself by the name Solo and refered to 9/11 conspiracy theories, writing, "US foreign policy is akin to Government-sponsored terrorism these days. . . . It was not a mistake that there was a huge security stand down on September 11 last year. . . . I am SOLO. I will continue to disrupt at the highest levels."

At the MUFON conference years later, McKinnon delivered a talk via Skype from his home in London in which he told the crowd dryly,

"It was an extreme act, I can see that now." He believed that the US authorities were covering up critical information not just about alien contact, but about "free energy" and other alien technologies that could make human life immeasurably better. He was vividly aware of what Britons call "fuel poverty," where thousands of people die each bitter winter because they can't afford heating fuel. Free energy, he thought, would directly alleviate suffering and save lives.

The government saw it differently, saying McKinnon had deleted critical files, caused $566,000 in damage, and shut down for three days a computer network that served the military in Washington. He was indicted for computer fraud in November 2002.

At first, the government tried carrot over stick, saying that if he voluntarily came to the United States to face charges, he would get "six months community service," he told the MUFON crowd. "That turned out to be an inaccurate estimate." McKinnon learned that he was more likely to face seventy years. "I lost my career in IT due to this," he said. "I got my forklift license and got a job in a local luggage warehouse. Lost that job due to publicity, lost the room I rented, lost my girlfriend of twelve years. I was feeling pretty crappy, to understate it hugely."

In 2005, McKinnon managed to get a job with the London branch of an American company called—of all things—Electronic Data Systems. He completed one day at work, then returned home to find what he calls "three gigantic men" who identified themselves as the Scotland Yard extradition squad. McKinnon told the British journalist Jon Ronson that the charges terrified him due to the brutality of American jails, where he feared he would be raped.

The British courts granted an order for McKinnon's extradition in July 2006, but he and his family fought it. In 2008, his lawyers announced that he'd been medically assessed and formally diagnosed with Asperger's. "Nobody likes being diagnosed of any kind of syndrome, but it did explain a lot," he said to the MUFON audience. "It's a medical condition. People tend to have a hyper-inflated sense of truth and justice."

In 2012, after an exhausting game of extradition tennis, then–home secretary Theresa May announced that the extradition request would be blocked. "Mr. McKinnon is accused of serious crimes," she told the House of Commons. "But there is also no doubt that he is seriously ill. . . . He has Asperger's syndrome, and suffers from depressive illness. Mr. McKinnon's extradition would give rise to such a high risk of him ending his life that a decision to extradite would be incompatible with Mr. McKinnon's human rights." The Obama administration was "disappointed" with the decision but would respect it. McKinnon would still be arrested and brought to trial if he ever stepped foot in the U.S.

Years later, peering through a webcam into a country he can never visit, McKinnon knew how it all sounded. "To many people it seemed like a mad idea, but to me it seemed like a noble cause," he said. "It was very easy—I wish it hadn't been so easy."

In the end, McKinnon was still frustrated that it was even necessary, in his eyes, to do what he did. "Secrets are never good in any relationship," he told the MUFON crowd, and I caught myself nodding. "But secrets kept from both the people and the state by forces unknown are the worst kind of secrets."

10

CONSPIRACISM IS FOR EVERYONE:
THE DEEP STATE AND RUSSIAGATE

MOST OF THIS COUNTRY'S POPULAR CONSPIRACY THEORIES ARE focused on a specific incident, person, or place: JFK's assassination, 9/11, vaccines. But conspiracy thinking can sometimes be harder to identify, more amorphous, thoroughly mixed in with the trappings of our daily lives, the TV we watch, the newspapers we read, the politics in which we engage. The discomfiting truth is that when history is still in the writing, it can be hard to distinguish between a theory and a genuine conspiracy and avoid falling for the one that is fake.

The first, chaotic year of the Trump presidency proved that notion in spades, and it started early. If you turned on MSNBC on the evening of January 12, 2017, you might have seen host Rachel Maddow take her viewers on a conspiracy-tinged tour of a power blackout.

Maddow, her usually quizzical dark eyebrows hiked up to her hairline, focused her show that night on the confirmation hearing of Mike Pompeo, Trump's pick at that time for CIA director. Pompeo had earlier appeared before the Senate Intelligence Committee, where Senator Mark Warner, a Virginia Democrat, concluded his opening remarks by talking about Russia's possible interference in the US elections. "As you know," Warner told Pompeo, "Chairman Burr and I have committed to conduct a review of the intelligence supporting the intelligence committee's assessment that Russia, at the direction—"

Warner was cut off. The committee's hearing room was plunged into darkness: the horseshoe of senators, Pompeo at his table, the galleries full of people watching, reporters peering at their now-invisible notepads. A C-SPAN camera capturing the incident bobbled unsteadily.

"Okay," Maddow said, exhaling in wonderment in her recap of the incident. "*Yeah*. Do not adjust your set. This is not going wrong right now. This is what happened today at the hearing for the new head of the CIA, right after the topic of Russian hacking was broached for the first time. This is what happened. This is what we all saw. What happened in the room was a complete power cut. All the lights in the room went out, without warning, in that room."

Maddow was clearly shocked by the power outage—the "cut," as she called it, implying a deliberate action. And she wasn't alone in intimating that the timing was suspicious; Republican senator John Cornyn tweeted about it ("Lights suspiciously went off in hearing room for new CIA director, Mike Pompeo," he wrote. "Hmmmm"). Chairman Burr joked that it was "a conspiracy" to draw attention to the sorry state of American infrastructure. But on her show, Maddow took it further, linking the power outage to another weird incident that had happened later the same day, when California representative Maxine Waters was testifying on the House floor.

At the time, Waters was speaking against a Republican-backed bill that she said would strip oversight of the SEC. "As President-elect Trump takes office next week, beginning what is the most conflicted administration in US history, I urge my colleagues to join me . . . in opposing H.R. 78," she told the room. "To ensure that the actions of Trump's SEC are in the interest of Americans' economic stability, and not in Russia's or Wall Street's interests."

Viewers in the House gallery would have seen nothing amiss. But anyone watching C-SPAN witnessed something legitimately strange. C-SPAN's feed was bizarrely interrupted, and Waters's remarks were replaced by a broadcast of Russia Today, the Kremlin-backed news organization accused of functioning as a mouthpiece for Putin's government.

Maddow found the timing of both incidents darkly meaningful. "Welcome to your whole new world," she told her viewers. "Who knows what any of that was about?" Waters herself found the incident "unusual and curious," too. "Placed in the context of current events concerning cyberattacks and foreign interference in our elections," she wrote in a statement, "it is very important that C-SPAN provide a clear and concise explanation for the interruption of its online broadcast before we can reach any conclusions or establish the basis for additional inquiry."

Both incidents were rather quickly explained, in fact. The Pompeo hearing blackout was attributed to planned work an electrical company was doing in the neighborhood. C-SPAN stated definitively that the network wasn't hacked but had suffered a malfunction while testing for the inauguration. "RT's signal was mistakenly routed onto the primary encoder feeding C-SPAN1's signal to the Internet, rather than to an unused backup," a spokesman wrote.

Yet neither explanation got nearly as much attention as the incidents themselves. Maddow's overheated reaction presaged a particular kind of Russia-centric paranoia, mostly visible among liberals and the left, which feared that the Kremlin's spies and agents were everywhere, that the president himself was little more than a Creamsicle-hued puppet dancing to Vladimir Putin's tune, and that anyone skeptical was probably *in on the whole thing.*

Often outlandish theories begin at the fringes and gradually work their way inward. But in the case of Russiagate—as the panic was inevitably called—within the first year of Trump's presidency, both major political parties and the mainstream media embraced grand nationwide theories about how democracy had been undermined by the enemy. As if in response to Russia fever, right-wing media and politicians, first fed by conspiracy sites and quickly picking up their own speed, started to fret about the Deep State: a sinister cadre of unelected power brokers they claimed was buried within the federal government, working to bring the Trump administration down.

The speculation at the far edge of the right reached far more colorful proportions than anything the left could produce, with Alex Jones suggesting that government actors were spiking Trump's drinks. "I've talked to people, multiple ones, and they believe that they are putting a slow sedative that they're building up that's also addictive in his Diet Cokes and in his iced tea," Jones declared. "And that the president by six or seven at night is basically slurring his words and is drugged."

Poisoned Cokes aside, Russiagate and the Deep State are new incarnations of an old, familiar fear: the suspicion that subversive, nefarious elites or foreign elements have seized the reins of power. Americans periodically believe that the federal government has been undermined by villains, what author and political journalist Jesse Walker calls the "Enemy Above" mode of conspiracy theory. Author Kathryn Olmsted points out that this type of suspicion has erupted regularly since the nineteenth century, intensifying as the size of the government has increased. In a way, it's the most sympathetic, common, and understandable type of conspiracy theory. Who, after all, really trusts their government?

In this most recent eruption, the fear and suspicion closely reflect the real fragility of American democracy. Our system has shown itself to be profoundly vulnerable to outside influences: dark money, untraceable super PACs, gerrymandering, the persistent disenfranchisement of voters of color, and the Supreme Court's intervention in the 2000 presidential election spring to mind. There was fertile territory here, ready and waiting for Russiagate and the Deep State alike. As so often in American history, concrete conditions paved a wide, straight road for imagined ones, and real losses of power carved a path for the more fantastical scenarios that followed.

Sometimes paranoia around the government and the White House turns out to be well founded: Nixon and Watergate, for one, or Reagan and the Iran-Contra scandal. Sometimes, not so much. As researcher Chip Berlet writes, Bill Clinton, it was claimed, "assisted drug smugglers, ran a hit squad that killed his political enemies, and covered up the assassination of his aide Vincent Foster." The "Clinton body count" conspiracy, that Bill and Hillary kill their opponents, continues to this day.

This new set of conspiracy theories, founded and unfounded, around Russian interference in our elections and a Deep State campaign against Trump, mirroring each other across the aisle, involved one difference: one was real and the other was not. Despite much scoffing from the right, a persuasive case was made that the Russian government did meddle in the 2016 elections. The CIA, FBI, and NSA—not the most left-wing institutions, traditionally—jointly issued a report in January 2017 stating that Russian president Vladimir Putin ordered the meddling efforts to harm Hillary Clinton's presidential bid and undermine American democratic processes.

The Kremlin has implied that all this is payback. In the mid-2000s, as a series of "color revolutions" against Russian influence swept across eastern Europe, the Russian government claimed they were funded by the United States. Putin has long maintained that Clinton, as secretary of state, was also responsible for protests in Moscow in 2011, in which thousands of demonstrators accused him of electoral fraud. So, according to the best US intelligence information, came a round of retributive meddling, which experts speculated is meant to not just disrupt the electoral process, but create a general climate of uncertainty and instability.

Inevitably, the fact of this meddling led directly to the question of Donald Trump's role: Was he a hapless dupe? An enthusiastic participant? A blackmail victim working off his debt? The gravity of possible collusion by the Trump campaign with the Russian government led to the appointment of a special investigator under the Justice Department, former FBI director Robert Mueller. He soon began investigating whether Trump obstructed justice by firing FBI director James Comey and by his numerous tweets about the inquiry itself, in which he called on Congress, members of the administration, and law enforcement to end it.

At the very least, it was quickly established, the Russian government did indeed attempt to draw the Trump campaign into the meddling. We knew this because we had the deeply idiotic emails between Trump son-in-chief Donald Trump, Jr., and a Russian lawyer with ties to the Kremlin in which the latter bluntly offered the campaign dirt on Clinton. The lawyer said the documents "would incriminate Hillary and her dealings with Russia and would be very useful to your father." These would be "obviously very high level and sensitive information but is part of Russia and its government's support for Mr. Trump."

"If it's what you say," Trump Jr. responded, with the irrepressible exuberance of a man with an excess of hair and a dearth of forethought, "I love it."

In fact, well before a Trump son took an ill-advised, well-documented meeting with Kremlin lawyers, Russian-backed disinformation had already made itself felt in the United States. In 2010, there was evidence that Russian sources tried to create conspiracy theories around the Deepwater Horizon oil spill, a wellhead explosion in which eleven people died and nearly five million gallons of oil was dumped into the Gulf of Mexico. Kate Starbird, the researcher at the University of Washington who studies the way false flag stories and hoaxes spread online, noticed something odd. "Politically focused" Twitter accounts, as the *Washington Post* put it, aimed at sowing chaos and panic about the spill by tweeting a wave of links to articles detailing disastrous fake outcomes: a tsunami of oil washing ashore, the ocean floor collapsing. People who lived in the area were confused and scared, Starbird told the *Post* in 2017.

After the 2016 election, she became newly curious about how those tweets had spread. She realized that all the articles cited Russian scientists and had originated on what we might now call "alt-right" or far-right blogs. "At the time, I didn't notice what was going on," Starbird said. "But with the benefit of hindsight, you notice that this stuff was happening for a long time."

During the 2016 election, journalist Adrian Chen noticed something new and bizarre. Some of the Russian-troll Twitter accounts he'd been following for years, ones tied to the Russian-based Internet Research Agency and dedicated to spreading disinformation and discontent, had shifted identities. They had "begun to promote right-wing news outlets, portraying themselves as conservative voters who were, increasingly, fans of Donald Trump." Donald Trump himself resolutely denied any suggestion of Russian intervention on his behalf, dismissing the assertion that Russian-backed hackers were responsible for hacking into DNC emails and memorably proposing instead that the culprit could be China or "somebody sitting on their bed that weighs four hundred pounds, okay?"

There was conjecture that his family's business interests in Russia lay behind Trump's desire to brush off anything suspicious about Russian involvement in the elections. Or perhaps, as British ex-spy Christopher Steele suggested in a salacious dossier, the Russians held embarrassing material, including a tape of sex workers in Moscow urinating on a hotel bed for Trump's pleasure.

The notion of collusion tapped into a real and receptive well of left-wing angst. Masha Gessen, a Russian-American author and political observer, wrote in the *New York Review of Books* that Russian fever stemmed from a desperate liberal fantasy of a speedy Trump impeach-ment. "The dream fueling the Russia frenzy is that it will eventually create a dark enough cloud of suspicion around Trump that Congress will find the will and the grounds to impeach him."

Even before Trump took office, liberals sought to comfort themselves with paranoid imaginings of a swift downfall. There was the idea that "faithless electors" in the Electoral College would prevent him from being inaugurated by transferring their vote to someone else, a technically legal thing that has never happened in American history. (Seven faith-less electors in the Electoral College did vote for people besides Trump, but not enough to overturn his election. Only two of them were pledged to vote for him in the first place; the rest had actually been pledged to vote for Clinton.) And Green Party presidential candidate Jill Stein raised millions of dollars from desperate liberals for a recount effort, spurred by a conviction that the vote had been somehow, someway, rigged. It was a sad irony. People who the day before the election mocked Trump for his tweets decrying a rigged system were themselves claiming the same thing only twenty-four hours later.

Gessen was profoundly concerned by the Russiagate frenzy. If it should lead to impeachment, they wrote, that "will have resulted largely from a media campaign orchestrated by members of the intelligence community—setting a dangerous political precedent that will have cor-rupted the public sphere and promoted paranoia. And that is the best-case outcome."

A "CAMPAIGN ORCHESTRATED BY MEMBERS OF THE INTELLIGENCE community": that quickly became the right-wing cause. Russian med-dling allegations were the result of intelligence agencies gone rogue, intent on devouring a legitimately elected president. At its core, the right's preoccupation with the Deep State began as a defensive response to liberal claims of an illegitimate, enemy-backed government. But what exactly is the Deep State, and how did it come to be blamed for all the woes of the Trump administration?

The concept is not new, either in the United States or abroad; in some countries it is a very real phenomenon—a permanent ruling class within the military, the judiciary, and intelligence agencies that remains in power no matter which party is elected. In Turkey, the best-known example, the Deep State, which likely became active during the 1970s, might have had ties to organized crime and was willing to use violence and even extrajudicial killings to stay in control.

In the United States, the Deep State or "state within a state" concept sometimes refers to the extensive power of the military-industrial complex or to the nation's sprawling national security bureaucracy. The term illustrates an unpleasant, intractable political and economic status quo, what Mike Lofgren, a former Republican congressional staffer, has called "a casino with a tilted wheel," where billion-dollar industries and the government agencies that regulate them are staffed by the same people in an endless revolving door, greased in dollar bills. The Deep State is where highly secretive agencies like the NSA function, with the cooperation of ethics-neutral Silicon Valley tech companies. It is where an electoral system is so awash in dark money that most Americans despair of ever truly fixing it.

The term can also refer to the government's secret engagement in activities abroad that our elected officials publicly denounced: the CIA's intervention to overthrow the democratically elected leaders of other countries and back opposition forces—Iran in 1953, Guatemala in 1954, Congo in 1960, the Dominican Republic in 1961, South Vietnam in 1963, Brazil in 1964, and Chile in 1972. The list includes attempts to assassinate Fidel Castro with a series of increasingly absurd plots and devices. (One of Castro's deputies estimated the number of US assassination attempts at six hundred thirty-four, which seems high but perhaps not wildly off base.)

The great power of the military-industrial complex, as President Dwight Eisenhower, who coined the term, argued, lay in the new conjunction of an "immense military establishment and a large arms industry," which could be said to amount to a Deep State actor. "The total influence—economic, political, even spiritual—is felt in every city," Eisenhower said, "every statehouse, every office of the federal government. We recognize the imperative need for this development. Yet, we must not fail to comprehend its grave implications. Our toil, resources, and livelihood are all involved. So is the very structure of our society." Americans had to guard, he said, against "the acquisition of unwarranted influence, whether sought or unsought, by the military-industrial complex."

For these reasons, well before it became a fixture on far-right sites, the Deep State or "permanent state" was thus a subject of concern for both liberal and centrist writers and academics. In his book *The Deep State*, Mike Lofgren paints a picture of an army of federal agencies that have come to function more or less independently of who is in power, in a permanent, lusty liplock with such powerful private companies as Boeing and Northrop Grumman and Lockheed Martin, all of which earn billions in government contracts every year, building the weapons that arm the United States, its allies, and often enough, its adversaries.

"It is a hybrid of national security and law enforcement agencies," he told host Bill Moyers in a television appearance. "The Department of Defense, the Department of State, the Department of Homeland Security, the Central Intelligence Agency, and the Justice Department. I also include the Department of the Treasury because of its jurisdiction over financial flows, its enforcement of international sanctions, and its organic symbiosis with Wall Street."

Echoing Lofgren, the *Washington Post*'s Dana Priest and Bill Arkin published "Top Secret America," a four-part series in 2010 on the military intelligence community that had grown staggeringly since September 11. The reporters found that a mind-boggling number of Americans held high-level security clearances and that in general, the nation's national security apparatus "has become so large, so unwieldy and so secretive that no one knows how much money it costs, how many people it employs, how many programs exist within it or exactly how many agencies do the same work." The *Post* concluded that the system "amounts to an alternative geography of the United States," a warren of agencies and programs shrouded from public view and public oversight.

Given those very real elements and their undeniable influence on American lives, Glenn Greenwald, The Intercept's editor and frequent critic of government powers, expressed frustration that the notion of Deep State interference was dismissed so easily. "That the U.S. has a shadowy, secretive world of intelligence and military operatives who exercise great power outside of elections and democratic accountability is not some exotic, alt-right conspiracy theory," he wrote. "It's utterly elemental to understanding anything about how Washington works. It's hard to believe that anyone on this side of a sixth-grade civics class would seek to deny that."

Nonetheless in the Trump era, Deep State theorizing extended well beyond a sober assessment of extragovernmental power. Even outside of Alex Jones and his predictably absurd speculations about drugged sodas, the concept of the Deep State was weaponized by Trump partisans and right-wing politicians leaping from a little-used term to a ubiquitous one. (According to Google Trends, searches for the phrase spiked modestly around May 2017 and then extraordinarily in January 2018.)

Deep State paranoia was prefaced by a concern on the far right that President Obama had a sinister amount of power and would perhaps, when the time came, refuse to give it up. Obama rode out the last of his presidency on a tide of conspiratorial suspicions about his supposed iron grip. During the 2016 election's campaign season, WorldNetDaily founder Joseph Farah found it highly suspect that Obama called Trump unfit for the presidency. He implied that Obama wouldn't leave office if Trump were elected. "Should we not be concerned about what Obama might do?" he wrote. "Should he not be asked pointedly about the implications of his stunning statements?" Other sites were more explicit, claiming that Obama planned to declare martial law to block Trump.

But when Inauguration Day went off without incident—other than the fact of Donald Trump becoming president—the Deep State idea persisted. Obama was still held responsible. Dozens of far-right and conspiracy-leaning websites insisted that he had continued working as a "shadow president," snarling the gears of the Trump White House, directing his minions to stand in its way, even perhaps directing the

Russia-collusion inquiry. But that claim wasn't just relegated to the fringes; it was espoused and repeated by elected officials and White House staffers on national TV.

Jay Sekulow, a member of Trump's personal legal team, used the words "shadow government" outright in an appearance on Sean Hannity's show on Fox. "You've got a shadow government that is leaking . . . information" about Trump, he said, and it includes "people that were in step with the previous administration." Sekulow also speculated about whether Clinton was "leading the shadow government while Obama's giving $400,000 speeches," or if Obama was leading it directly.

"If there was ever confirmation that the Deep State is real, illegal & endangers national security, it's this," Donald Trump, Jr., tweeted about yet another White House leak. "Their interests above all else." Western Pennsylvania congressman Mike Kelly claimed that Obama continued living in Washington, DC, with his family for "one purpose and one purpose only." He planned "to run a shadow government that is going to totally upset the new agenda." In a later qualification, Kelly's spokesperson walked back the comment, saying that Kelly "was sharing the frustration of everyone in the room over how they believe certain Obama administration holdovers within the federal bureaucracy are attempting to upset President Trump's agenda."

"Holdovers" is in itself a revealing term, used by people who don't want to say "shadow government" outright. Former Trump campaign manager Corey Lewandowski added the word in a tweet in which he proclaimed "The deep state is real." All "Obama hold overs in the Gov't need to go to allow @realDonaldTrump to Make America Great Again!" The holdovers were frequently blamed for leaking or fabricating anything unflattering about the Trump administration. (Sometimes—for example, in the president's volleys of outraged early morning tweets—a piece of news is denounced as both leaked *and* fabricated, which is a neat semiotic trick.)

In one thing, however, the people fretting about leaks were correct. There were an unprecedented number of them in the first years of the Trump administration, particularly in the West Wing, where it sometimes seemed as though everyone was secretly recording each other. They were astounding in their breadth (fired White House aide Omarosa

Manigault released numerous recordings she'd made, including one of Chief of Staff John Kelly firing her) and their pettiness. When First Lady Melania Trump had kidney surgery, her staff didn't inform West Wing personnel about when she'd return to work, for fear that would leak, too. In the West Wing, the leaks were part of constant backstabbing and palace intrigue, which seemed endemic to working for the Trump administration. But elsewhere, at the Environmental Protection Agency, for example, they seemed to occur out of a sense of defiance: when EPA staffers were ordered in the fall of 2017 to take a mandatory course on preventing leaks, news of that leaked, as well.

Actual opposition forces within the government allowed the Deep State conspiracy theory to flourish, buoyed by inarguably real events. Similarly, a raft of Twitter accounts dispensing "rogue" tweets spurred paranoia over leakage as evidence of malicious moles inside the government. The tweets were presented as uncensored reports from staffers within various federal agencies, including the EPA and the National Park Service. It is possible that some of the accounts, at least in the administration's early days, really were manned by dissatisfied employees at agencies that would likely undergo profound changes under the new regime. But soon enough, some of the accounts looked more like liberal fan fiction. One appeared calling itself "Rogue POTUS Staffer."

"The unofficial resistance team inside the White House," the account's bio read at one point. "We pull back the curtain to expose the real workings inside this disastrous, frightening Administration." Rogue POTUS Staffer managed to garner thousands of credulous retweets by writing, essentially, what liberals wished to hear. Most of the dispatches featured Trump panicking or melting down in absurd ways.

"POTUS suddenly angry watching Ryan press conference," one tweet read. "Apparently shouted '—off' and threw book at a TV which may be broken now." In another, "Reportedly, POTUS just became so angry he tried to tip over his desk. Tried three times before giving up. Now, angry and embarrassed."

Tellingly, this insider account never managed to predict any of the numerous administration departures or produce any information that convincingly showed the missives were coming from inside the White House. Still, the tweets generated a satisfying, narcotizing stream of likes and retweets by delivering constant, impassioned indictments against the administration and dark warnings about where it was headed.

SMALL ENOUGH TO FIT IN A SODA CAN OR LARGE ENOUGH TO encompass a violent plot against America, in the hands of Trump partisans, the Deep State functioned like Silly Putty, stretching in all directions to cover anything that might need explaining away. It might be the Russian collusion investigation or Hillary Clinton not being jailed over her private email servers. ("Why aren't our deep state authorities looking at this?" Trump groused on Twitter in November 2017, referring to Clinton's emails, more than a year after the FBI elected to not charge her. "Rigged & corrupt?")

At the farcical end of the spectrum, Deep Statism was deployed as exculpation in the legal scrapes of a bunch of low-level political actors. In Montana, for example, a Republican candidate for Senate named Troy Downing blasted the Deep State for its "witch hunt" against him—specifically the Montana Department of Fish, Wildlife and Parks, which looked into suspected violations of his hunting license. Then there was Trump advisor Roger Stone, who told Alex Jones in an interview that the Deep State had sent some villains to T-bone his car in a hit-and-run. "They have poisoned me, they have smeared me, and someone in a car tried to kill me," Stone said, appearing via satellite unharmed and quite chipper after the alleged incident. (According to the *Washington Post*, Stone claimed to have been a passenger in the car, but he left the scene by the time the police arrived to take a report.) Stone had previously complained in late 2016 that someone had poisoned him with polonium, the deadly radioactive material that was used to kill a Russian spy a decade earlier. Then, too, he appeared to recover in miraculous fashion.

In its more serious guise, Deep Statism represented an alarming new development: a ruling party and a presidential administration that claimed to be under attack even as they held the bulk of power in the United States, that used the language of victimhood even as they were the victors, the history-makers. That is a worrisome phenomenon: claiming that an external enemy threatens the sovereignty of the state—an enemy to be repelled by any means necessary—is historically a hallmark of authoritarian leaders.

Demonstrating the extent to which besieged thinking seeped into the Trump administration was a memo sent out by a staffer at the National Security Council, Rich Higgins, which was so alarming that it became minor national news. Working in the NSC's strategic planning office, Higgins was one of a group hired by quickly ousted and criminally charged National Security Advisor Michael Flynn. (Flynn pleaded guilty to lying to the FBI about his contacts with Russian government officials before Trump had been inaugurated.) Higgins's memo, titled "POTUS & Political Warfare," contained a long list of the president's supposed enemies, among them "deep state actors, globalists, bankers, Islamists, and establishment Republicans." It went on to present a Trumpian view of how the administration should respond to its foes.

"The administration has been maneuvered into a constant back-pedal by relentless political warfare attacks structured to force him to assume a reactive posture that assures inadequate responses," part of it reads. "The president can either drive or be driven by events; it's time for him to drive them."

Higgins was fired by Flynn's saner replacement H. R. McMaster, but one administration official went on the record agreeing with him. A government source told *Foreign Policy* magazine, which published the memo, that its purpose was to warn Trump. "The memo maybe reads a little crazy, sure, but it's not wrong and Rich isn't crazy," the official said.

At its extreme edge, Deep Statism looks a lot like the New World Order suspicions that came before it: a fear of total domination, subjugation, literal slavery. "The goals of the deep state are simple," wrote the conspiracy-addled finance site Zero Hedge. "The complete enslavement of mankind by political elites." The site is run by a former hedge fund analyst named Daniel Ivandjiiski, who was barred from Wall Street for insider trading in 2008 and, like a lot of people who are out of better ideas, started blogging. Ivandjiiski and other contributors to the site wrote under the pseudonym "Tyler Durden." He, or they, fretted with increasing zeal about Trump being impeached by the Deep State, a pit stop on the journey to global enslavement.

"It has been apparent to those not blinded by partisan politics that something is going on in the government right now," offered one post. "Yet most simply call it a 'witch hunt,' simply for lack of wanting to admit the deep state exists. It certainly looks like a battle between democracy and the deep state. And we aren't sure we'd put money on democracy at this point in history."

Along these lines, Stone, in an interview with the *Harvard Political Review*, blamed the Deep State for a looming coup attempt (and for the president's ignorance about world events). "I have come to this conclusion that we are witnessing a slow-motion coup by the deep state, the very people that opposed the presidential election," Stone told the journal. "They have used illegal and unconstitutional leaks to destabilize his presidency. The generals have pretty much taken control of the White House and are seeking to isolate the president and limit his access to information. I am surprised how much he does not know."

Right-wing gasbag Rush Limbaugh echoed Stone. "There is already a silent coup," he told his audience, perhaps misunderstanding what a coup is, "and it's been under way for quite a while to get rid of Donald Trump." And Mike Cernovich predicted that the Deep State would eventually turn deadly. "Trump will be killed," he told Jones. "They're going to kill us. They're going to kill him, they're going to kill everybody."

That kind of language—setting up an immediate, apocalyptic battle between the meager forces of good and the pervasive foot soldiers of evil—is a hallmark of conspiracism (and again, has often served as a justification for authoritarianism). The ultraconservative legal activist group Judicial Watch released a report awash with such language, claiming that the Deep State comprised the EPA, the IRS, law enforcement agencies, and, of course, career civil servants throughout the government. "No matter who's in power, they exert control," Judicial Watch wrote. The organization also called the Deep State "dangerously malignant," suggesting a cancer needing to be cut out by any means necessary—an immediate kill-or-be-killed scenario for Trump.

"Sometimes, as it has with the Trump presidency, the Deep State rises to the surface in rebellion," the report stated, "taking aggressive, seditious measures against a president whose election it opposed and who it perceives to be a threat to its own agenda and, perhaps, its very survival.

As already is clear with the Trump presidency, the Deep State can turn on any president that threatens its interests and survival. And left unchecked, it may illegally destroy him."

As those on the far right fulminated about imminent global takeovers, they were matched on the left by its own paranoia. The left's fears of conspiracies and collusion made for some very strange bedfellows. Elements of the anti-Trump resistance saw the Kremlin's agents everywhere and so found themselves cheering on the intelligence institutions doing battle in Russiagate—the same institutions historically distrusted by the left, and with good reason. People like James Comey, the FBI director fired by Trump, became a hero to liberals, although they reviled him during the elections for his role in the scandal over Hillary Clinton's use of a private email server during her time as secretary of state.

The Russia frenzy produced rhetoric that replicated that on the conspiratorial far right, along with conspiracy stars to espouse it. Eric Garland, a small-time economic consultant and self-described "futurist" (how he actually earned a living was opaque), became well known overnight for a one-hundred-twenty-seven-tweet thread. His exhausting missive began with the words "Time for some game theory" and culminated in a sweeping, not-altogether-coherent account of Russian interference in the 2016 election. The tweetstorm garnered sincere praise from legitimate reporters; *Mother Jones* editor Clara Jeffrey called it the "single greatest thread I have ever read on Twitter. And in its way a Federalist Paper for 2016."

Praise from such credible journalists encouraged Garland to spend the next year identifying various people he thought were in league with the Russians, which came to encompass a long list. At one point, Garland condemned Bernie Sanders as a Russian simp in terms that seemed borderline anti-Semitic. "Sanders is not a son of Vermont—he is not an inheritor of our values of inviolable liberty, sovereignty, justice, and law," Garland declared of the state's senator. "If Sanders will not stand with America—much less Vermont, my ancestral home—against Russia, he has betrayed both Republic and Country."

Garland reached extremes that put him in the front ranks of the conspiracy-minded. "Let's talk about this weeks [*sic*] events that already show that we're in hyperdrive to expose a global criminal conspiracy," he tweeted. He also sounded alarmingly unhinged, vowing, with a signature mix of all-caps and exaggeration, "I WON'T BE THE FIRST GARLAND OF MY LINE TO SPILL BLOOD FOR AMERICA AND THE RIGHT SIDE OF HISTORY AND NEVER THE LAST, YOU FUCKERS." Seth Abramson, an English professor and former lawyer who identified himself on social media as a political expert, wrote in November 2017, also on Twitter, "While the final pieces of proof must still be put into place, every indication we have *so far* is that the President has been and continues to be a Russian asset."

In line with the conspiracist playbook, Russiagate even yielded false flag accusations. In an account called "A Hamilton Spirit," a person claiming to be a psychiatrist garnered close to sixty thousand followers with rants connecting every event in the visible universe to Trump's Russian ties. He implied that a mass shooting at a Las Vegas music festival might have been staged—by whom, it wasn't clear—in order to distract Democrats and somehow prevent them from filing articles of impeachment against Trump. A Hamilton Spirit seemed proud of the fact that he made logical connections no one else had. "I've always been really good at puzzles," he explained.

DEEP STATERS AND RUSSIAGATERS REVEALED AN ENTIRE COUNTRY IN the grips of conspiracy thinking. Both sides considered themselves eminently reasonable, though, following the habits of the conspiracy-verse: they insisted they had done their research and arrived at the only sensible conclusion, and that their enemies were bought and paid for, and probably actors, plants, or spies. Left-wing comedian Jen Kirkman called Bernie Sanders a "Russian chaos agent," while right-winger Steven Seagal, the partially fossilized action hero, wrote an entire novel based on his purported encounters with the Deep State, titled *The Way of the Shadow Wolves*. Referring to himself and coauthor Joe Morrissey, part of the novel's introduction reads, "*Shadow Wolves* is a book of fiction based on reality. Both authors have worked with, confronted, and seen the power of the Deep State and the manner in which many federal government agencies willfully violate the Constitution and the laws of the land in service to special interests."

The two camps operate with a specific kind of linguistic grandiosity, an overheated rhetorical style where every event, no matter how mundane, is part of a showdown between good and evil. The speaker/writer/tweeter is always standing alone at the gate, bravely pushing back the demonic hordes. And even thoughtful believers on the left also express their fear in terms of a coup.

The essay "Trial Balloon for a Coup," published in Medium by a writer named Yonatan Zunger, went viral with claims that the Trump administration, in passing bans on immigration, was testing the resolve of the American populace to pave the way for a military coup. "It wouldn't surprise me if the goal is to create 'resistance fatigue,'" the author wrote, "to get Americans to the point where they're more likely to say 'Oh, *another* protest? Don't you guys ever stop?' relatively quickly." Another essay in Medium also declared the immigration ban a "headfake," designed to test whether the Trump administration could attempt a full-scale government takeover. It didn't use the word "coup," but came very close. "The administration," the author, a San Francisco entrepreneur named Jake Fuentes, wrote, "is deliberately testing the limits of governmental checks and balances to set up a self-serving, dangerous consolidation of power."

The Russiagate coup theory was stated explicitly on Patriobotics, a site that traffics in heated Trump–Putin conspiracizing. The site was set up by Louise Mensch, a former Conservative politician in Britain turned romance novelist who moved to New York in 2012 and became a journalist of sorts. Mensch was frequently joined by former NSA staffer John Schindler, as well as Claude Taylor, a freelance photographer who describes himself as a "former staffer" in the Clinton White House. (He worked in the volunteer office in 1993.) All three have generated devoted, almost fanatical followings, alongside a larger number of people calling them cranks and liars.

Among other things, Mensch suggested that Trump had been secretly indicted and handed a copy of that indictment on an airplane runway by the "Marshal of the Supreme Court," which is not how indictments work. At one point she said that teams backed by Trump advisor Steve Bannon were behind a series of bomb threats phoned into Jewish community centers. (The threats were traced to a disgraced journalist trying to terrorize his ex and a disturbed Jewish teenager in Israel.)

In other Mensch assertions, Bannon was in for a pretty dark fate: "My sources say the death penalty, for espionage, being considered for @StevenKBannon," she tweeted. "I am pro-life and take no pleasure in reporting this." Additionally, Black Lives Matter was a Russian operation, for instance, directly funding protests in Ferguson, Missouri. Taylor reported on a criminal probe into Trump Models Management by the New York Attorney General based on a tip from an insider at the AG's office. Separately, Mensch claimed that according to her sources, Trump "is linked to a Russian-based human trafficking enterprise, where girls and women were kidnapped into sexual slavery. This includes underage girls and minors." Except there was no probe or source at the Attorney General's office; Taylor was fed information by a hoaxer who told the *Guardian* she'd acted out of frustration at the "fake news" disseminated by Taylor and Mensch.

Despite the bizarre nature of her reports, Mensch had a sizable Twitter following, and people outside journalism were not always aware that she was not a credible political journalist. This in turn helped generate more uncertainty about what is real, who can be trusted, and who is a real journalist. And, to complicate matters further, Mensch did once get her hands on a genuine, newsworthy piece of information. In February 2017, she learned that the FISA court had granted a warrant to surveil two Trump aides who were suspected of having communications with banks linked to the Russian government. The reporting was confirmed by other outlets, which allowed Mensch and her followers to declare her legitimacy.

In a delicious irony, conspiracy theories emerged about Mensch herself: she was a Trump-backed plant, paid to make the Trump resistance look stupid. She was a Russian plant, paid to make the anti-Russia resistance look stupid. Meanwhile, Mensch argued that the resistance movement against Trump itself *is a Russian plot*.

If Russiagate is an example of citizens' deep suspicion toward their government, it also prompted concern that it could lead to the reverse: the government's suspicion of its citizens, which has resulted in some of the darkest periods in American history. A mania for ferreting out secret domestic enemies brought us McCarthysim and the life-ruining inquisitions of the House Un-American Activities Committee, and thousands of Japanese Americans being imprisoned in internment camps during the latter days of the Second World War.

Masha Gessen, for one, feared that anti-Russia paranoia could lead to a climate of McCarthy-esque persecution, suspicion, and witch hunts. Gessen warned that Russiagate was "promoting a xenophobic conspiracy theory in the cause of removing a xenophobic conspiracy theorist from office." Press freedom organizations also worried that Russia-collusion panic could have a chilling effect on free speech. In September 2017, the FBI investigated whether Sputnik and RT were illegally spreading Russian propaganda without having registered under the Foreign Agents Registration Act. In November, RT did register as a foreign agent but planned to challenge the Justice Department's order to do so in court.

Trevor Timm, executive director of the Freedom of the Press Foundation, wrote that government control over news organizations is a bad idea. "No matter one's feelings on Russia or Sputnik," he wrote, "I think it's concerning anytime the FBI gets involved in defining who is and isn't a journalist."

In any case, Sputnik and RT's activities post-2016 were not new. They have long focused on true but unflattering aspects of American government to shape a narrative. They had plenty of material to work from: police violence, gun violence, government repression, enthusiastic drone use. With the exception of reporting by Sean Stone—director Oliver Stone's adult son and an enthusiastic conspiracy theorist—a lot of their coverage looked like typical journalism. And the government's response to Sputnik and RT gave both organizations grist for their mills. One Sputnik columnist condemned the suspicion against his outlet as part of the mainstream media plot against Trump. "Anyone, anywhere, who might be linked to Russia in any whichever way no matter how direct or indirect is suspected of being a 'Kremlin agent,'" he wrote. "And that their interactions with American political campaigns constitute, at the very least, some form or another of 'meddling.'"

In fairness, Russia did not by any means corner the market on state-sponsored propaganda pushing its message overseas. The Voice of America, a government-funded station that broadcasts around the globe—in more than one hundred countries and sixty-one languages—has done so since the Cold War. The United States always insisted that VOA was created to *counter* Soviet propaganda, not create our own, but that distinction has seemed awfully fuzzy.

The Deep State and Russiagate shared one other important characteristic. They both speedily took on the nature of something of great benefit to conspiracy sellers: formless, vast, amorphous modes of suspicion. They cast shadows that could grow to encompass any event, any discovery, or shrink to reveal a sunny, bright nothing. Conspiracist politicians and pundits only profit from an environment in which nothing is certain, everything is clouded by suspicion, and no source of information can be trusted.

If that sounds too, well, conspiratorial, consider one of Trump's early and few press conferences, held in the first year of his presidency. He called the Russia collusion story "fake news put out by the media" and said that the reporters gathered were part of a press corps that was "out of control." But, he suggested, soon it wouldn't much matter. "The press, the public doesn't believe you people anymore," Trump told the room, beaming contentedly. "Now maybe I had something to do with that. I don't know. But they don't believe you."

EPILOGUE

When the anonymous high-level government employee decided to reveal what she knew, she (or he) went where anyone would go if they had urgent information to reveal: 4chan. The "crumbs," as the clues were called, first appeared in the thread "The Calm before the Storm," posted to the 4chan board /pol/ in October 2017. The employee, known only as "Q," threw out possible hints about a massive—yet entirely covert—counterattack being waged by President Donald Trump against the Deep State, the government pedophiles, the Clintons, Satanists—anyone and everyone dedicated to keeping him down.

In a way, the whole idea was almost charmingly naive: that Trump was secretly doing a really good job and all his faithful needed to do was wait patiently for justice and vindication. Many were thrilled by the idea that the investigation by Special Counsel Robert Mueller into Trump's possible collusion with Russia during the 2016 election was really an inquiry into Hillary Clinton and other Democrats, and soon he would sweep out of his office and arrest them all.

With a message of hope and the suggestion of impending, possibly violent, justice, Q garnered a breathless online following dedicated to decoding every missive. By the summer of 2018, people waving Q signs and wearing Q T-shirts were seen popping up at Trump rallies. Mainstream media ran endless QAnon explainers, triggering a wave of public ridicule and backlash that only further convinced Q's followers they were on the right track. It was a classic conspiracy theory, and it was harmless—a gigantic, increasingly contorted online community, essentially—until it wasn't. Soon, as so often happens, the mission started to leak offline, and people took matters into their own hands.

In June 2018, Matthew P. Wright of Nevada drove a self-made armored car halfway across a bridge near the Hoover Dam, stopped there, and held up a sign: "RELEASE THE OIG REPORT!" QAnon followers were convinced that a report released by the FBI's Office of the Inspector General—a six-hundred-page examination of the FBI's actions leading up to the 2016 election—wasn't a true report. The real one, they knew, fully exonerated Trump of meddling in the vote or obstructing justice. Wright, armed with an AR-15 rifle and a handgun, complained in a video shot on his phone that Trump himself had also betrayed his followers. "We the people demand full disclosure," Wright said. "We elected you to do a duty. You said you were going to lock certain people up if you were elected. You have yet to do that. Uphold your oath!"

Wright fled after blocking the bridge for an hour and was later arrested on a rich variety of criminal charges. In letters he wrote to the president and other public officials from jail, he referred to the "Great Awakening"—a popular QAnon phrase—and apologized, in a way, for his impulsivity. "I am no seditionist, nor do I wish to fight the government. I understand that the evil and corruption is limited to a select few in power and that the greater good is doing its best to combat this," he wrote. "I never meant harm to my brothers and sisters. I simply wanted the truth on behalf of all Americans, all of humanity for that matter." He signed off with another QAnon slogan: "Where we go one, we go all" (sometimes shortened to #WWG1WGA).

With unmistakable shades of Pizzagate and a significant overlap in followers, Q's adherents also believed the Trump administration was poised to arrest dozens of high-level pedophiles in government. An armed vigilante group in Arizona called Veterans on Patrol came across an abandoned homeless encampment in the summer of 2018. VOP's leader, Michael Meyer—who is not actually a veteran—claimed they had in fact stumbled upon a property being used as a "child sex camp." Sex-trafficking cartels, backed by the Clinton family and other elites, were purportedly involved with the Cemex cement company, which had a plant not far from the abandoned encampment. In protest, Meyer climbed a tower at the Cemex plant and refused to come down for nine days. He was arrested for trespassing; soon after his release, he posted the hashtag #WWG1WGA on his Facebook page.

QAnon was illustrative of two things. It showed how conspiracy theories reliably change form to encompass the anxieties of the day, which is why Trump supporters, in the middle of an intensifying investigation into Russian collusion, adopted the idea as an alternate narrative of the president's secret competence and success. And conspiracy theories are, in the end, not so much an explanation of events as they are an effort to assign blame. More than questioning an official narrative, they are aimed at identifying the *real* perpetrators, the true power behind the throne, the hidden hand pulling beneath the surface. QAnon shifted in the way that conspiracy theories always do, from trying to solve a mystery to nailing the real villains and bringing them to justice.

The impulse is understandable, and it is an extension of our normal desire to hold power accountable. Often the motivations of ordinary conspiracy theorists are harmless: a desire to improve the world, to explain suffering—one's own and that of others—and to remedy injustice. People join the "truth community" to help expose the inner workings and also to be part of something, to be one of the select few who *know what's really going on.*

But in the early years of the twenty-first century, people feel particularly dispossessed by a political process bound by two unresponsive parties, an ever-growing ocean of dark money, and representatives who become more inaccessible with each passing year. They feel that our lives are controlled by corporations and federal agencies they cannot see or appeal to. They want to fight back. And once you see the truth, in fact—once the light has penetrated the life you previously led and the lies you previously believed—who could do otherwise? For some, inaction feels morally intolerable. Think of Edgar Welch, the Pizzagate gunman, grimly dressing in the dark, leaving his sleeping children, and climbing into his car.

What's more: we *like* conspiracies and seem to genuinely enjoy sharing them. These murky real-world mysteries can feel like the junk food of entertainment, and we cram them into our mouths as fast as they are produced. This observation is not sanctimony; the data affirms the greedy consumption of conspiracy. A study by researchers at Oxford University noted that during the 2016 election, Twitter users were just as likely to share links to "polarizing and conspiratorial junk news" as they were to share professionally produced news created by journalists. "The number of links to Russian news stories, unverified or irrelevant links to WikiLeaks pages, or junk news was greater than the number of links to professional researched and published news," the study claimed.

"Indeed," it added, "the proportion of misinformation was twice that of the content from experts and the candidates themselves. Second, a worryingly large proportion of all the successfully catalogued content provides links to polarizing content from Russian, WikiLeaks, and junk news sources." The word "polarizing" has a specific, and alarming, meaning, the authors noted. "This content uses divisive and inflammatory rhetoric and presents faulty reasoning or misleading information to manipulate the reader's understanding of public issues and feed conspiracy theories." Truth and fact-checking travel along the same paths that conspiracies do. But the truth is often complicated, shaded, and demanding, and there's no denying that it often lacks the powerful, emotional, gut-level appeal of a conspiracy.

Furthermore, by creating a legible moral map of the universe, conspiracism can lead to a particular lack of empathy, a route so simple and straight and perilously narrow it points, at times, directly to hatred. If you have found a genuine foe, you are free to loathe him or her as expansively as necessary. The self-investigators cannot feel compassion for Seth Rich's family or the families of the Sandy Hook children or the Las Vegas shooting victims, because in a universe peopled with false-flag attacks and crisis actors, they are on the wrong side of truth. The world is divided into secretive, shadowy perpetrators and the few righteous detectives, hellhounds on the trail of an explosive secret.

Beyond building an environment of misinformation and secrecy, conspiracy theories also have the worrisome effect of inducing paralysis, even as they galvanize those at the extreme end to extreme action. Two social psychology researchers at the University of Kent in England found that exposure to anti-government theories made people less likely to want to vote. People subjected to climate change conspiracy theories were less motivated to reduce their carbon footprint. The theories, according to one of the researchers, Karen Douglas, writing in the *New York Times*, can work directly and subtly to "decrease social engagement" because "they left people feeling powerless." These findings suggest a troubling symbiosis. As conspiracy sellers become more energized, more profitable, and more politically committed, they feed what seems to be a strength-sapping potion to viewers and listeners.

As we have seen, there is no shortage of people willing to profit from a population's distrust and disengagement, from the impulse to expose evil and the desire to right wrongs. Thus ordinary people become the willing foot soldiers of a mob of fame-hungry provocateurs such as Mike Cernovich and Alex Jones, whose paranoid fantasies then ripple outward and touch us all. As a result, the Rich family and the Pozners, having suffered the most profound and wrenching of losses, have to contend with harassment and threats to their safety.

THERE ARE NO IMMEDIATELY OBVIOUS, FOOLPROOF BRAKES AVAILABLE. There is no mechanism to prevent another Edgar Welch storming into a pizza place or another James Fields getting behind the wheel, speeding toward Heather Heyer. Welch's fiancée and his closest friends couldn't talk him out of taking that drive. People who have journeyed to the dangerous far end of conspiratorial extremism are not amenable to the reason that might resonate with the rest of us. Countering an idea that has taken root is incredibly hard. Studies suggest that trying to argue someone out of a conspiratorial belief does not work, likening conspiracy theories to religious faith, which helps us see how they can be similarly fixed in the mind.

In a 2018 study, Virginia Tech researchers Mattia Samory and Tanushree Mitra looked at the contents of several conspiratorial Reddit boards and, among other recommendations, suggested that dissuading someone from a conspiracy theory would be more successful if the believer were a recent convert. "A good course of action to mitigate the problem is to catch new conspiracy theorists early," Samory told *Wired*. "They're the fastest to radicalize, they're the ones that remain the most engaged, but they also have the highest amount of distrust" before they're fully invested.

The popularity and durability of conspiracism means that it will always have its huckster street preachers such as Jones and Cernovich. But beyond the individuals, we need to look at the systems that made them so influential. Social media has created the world's most efficient vehicle of delivery for conspiracy theories. Combined with the hyper-polarized state of American politics and the resurgence of white suprem-acist and nationalist movements, social media provides a virtual assembly line for scapegoats, a systematized and lightning-fast way to spread blame, doubt, enmity, and politically expedient rumormongering.

The bandage responses proposed by social media companies have largely been late, muddled, and inconsistent: banning Alex Jones from Twitter and Facebook or asking him to delete individual tweets cannot be a wholesale solution to the problem of his immense reach. Such mea-sures were not even intended as solutions; their goal was to lessen the companies' legal exposure and their chance of being held liable in a civil lawsuit, and probably to relieve the pressure of consumers calling for sponsors to pull advertising money.

The consequences of these small steps might help to diminish the power of some individual conspiracists, and the mainstream attention has had an unintentional benefit: Alex Jones had been making some truly vile arguments for decades; once he began receiving broad atten-tion, the negative consequences for him also grew. (Besides social media bans, he was sued in the spring of 2018 by three Sandy Hook parents, including Lenny Pozner, for defamation.) In the case of Milo Yiannopou-los, the anti-feminist troll who flirted with white nationalism, his perma-nent ban from Twitter in 2016 (for directing an online mob to harass actress Leslie Jones) and the cancellation of a lucrative book contract certainly curtailed his power.

Ultimately, social media cannot be held directly responsible for the virulence of conspiracy theories. The same Internet that spreads garbage has also toppled regimes, created a megaphone for marginalized voices, exposed injustice, fomented discussion, and held power to account. Free speech is a social good and an American value, and the Internet should be allowed to function in a way that enhances that value.

People such as Lenny Pozner, the father of a child killed in Sandy Hook, have called for more stringent regulation of the Internet, which has undeniably been used as an instrument of torture against his family. Yet some proposals—like pressuring social media platforms to flag conspiracy theories as hate speech and remove the pages spreading them on those grounds—involve trusting companies like Facebook to distinguish between constitutionally protected speech and other kinds. Those companies, tasked with such a mammoth and nuanced task in a chaotic media environment, are inevitably going to make some incorrect calls. The exploitation of intellectual property, though, like the photos Pozner took of his son now used without his permission, should elicit a better, swifter response than a form letter from Google or YouTube. There are rules in place to prevent that exploitation, rules that need only to be enforced.

Social media aside, it is our job to counter bad speech with better speech. We have to find a way to flag and debunk disinformation even as we try to avoid promoting it. And we should provide as much information as possible about the pipelines that carry misinformation to effectively disable them. We have to figure out better ways to confront directly the propaganda and outright lies crowding the media ecosystem, as reporter Sarah Jones wrote in the *New Republic* in the summer of 2017. We cannot simply scoff at it as fake and turn our backs, because millions of people across the country are not doing the same.

"The alternative," Jones wrote, "is to allow conservative propaganda to fester. An impenetrable bloc of voters will continue to blame Latinos for their woes, to ignore basic facts that are staring them in the face, to trumpet American exceptionalism while neo-Nazis roam the streets, and to look to a strongman in their image to save them. We will have an unfree country, ruled by fear, and if we do not act we will bear some of the blame."

Reporters have a specific task: to gain public trust by showing, as transparently as possible, the process by which they engage in fact-finding and investigating. They must engage with their critics, even as these critics deride journalists as fake news peddlers. There is a direct relationship between media distrust and conspiracy theorizing, which is evident beyond the United States. A 2016 study in Sweden found that half the country gets their news from alternative, heavily partisan sites, and one in five said they don't trust "traditional media" at all. (The Digital News Report, a yearly publication from the Reuters Institute and Oxford University, found the same thing in 2017: "Amid intensified discussions on the prevalence of fake news, there is concern [in Sweden] about so-called news avoiders and also right-wing sympathisers deserting news media in favour of so-called alternative media.") Sweden is also the European country in which the alt-right has most heavily taken root—probably not a coincidence—and where conspiracy theories about immigrants are most visible and virulent. The news that Swedes were avoiding mainstream media was covered triumphantly on the far-right site Breitbart, which is also not a coincidence.

There is much at stake. In Europe, racist conspiracy theorists have tried to grasp at lasting political power. Those in the west—Marine Le Pen and her anti-Semitic dog whistles in France, the Netherlands' Geert Wilders and his racist, Islamophobic rhetoric and alarming white-blond hair helmet—have largely failed, thus far. In Central and Eastern Europe, though, they have often succeeded. In Hungary, the far-right, racist Jobbik party has moved ever closer to the mainstream, and ultra-nationalist groups in Poland are on the rise. In the United States, conspiracy theorists and white nationalists are attempting to breach the political system and there's no understating the cause for concern.

In the end, though, conspiracy theories are the symptom, not the disease; they are a function of the society in which they breed. The worst conspiracy impulses, it seems, flourish in isolation. That, in a way, is the hardest condition to counter. Across the United States, there is an army of QAnon detectives or Sandy Hook deniers who sit at home, scrolling endlessly, sinking further and further into a construct of lies designed to provoke fear and fury. The bars maintaining their solitude are extremely sturdy; in a country of vast distances and weak social supports and community institutions, we have designed them that way.

Conspiracy theories can lose their draw if we turn to the work of improving the environment in which they grow by creating a more just, equitable, economically secure, and politically representative society. Conspiracism, like the xenophobia and suspicion that grow from the same gnarled roots, is fed by social instability. We will not be a less paranoid country until we are a fairer one. We need genuinely representative elections, better education in science and media literacy, a less moneyed system of democracy, true and permanent government transparency. Banishing some types of conspiracism will also involve grappling with our past, which is replete with actual cover-ups and human rights abuses.

For the moment, though, we must challenge the hypocrisy, contradictions, and opportunism of our better-known conspiracists and call to reason even the most virulent of them, the people who have pointed the fire hose of misinformation most profitably. Days before Hurricane Irma struck Cuba and Florida, Rush Limbaugh opined that news coverage of the storm was hyped up by people bent on pushing the "climate change agenda," as he called it.

"There is a desire to advance this climate change agenda, and hurricanes are one of the fastest and best ways to do it," he told his listeners, alone in his soundproof booth. "You don't need a hurricane to hit anywhere. All you need is to create the fear and panic accompanied by talk that climate change is causing hurricanes to become more frequent and bigger and more dangerous, and you create the panic, and it's mission accomplished, agenda advanced."

As with so many conspiracy peddlers, Limbaugh's desire to sell lies to his audience was only outmatched by his self-interest. A day after his impassioned denunciation of Hurricane Irma as a hoax tool of a lying government, Limbaugh did something quietly reasonable. He evacuated Florida, steering himself out of the path of the fake storm. Irma made landfall soon after, creating a path of chaos and destruction that was all too real.

SOURCES

GENERAL:

David Aaronovitch, *Voodoo Histories: The Role of Conspiracy Theory in Shaping Modern History* (New York: Riverhead, 2011).

Kurt Andersen, *Fantasyland: How America Went Haywire: A 500-Year History* (New York: Random House, 2017).

Jack Z. Bratich, *Conspiracy Panics: Political Rationality and Popular Culture* (New York: State University of New York Press, 2008).

Rob Brotherton, *Suspicious Minds: Why We Believe in Conspiracy Theories* (New York: Bloomsbury Sigma, reprint 2017).

Mark Fenster, *Conspiracy Theories: Secrecy and Power in American Culture*, 2nd ed. (Minneapolis: University of Minnesota Press, 2008).

G. Edward Griffin, *The Creature from Jekyll Island: A Second Look at the Federal Reserve*, 5th ed. (New York: American Media, 2010).

Emma A. Jane and Chris Fleming, *Modern Conspiracy: The Importance of Being Paranoid* (New York: Bloomsbury Academic, 2014).

Mike Lofgren, *The Deep State: The Fall of the Constitution and the Rise of a Shadow Government* (New York: Viking, 2016).

Kathryn S. Olmsted, *Real Enemies: Conspiracy Theories and American Democracy, World War I to 9/11* (New York: Oxford University Press, 2009).

Jon Ronson, *Them: Adventures with Extremists* (New York: Simon & Schuster, reprint 2003).

Vegas Tenold, *Everything You Love Will Burn: Inside the Rebirth of White Nationalism in America* (New York: Nation Books, 2018).

Jesse Walker, *The United States of Paranoia: A Conspiracy Theory* (New York: Harper, 2013).

Lawrence Wright, *Remembering Satan: A Tragic Case of Recovered Memory* (New York: Alfred A. Knopf, 1994).

Ilya Yablokov, *Fortress Russia: Conspiracy Theories in the Post-Soviet World* (Boston: Polity, 2018).

Kevin Young, *Bunk: The Rise of Hoaxes, Humbug, Plagiarists, Phonies, Post-Facts, and Fake News* (Minneapolis: Graywolf Press, 2017).

PROLOGUE

Marc Fisher, John Woodrow Cox, and Peter Hermann, "Pizzagate: From Rumor, to Hashtag, to Gunfire in D.C.," *Washington Post*, December 6, 2016.

Dark Secrets: Inside Bohemian Grove (film, 2000), dir. Alex Jones.

"UFOs Exist, Say 36 Percent in National Survey," ABC News, June 27, 2012.

1: FALSE TIMES

Sean David Morton, interview with the author, February 11, 2016.

Kathryn S. Olmsted, interview with the author, August 31, 2017.

Richard Hofstadter, "The Paranoid Style in American Politics," *Harper's*, November 1964.

Joseph E. Uscinski, Casey Klofstad, and Matthew D. Atkinson, "What Drives Conspiratorial Beliefs? The Role of Informational Cues and Predispositions." *Political Research Quarterly* 69, no. 1 (March 2016): 57–71.

Michael J. Wood, Karen M. Douglas, and Robbie M. Sutton, "Dead and Alive: Beliefs in Contradictory Conspiracy Theories," *Social Psychological and Personality Science*, January 25, 2012.

2: "NONE OF IT IS CRAZY"

Michael Harriott, interview with the author, November 16, 2017.

Dr. John L. Jackson, interview with the author, November 16, 2017.

Minister Tony Muhammad, interview with the author, June 21, 2017.

"Hurricane Katrina: Voices from Inside the Storm," hearing from the Select Bipartisan

Committee to Investigate the Preparation for and Response to Hurricane
Katrina, December 6, 2005, accessed via C-SPAN.org.

Lisa Meyers, "Were the Levees Bombed in New Orleans?: Ninth Ward Residents
Give Voice to a Conspiracy Theory," NBC News, December 7, 2005.

"Looking Back at the Blasting of the Mississippi River Levee at Caernarvon," *New
Orleans Times-Picayune*, April 9, 2012.

The Great Mississippi River Flood of 1927: Ain't Got No Place to Go, online inter-
active exhibit, National Museum of African American History and Culture,
undated, accessed 2017.

"The Mississippi Valley Flood Disaster of 1927; Official Report," American National
Red Cross, 1929, accessed 2018 through Hathi Trust Digital Library.

Susan Scott Parrish, "The Great Mississippi Flood of 1927 Laid Bare the Divide
Between the North and the South," Smithsonianmag.com, April 11, 2017.

William Howard, "Richard Wright's Flood Stories and the Great Mississippi River
Flood of 1927: Social and Historical Backgrounds," *Southern Literary Journal*
16, no. 2 (Spring 1984): 44, accessed via RichGibson.com.

"When the Levee Breaks: Ripples of the Great Flood," NPR, May 18, 2011.

Eric Konigsberg, "Who Killed Anna Mae?" *New York Times Magazine*, April 25, 2014.

*STATE of South Dakota, Plaintiff and Appellee, v. John GRAHAM a/k/a John Boy
Patton, Defendant and Appellant*, No. 25899. Decided: May 30, 2012.

Alleen Brown, Will Parrish, and Alice Speri, "Leaked Documents Reveal Counterterrorism Tactics Used at Standing Rock to 'Defeat Pipeline Insurgencies,'" The
Intercept, May 27, 2017.

Peter Aldhous and Charles Seife, "Spies in the Skies," Buzzfeed News, April 6, 2016.

"Reproductive Health of Urban American Indian and Alaska Native Women: Exam-
ining Unintended Pregnancy, Contraception, Sexual History and Behavior, and
Non-Voluntary Sexual Intercourse," Urban Indian Health Institute, May 2010.

Ted Goertzel, "Belief in Conspiracy Theories," *Political Psychology* 15, no. 4
(December 1994).

L. M. Bogart and S. Thorburn, "Are HIV/AIDS Conspiracy Beliefs a Barrier to HIV
Prevention Among African Americans?" *Journal of Acquired Immune Deficiency
Syndromes*, February 2005.

Jacob Heller, "Rumors and Realities: Making Sense of HIV/AIDS Conspiracy Narratives
and Contemporary Legends," *American Journal of Public Health*, January 2015.

Mike Adams, "And Now the Cover-up Murders Begin in Flint, Michigan: Water Treatment Plant Foreman Found Dead . . . Young Mom Murdered in Her Home After
Filing Lawsuit against Michigan Government," *Natural News*, April 24, 2016.

Merrit Kennedy, "Lead-Laced Water in Flint: A Step-by-Step Look at the Makings
of a Crisis," NPR, April 20, 2016.

3: NOCTURNAL RITUAL PIZZA PARTY

David Seaman, interview with the author, March 25, 2017.

Bryce Reh, interview with the author, March 25, 2017.

Amanda Robb, "Pizzagate: Anatomy of a Fake News Scandal," *Rolling Stone*, November 16, 2017.

Lorenzo Franceschi-Bicchierai, "How Hackers Broke into John Podesta and Colin Powell's Gmail Accounts," Vice News, October 20, 2016.

Nick Bryant, "Flight Logs Put Clinton, Dershowitz on Pedophile Billionaire's Sex Jet," Gawker, January 22, 2015.

United States of America v. Edgar Maddison Welch, federal complaint, December 12, 2016.

Bryan Menegus, "What We Learned From the Pizzagate Shooter's Latest Court Docs," Gizmodo, June 14, 2017.

Adam Goldman, "The Comet Ping Pong Gunman Answers Our Reporter's Questions," *New York Times*, December 7, 2016.

James Doubek, "Conspiracy Theorist Alex Jones Apologizes for Promoting 'Pizzagate,'" NPR, March 26, 2017.

Paul Joseph Watson, "Ex-Banker Claims He Was Invited to Participate in Child Sacrifice Rituals," InfoWars, May 2, 2017.

Eric Hananoki, "Alex Jones Deletes Video in Which He Had Told His Audience to Personally 'Investigate' 'Pizzagate' Restaurant," Media Matters, December 16, 2016.

Dan Shewan, "Conviction of Things Not Seen: The Uniquely American Myth of Satanic Cults," *Pacific Standard*, September 8, 2015.

Ken Huff, "The Lonely Life of 'Latchkey' Children, Say Two Experts, Is a National Disgrace," *People*, September 20, 1982.

Steven R. Churm, "Parents Dig Persistently for Evidence: McMartin School," *Los Angeles Times*, June 5, 1990.

4: FALSE FLAGS

Lenny Pozner, interview with the author, March 15, 2017.

Louis Leo IV, interview with the author, June 10, 2017.

Silvia Foster-Frau, "Pair Arrested After Harassing Pastor in Sutherland Springs," *San Antonio Express-News*, March 5, 2018.

Mike Schneider, "Ibragim Todashev's Family Sues Agents over His Death," Associated Press, May 24, 2017.

"Zionist Jews Strike Again, Murdering Three in Boston," NoDisInfo.com, April 15, 2013.

"SWAT Team Head Behind Attack on Dzhokhar Busted as a Zionist Jew," NoDisinfo.com, July 22, 2013.

Dave Hodges, "The Globalist Brainwashing of Your Children," Common Sense Show, April 1, 2014.

"Extremists and Conspiracy Theorists React to Boston Marathon Terrorist Attack," Anti-Defamation League, April 18, 2013.

Kate Starbird et al., "Ecosystem or Echo-System? Exploring Content Sharing Across Alternative Media Domains," University of Washington and Harvard T. H. Chan School of Public Health, 2017.

5: USEFUL MURDERS

Joseph Uscinski, interview with the author, February 1, 2017.

Aaron Rich, interview with the author, April 21, 2017.

Manuel Roig-Franzia, "Seth Rich Wasn't Just Another D.C. Murder Victim. He Was a Meme in the Weirdest Presidential Election of Our Times," *Washington Post*, January 17, 2018.

David Folkenflik, "Behind Fox News' Baseless Seth Rich Story: The Untold Tale," NPR, August 1, 2017.

Jonathan Mahler, "The Problem with 'Self-Investigation' in a Post-Truth Era," *New York Times Magazine*, December 27, 2016.

Adam Shrier, "Democratic National Committee Staffer Killed in Washington, D.C. Shooting," *New York Daily News*, July 11, 2016.

Aaron Rich v. Edward Butowsky, Matthew Couch, America First Media, and the Washington Times, federal complaint, filed March 26, 2018.

Sorcha Faal, "Assassination of Top US Democratic Party Official Leads to FBI Capture of Clinton 'Hit Team,'" WhatDoesItMean.com, July 13, 2016.

Peter Hermann and Clarence Williams, "WikiLeaks Offers Reward for Help Finding DNC Staffer's Killer," *Washington Post*, August 9, 2016.

Danielle Kurtzleben, "Unproved Claims Re-Emerge Around DNC Staffer's Death: Here's What You Should Know," NPR, May 11, 2017.

Jeremy W. Peters, "A Pro-Trump Conspiracy Theorist, a False Tweet and a Runaway Story," *New York Times*, June 10, 2017.

Cass R. Sunstein and Adrian Vermeule, "Conspiracy Theories," University of Chicago Law School, Coase-Sandor Working Paper Series in Law and Economics, 2008.

Rosie Gray, "D.C. Lobbyist Who Once Supported Trump Now Says He'll Raise Money for Anti-Trump Effort," Buzzfeed News, July 7, 2016.

Jonathan Valania, "How Jack Posobiec Became the King of Fake News," *Philadelphia Magazine*, September 16, 2017.

"Roger Stone Uses Vince Foster Conspiracy Theory to Promote Upcoming Book on Hannity's Radio Show," Media Matters, September 18, 2015.

"Rod Wheeler Backtracks Statements About Seth Rich Investigation," Fox News 5 DC, May 17, 2017.

Mary Rich and Joel Rich, "We're Seth Rich's Parents. Stop Politicizing Our Son's Murder," *Washington Post*, May 23, 2017.

Emily Steel, "Lawsuit Asserts White House Role in Fox News Article on Seth Rich," *New York Times*, August 1, 2017.

David Weigel, "Gingrich Spreads Conspiracy Theory About Slain DNC Staffer," *Washington Post*, May 21, 2017.

Caitlin Johnstone, "Why You Should Definitely Keep Talking About Seth Rich," Medium, May 24, 2017.

David Folkenflik, "Judge Dismisses Suits Against Fox News over Seth Rich Story," NPR, August 3, 2018.

6: MEDICAL ODDITIES

Andrew Wakefield et al., "RETRACTED: Ileal-Lymphoid-Nodular Hyperplasia, Non-Specific Colitis, and Pervasive Developmental Disorder in Children," *Lancet*, February 28, 1998.

Brian Deer, "How the Case Against the MMR Vaccine Was Fixed," *British Medical Journal*, January 6, 2011.

Y. Tony Yang et al., "Sociodemographic Predictors of Vaccination Exemptions on the Basis of Personal Belief in California," *American Journal of Public Health*, January 2016.

Mary Ann Roser, "Discredited Autism Guru Andrew Wakefield Takes Aim at CDC," *Austin American-Statesman*, September 23, 2016.

Linda A. Johnson, "FDA: Avoid Fake 'Miracle' Cancer Treatments Sold on Internet," Associated Press, April 25, 2017.

David A. Broniatowski et al., "Weaponized Health Communication: Twitter Bots and Russian Trolls Amplify the Vaccine Debate," *American Journal of Public Health*, August 23, 2018.

J. Eric Oliver and Thomas Wood, "Medical Conspiracy Theories and Health Behaviors in the United States," *JAMA Internal Medicine*, May 2014.

Rong-Gong Lin II, "How California Got More Children Vaccinated After the Disneyland Measles Outbreak," *Los Angeles Times*, April 13, 2017.

Laurie Wilson, "Family of Radiation Test Victim Angered by Government's Deceit," *Washington Post*, January 2, 1994.

"Settlement Reached in Suit over Radioactive Oatmeal Experiment," *New York Times*, January 1, 1998.

Arnold H. Lubasch, "$700,000 Award Is Made in '53 Secret Test Death," *New York Times*, May 6, 1987.

Tim Weiner, "Sidney Gottlieb, 80, Dies; Took LSD to C.I.A.," *New York Times*, March 10, 1999.

Nikhil Sonnad, "All the 'Wellness' Products Americans Love to Buy Are Sold on Both InfoWars and Goop," Quartz, June 29, 2017.

7: A NATURAL MAN

Sean David Morton, interview with the author, April 7, 2017.

Colleen Morton Anderson, interview with the author, August 30, 2017.

"Tax Protester Movement," Anti-Defamation League, undated/archived.

"The Truth About Frivolous Tax Arguments," IRS.gov, March 13, 2018.

Sean David Morton, letter to potential investors, UFO Watchdog, undated.

Shannon Sands, "Believers Are Not Alone: Outer Space: A Nevada Military Base Lures the Faithful Seeking Close Encounters of Any Kind with the UFOs They Believe Frequent the Area," *Los Angeles Times*, March 20, 1991.

Robert Anglen, "Gordon Hall Trades Millions, Mansion for Prison Cell," *Arizona Republic*, June 25, 2015.

8: WHITE NATIONALIST COOKOUT

Matthew Heimbach, interview with the author, April 17, 2017.

Chip Berlet, interview with the author, November 9, 2017.

Ryan Lenz, interview with the author, May 21, 2017.

"TradWorker 25 Points," Traditionalist Worker Party Tennessee website, undated.

Sarah Viets, "Meet the Aryan Nationalist Alliance, a Racist Hodgepodge Doomed to Fail," Southern Poverty Law Center, July 21, 2016.

Sarah Viets, "Nationalist Front Chumming Up to Klan Members Once Again," Southern Poverty Law Center, May 30, 2017.

Josh Little, "Pike's Population on the Decline," *Appalachian News-Express*, April 9, 2016.

2016 Kentucky Presidential Election Results, *Politico*, December 13, 2016.

"The Enemy Within," Original Knights of America, Knights of the Ku Klux Klan, undated.

Kathryn Flett, "We're Off to See the Lizards," *Guardian*, May 12, 2001.

Jon Ronson, "Beset by Lizards," *Guardian*, March 17, 2001.

Marlon Solomon, "Forget the Lizards: David Icke Is Dangerous and We Should Take Him Seriously," Half Chips/Half Rice, January 4, 2017.

Mansfield v. Church of the Creator, Case Background and Federal Complaint, Southern Poverty Law Center.

"Ku Klux Klan: A History of Racism," Southern Poverty Law Center, February 28, 2011.

Alexander Zaitchik, "Patriot Paranoia: A Look at the Top Ten Conspiracy Theories," Southern Poverty Law Center, August 1, 2010.

"Ctrl-Alt-Delete: The Origins and Ideology of the Alt Right," Political Research Associates, January 20, 2017.

"Identity Evropa and Arktos Media—Likely Bedfellows," Southern Poverty Law Center, September 26, 2017.

J. Lester Feder and Edgar Mannheimer, "How Sweden Became 'The Most Alt-Right Country in Europe,'" Buzzfeed News, May 3, 2017.

Tom Batchelor, "Anti-Fascist Activist Goes Undercover with 'Alt Right' to Expose Movement's Rapid European Expansion," *Independent*, September 20, 2017.

"The International Alternative Right," Hope Not Hate.

Jessi Balmert, "Lawmaker Keller Spoke on White Power Advocate's Show," *Cincinnati Enquirer*, April 18, 2017.

Zachary Roth, "Local Tea Party Leader Who Suggested Shooting Hispanics Now Is Wanted by Cops—Tweets: 'Arm Yourself,'" Talking Points Memo, April 14, 2010.

Grant Pick, "Bigot for Hire," *Chicago Reader*, July 21, 1994.

Lauren Carroll, "Fact-Checking Trump's Claim That Thousands in New Jersey Cheered When World Trade Center Tumbled," Politifact, November 22, 2015.

"ADL Urges Donald Trump to Reconsider 'America First' in Foreign Policy Approach," Anti-Defamation League, April 28, 2016.

Zack Beauchamp, "Study: 11 Million White Americans Think Like the Alt-Right," Vox, August 10, 2018.

Gary Langer, "1 in 10 Say It's Acceptable to Hold Neo-Nazi Views (POLL)," ABC News, August 21, 2017.

"Extremist Info: Frank Gaffney Jr.," Southern Poverty Law Center.

Natasha Korecki, "'I Snookered Them': Illinois Nazi Candidate Creates GOP Dumpster Fire," Politico, June 29, 2018.

Lois Beckett, "White Nationalist Leader Charged with Harassing Black Protester at Trump Rally," *Guardian,* May 1, 2017.

Luke O'Brien, "The Making of an American Nazi," *The Atlantic*, December 2017.

Anna Merlan, "Leader of the Hate Group Linked to Charlottesville Attacker Was a Recruiter for the U.S. Marines," Splinter News, August 14, 2017.

Brennan Gilmore, "How I Became Fake News," Politico, August 21, 2017.

A. C. Thompson, Ali Winston, and Jake Hanrahan, "Inside Atomwaffen As It Celebrates a Member for Allegedly Killing a Gay Jewish College Student," ProPublica, February 23, 2018.

9: THE POLITICS OF UFOS

Sharon Hill, "UFO Research Is Up in the Air: Can It Be Scientific?" Center for Skeptical Inquiry, August 28, 2013.

The Roswell Report: Fact vs. Fiction in the New Mexico Desert, Headquarters United States Air Force, 1995.

William J. Broad, "Air Force Details a New Theory in U.F.O. Case," *New York Times,* June 24, 1997.

Jason Colavito, "Top MUFON Official Quits over Organization's Continued Support of John Ventre a Year After Ventre's Racist Rant," JasonColavito.com, April 17, 2018.

10: CONSPIRACISM IS FOR EVERYONE: THE DEEP STATE AND RUSSIAGATE

Jonah Engel Bromwich, "C-Span Online Broadcast Interrupted by Russian Network," *New York Times*, January 12, 2017.

Amanda Taub and Max Fisher, "As Leaks Multiply, Fears of a 'Deep State' in America," *New York Times*, February 16, 2017.

Kate Starbird, "Tracing Disinformation Trajectories from the 2010 Deepwater Horizon Oil Spill," *Medium*, December 2, 2016.

Philip Bump, "The Web of Conspiracy Theorists That Was Ready for Donald Trump," *Washington Post*, April 4, 2017.

Masha Gessen, "Russia: The Conspiracy Trap," *New York Review of Books*, March 6, 2017.

Jana Winter and Elias Groll, "Here's the Memo That Blew Up the NSC," *Foreign Policy*, August 10, 2017.

Jon Swaine, "Lurid Trump Allegations Made by Louise Mensch and Co-Writer Came from Hoaxer," *Guardian*, August 28, 2017.

EPILOGUE

Brandy Zadrozny and Ben Collins, "Arizona Veterans Group Finds Homeless Camp—and Fuels a New 'Pizzagate'-Style Conspiracy," NBC News, June 7, 2018.

Matthew Gault, "#QAnon Conspiracy Theorists Are Hunting for 'Child Sex Camps' in the Arizona Desert," *Vice*, June 7, 2018.

Will Sommer, "QAnon, the Crazy Pro-Trump Conspiracy, Melts Down over OIG Report," Daily Beast, June 19, 2018.

Asawin Suebsaeng and Will Sommer, "Trump Meets QAnon Kook Who Believes Democrats Run Pedophile Cult," Daily Beast, August 24, 2018.

Sebastian Murdock, "Sandy Hook Parents Hit Alex Jones with Defamation Lawsuits," Huffington Post, April 17, 2018.

Henry Brean, "Suspect in Hoover Dam Standoff Writes Trump, Cites Conspiracy in Letters," *Las Vegas Review-Journal*, July 13, 2018.

Philip N. Howard et al., "Social Media, News and Political Information During the US Election: Was Polarizing Content Concentrated in Swing States?" Project on Computational Propaganda, Oxford University, September 28, 2017.

"Every Fifth Swede Does Not Trust Traditional Media," *Resumé*, December 15, 2017.

Reuters Institute Digital News Report 2017, Reuters Institute and Oxford University.

Daniel Jolley and Karen M. Douglas, "The Social Consequences of Conspiracism: Exposure to Conspiracy Theories Decreases Intentions to Engage in Politics and to Reduce One's Carbon Footprint," *British Journal of Psychology*, January 4, 2013.

Bradley Franks, Martin W. Bauer, and Adrian Bangerter, "Conspiracy Theories as Quasi-Religious Mentality: An Integrated Account from Cognitive Science, Social Representations Theory, and Frame Theory," *Frontiers in Psychology*, July 16, 2013.

ACKNOWLEDGMENTS

Writing a book has been one of the greatest privileges of my life. I'm so grateful to everyone who helped make it possible, starting with Metropolitan Books, my editor Riva Hocherman, and my agent David Patterson of the Stuart Krichevsky Literary Agency.

Thanks to the talented reporters, authors, and editors who read early drafts of individual chapters and provided edits, encouragement, feedback, corrections, and affirmations that aliens are real: Stephen Fried, Joe Tone, Nathan Tempey, Mehera Bonner, Brendan O'Connor, Greg Howard, Colin McRoberts, Bronwen Dickey, Dina Litovsky, and Tim Marchman.

Thank you to the people who were gracious enough to grant me interviews, especially those of you who were not particularly happy to see or hear from me but decided to speak anyway.

Thank you to the fellow journalists who talked to me about concepts in this book and helped refine my own thinking, making me sound smarter than I am, particularly everyone at Jezebel and the Special Projects Desk.

Thanks to everyone who helped me access academic studies and other materials: Mark A. Davidson, Stephanie Rains, Betsy Powell, Katie Martin, and Lucien Greaves.

Thank you to Patrick Crawford for designing my book cover, which is even better than I imagined.

Thank you to Spencer Sunshine, who fact-checked my chapter on white supremacist conspiracy theories, and to Laura Bullard, who miraculously fact-checked the rest of the book on a tight deadline and without having a nervous breakdown, somehow.

Thank you to Tessa Stuart, who talked to me about every single concept in this book and provided years of daily, sometimes hourly, encouragement and reassurance.

Thank you to Tod Seelie, for caring deeply about this project from the start, for editing the first draft of my proposal while we drove through a blizzard, for taking my author portrait, and for being present for the worst of these adventures.

Thank you to my brother, Steve, for helping me with research and sending snacks and UFO books, and to my parents, Tom and Fran, for everything, always, and for mailing backup tequila.

Finally, thank you to Megan Dooley Fisher, the Jezebel reader who suggested to my editors that I go on a conspiracy-themed cruise and who launched me down this road. I am grateful, and I will also never forgive you.

INDEX

ABOUT THE AUTHOR

ANNA MERLAN is a journalist specializing in politics, crime, religion, subcultures, and women's lives. She is a reporter at the Special Projects Desk, the investigative division of Gizmodo Media Group. She was previously a senior reporter at Jezebel and staff writer at the *Village Voice* and the *Dallas Observer*. She lives in New York.